THE HANDMAIDEN

TAKE NOT THY HOLY SPIRIT

BC Talbott

WORD & SPIRIT
PUBLISHING

THE HANDMAIDEN
TAKE NOT THY HOLY SPIRIT
Copyright © 2022 by BC Talbott.
ISBN: 978-1-949106-97-8

Published by Word and Spirit Publishing
P.O. Box 701403
Tulsa, Oklahoma 74170
wordandspiritpublishing.com

CONTENTS

DEDICATION

I give thanks to the Holy Spirit for guiding me through this journey to tell the story that Kathryn Kuhlman wanted to tell: a journey that started in 1997. God has brought the most wonderful and loving people into my life while writing Kathryn's story. Each one of them shared their time with me and entrusted me with their beautiful memories and stories about the woman they all loved, Kathryn Kuhlman. This book is dedicated to each of them: Ole Anthony, Ruth & Gene Martin, Tink Wilkerson, Sally O'Brien, Charles "Cappy" Cappleman, Dr. Richard Casdorph, Dr. Bill Loughridge, Fannie Mae, Burrows Waltrip Jr., Kim Renee, Sara O'Meara, Yvonne Fedderson, Roberts Liardon, and Tom Rutherford. To my husband Todd, thank you for encouraging me every day and always reminding me that in all things, God's timing is perfect timing. I pray that Kathryn's story will touch your heart and touch your life as it has done mine. Every day I am so thankful for the grace of God and for all the amazing and beautiful things He has done in my life. My life is a miracle, and in the words of The Handmaiden, Kathryn Kuhlman, "I Believe in Miracles Because I Believe in God."

PAPA'S LOVE

"Ah, what a lovely day, my dear." It was a breathtaking sight, the bright orange sun rising in a pale blue sky, clouds on which you could float to heaven. In Concordia, Missouri, at 1018 St. Louis Street, all was well, and the ease of the simple life surrounded Joseph Kuhlman and his pride and joy, daughter Kathryn. They stepped off the front porch, holding hands as they often did. It was easy to tell that she was a daddy's girl. Tall and slender with curly hair, strong German features, and bright blue eyes, she was the spitting image of her Papa.

"Kathryn, we have a lot of stops today, but I suppose if you need it, we can manage." They had mutual respect. Kathryn never asked for anything Papa could not give, so neither of them would have to be disappointed. Of course, there was not too much that Papa would not give.

They were almost to the bakery when Papa abruptly took Kathryn by the hand and crossed the street. Confused and wide-eyed that Papa would deprive her of a much-needed cherry sweet roll, she looked to the bakery, "Did you forget, Papa?"

He quickly reassured her, "Oh, no, baby. It is just that preacher man." He nodded toward him. "He would have rambled on before he asked for some kind of donation of something. I am not in the mood to ruin this beautiful morning. Let's go in here and pick up a few things, and then we will go right to the bakery."

Kathryn wondered why Papa felt that way about the preacher, but it was best she did not press for an explanation. The last thing she wanted was to upset Papa. He occasionally attended the Baptist church; Mama faithfully took Kathryn and the older children, Earl and Myrtle, to the Methodist church. Mama also taught Kathryn and the other children the King's Heralds Bible Study on Sunday afternoon. She played the piano for the evening service and taught the children hymns.

Finally, after what seemed like an eternity to Kathryn, Papa set a course to the bakery. Papa sipped on black coffee while Kathryn savored every bite of her cherry sweet roll, licking her fingers and jabbering to anyone who would listen. Two young girls came in and ran straight to Kathryn. "Friday night, we are having a sleepover, and you simply must come." And at the prospect of a captive audience, she looked to Papa, who simply raised an eyebrow and said, "Ask your mother." Kathryn sighed, rolled her eyes, and told her friends she would have to let them know.

Mama was a stern disciplinarian, but never in front of Papa. He could not stand it. Kathryn's mischievous behavior was not as endearing to her as it was to Papa. With boundless energy and curiosity, Kathryn embraced life and all it had to hold. It often led to outings that ended with Mama and a whipping in the basement. Neither was she proud of Kathryn's untamed curly red hair and freckled face, instructing her to put on her bonnet before she went outside. Mama had worked hard with Kathryn to develop proper speech and to slow down her "motor mouth" as "Kooley," Kathryn's brother Earl's nickname, so often called it. Being ten years older than Kathryn, Kooley's tolerance for Kathryn's childlike antics was extremely limited as well. Papa spoiled him too, with custom-made race cars and later, airplanes.

It was Myrtle, fifteen years older than Kathryn, who saw Kathryn's potential. While Kathryn was still in Mama's womb, Myrtle felt a special bond with her baby sister. Everyone was excited about having a new baby in the house. The Kuhlmans had everything now, and the timing was perfect for a new addition to the family. Joseph and Emma Kuhlman told his mother as she lay dying that their child, due in only three months, would be her namesake if it were a girl. They would, however, change the spelling. The name Kathryn is of Greek origin and means "one of purity; beloved." Her middle name came from Emma's mother, Johanna. Joseph's father's name also happened to be Johannes. Johanna is of Hebrew and German origin and means "God is gracious." In the years to follow, Kathryn would live up to her name. She strived to exemplify a life free from the corrupting things of this world. She was loved by the masses for the down-to-earth way she spoke from her heart about the Word of God.

From the day she was born, on May 9, 1907, Kathryn was the apple of her father's eye. His baby girl was at the center of his attention and would hold that for the rest of her life.

None is living to tell of her early childhood. The family photographs from her estate show and tell their own story. When Tink Wilkerson brought them to me, twenty-two years after her death, they were in the same shoebox she had probably kept them in for much longer. They were unorganized, and it took quite a while to recreate the childhood that brought new insight into this humble handmaiden of the Lord. If a picture is worth a thousand words, this shoebox spoke volumes. As you study Kathryn's childhood pictures, it is clear she grew up in a secure and loving environment. The first photograph of this daughter of destiny is telling. It is one of many black and white photos that were so popular in the early 1900s. Mother stands in profile proudly, holding and looking upon the child. Kathryn faces front and center in a long flowing white gown with a high neck and ruffled sleeve cuffs—her trademark pulpit attire in later years. She owned many such gowns, but Tink kept only the last one she wore and disposed of the others. What stands out, even in the black and white photo, are pale, piercing blue eyes that look right into the camera. With wisdom and intensity beyond their years, they pull you in, as if to say, come to me. Her mouth is open as though she is speaking to us already. Kathryn would say she was not a pretty child—one born with no hair, only red fuzz. It was partly true. The crown of her head was nearly transparent, but despite that temporary minor affliction, she was indeed a pretty baby.

Until she was four, Kathryn enjoyed the privileged life on a one hundred sixty-acre playground. Photos of the family farm, southwest of town, show the gathering place for festivities that included all of Papa's and Mama's family. A two-story white frame house with a gingerbread front porch, flower gardens, and a red brick chimney paint a picture-perfect world. It would appear, from the beginning, Kathryn had more than enough of everything—family, love, affection, and Papa.

On the farm, Mama was always busy, but Papa was home for breakfast, lunch, and dinner. Papa always took lunch at eleven o'clock. Kathryn was only two or three years old when Mama would watch the clock and say Papa would be here in just a few minutes. Kathryn's feet and curls flew in the wind to meet him, and he would pick her up and carry her in the house with him. Papa carried Kathryn until her feet were dragging the sidewalk. In the evenings, Kathryn would crawl up in his lap, secure in knowing that she was his greatest treasure.

When she was four years old, Papa sold the family farm and moved into town. Joe Kuhlman built his wife the two-story dream house she designed. Kathryn grew up playing on the front porch that ran the length of the house. In one photograph, Kathryn stands at the corner of the porch with a carriage containing several dolls and a teddy bear. In her arms is another doll half her size. It was the perfect viewpoint as she would eagerly wait for Papa to come home and shower her with affection that Mama was less inclined to give. When Kathryn spotted Papa, she ran and jumped in his arms, where she felt his unconditional love.

One evening, she was upstairs when she heard him in the kitchen with Mama. She ran downstairs and found him warming his hands by the stove. In her excitement, she stumbled and burnt her hands, trying to reach him. This pain was almost worth the comfort when he picked her up and rocked her in his arms until there were no more tears.

"I had a perfect father a girl ever had," Kathryn later said, "Papa could do no wrong. He was my ideal." Similarly, in Papa's eyes, Kathryn could do no wrong. Never once did he punish her; he did not have to. She so adored him that all he had to do was give her a look, and Kathryn responded. To disappoint Papa was worse than any discipline Mama could give. As a child, Kathryn frequently suffered from earaches. Mama's remedies did not help, but Papa's love did. Kathryn recalled, "The things that eased the pain the best was for Papa to stay home from work, take me on his lap, and let me put my aching ear on his shoulder."

Papa was the head of the house, as the Word of God instructs. He was one of the wealthiest men in town and later became mayor. Kathryn liked to say that Papa ran the house and the town, but Mama ran Papa. It was perfect. Papa always had several things going. He was a good business manager with a mind for numbers, adding in his head with no need for pencil or paper.

Every night he came home with a bag of candy. After dinner, the Kuhlman family gathered around the kitchen table and engaged in fun-filled games. The winner got to pass the candy around.

Before bedtime, Papa retired to his office and sorted the yellow freight and express bills. Kathryn helped Papa, as she quietly learned to count using dominos. Papa showed such patience and trust. Sometimes on collection day, the merchants on Main Street paid Kathryn for the invoices by letting her help herself to a cookie from the jar or a pickle out of the barrel while she waited. There were a lot of benefits to working with Papa; it was the beginning of Kathryn's business acumens, and she became quite proficient from these days of instruction with Papa.

To almost everyone's great relief, when Kathryn was fourteen years old, standing beside Mama at the little Methodist church, every-thing changed. There was no altar call, but at five minutes till twelve, Kathryn began to shake violently. Weeping uncontrollably, she laid the Methodist hymnal aside and stepped out of the pew toward the altar. A kind lady in the congregation handed her a handkerchief and tried to calm her, saying, "But Kathryn, you have always been such a good girl!" Kathryn knew it was not true. She was a spoiled brat, a showoff, mean, bad, always in trouble for some crazy prank. It was just her makeup, and the conviction of sin rolled over her.

On the way home, the entire world looked different. Colors were vibrant, and the gentle breeze against her face seemed to caress her head to toe. For the first time, she felt the peace of the Holy Spirit. She ran up the steps straight to the most important person in the world. "Papa, Jesus has come into my heart!" Without much emotion, he said he was glad and went back to his paper. Perhaps Papa's disdain for the preacher caused him to suspect that the man of God had manipulated his little girl.

Kathryn never knew it, but Papa had never felt the same way about preachers after the old Baptist church his family attended outside of town had a big split with some of the newer members. They forced a move into town where people who had more money might come. The membership chose a side and the church divided. It remained a sore spot among those involved for many years. Papa let his children make up their minds about church affiliation. He didn't try to influence them one way or the other. Only Earl inherited his father's dislike for preachers.

One Sunday, shortly after Kathryn's conversion, the preacher asked Kathryn what she was going to do with her life now that she was saved. Showing that she had not completely changed, "I am going to find me a good-looking preacher man and marry him!" Everyone but Emma Kuhlman laughed. Mothers have the innate sixth sense when anything is amiss with one of their children. Her oldest, Myrtle, had gotten married to a preacher man when Kathryn was six, and Emma sensed that all was not well. Papa, of course, was none too pleased to hear Kathryn's news, either.

At sixteen, she had just completed her sophomore year when Myrtle and her evangelist husband of ten years, Everett Parrott, came to visit. Myrtle had recognized qualities in Kathryn that might be an asset to their ministry. Mama recognized the need to get Kathryn away from temptation. After much discussion and prayer, it was agreed Kathryn could go and hit the road with Myrtle and Everett for the summer.

Only Kathryn's nine-year-old sister, Geneva, who was now at home, remained to fill the emptiness that had developed between Joe and Emma Kuhlman. Over the years, Papa had softened while Mama had hardened. Occasionally, Joe indulged in a drink of hard liquor, and when Emma smelled the foul liquor on his breath, she sent him to the stable to sleep. Papa loved Kathryn too much to hold her back, especially in the unhappy environment they called home.

She packed her bags and, before leaving, walked through the entryway with Papa; she would miss him more than anything. They embraced for the longest time with tears in their eyes, but neither said a word. Through each other, they both knew the unconditional love that soothes all pain.

We must never underestimate the impact a loving parent can make on a child's future. It is the most important gift we can impart to the development of faith in God. How can we expect a child to believe in the unconditional love of a heavenly Father if they know it not? It was easy for Kathryn to understand Father God's love. She had known it. She passed from the protective arms of the earthly father into the blessed assurance of her heavenly Father.

HARMONY, USA

"Welcome to Concordia, Missouri, a great place to raise your family," reads the cover of the 1998 city publication. The name "Concordia" is derived from a Latin word meaning harmony and peace.

In 1853, with high hopes, Papa's parents, Henry and Catherine Borgstadt Kuhlman, left Westphalia, Germany, behind. Showing great courage and faith, they sailed the ocean to settle in this small German community. Eastern and Western Europe were in shambles from decades of bitter battles between earthly kingdoms seeking more land and power. Thousands lost their lives. Food was extremely hard to come by, and tuberculosis was rampant. Three sons and three daughters made it to the land of promise. Two did not.

The name was given to the settlement in 1860 during the Civil War by Reverend F.J. Biltz. Reverend Biltz, who was the pastor of St. Paul's Lutheran Church, named the town after his sister and daughter, Concordia.

The Civil War was a great disappointment to the German people who came to America hoping to leave war far behind them.

The wisdom imparted by a Kuhlman family member who stayed in Germany rings true of the fine people Kathryn would call "the salt of the earth."

"They should be careful not to succumb to luxury and wealth, which have no final point but are always on the lookout for more. I wish with all my mind and heart they should grow more aware of the fact that caring for only themselves works out to be disastrous to them. After all, we long to be happy down here. There is but one way to be it. Love thyself last, so that all human beings should be treated as brothers and sisters. We will meet in an eternal spiritual abode with complex comprehension, total goodness, and love, not based on human appearances. We are all responsible for our complicated character and behavior thereof. Be sure God's balance cannot err, unlike all human views."

Dreams became a reality in Concordia. Since the Civil War, Concordia has been a place of harmony and peace, a perfect place to raise a family. Records show that in February 1909, Papa bought the corner lot at 1018 St. Louis Street and built the only house Kathryn remembers growing up in.

In the fifties, while ministering at Kansas City Municipal Auditorium, Kathryn invited a childhood friend, Roland Petering, to attend her service. She left his name at the door, granting easy access past those who lined the sidewalk. Kathryn's appearances drew a crowd. Folks drove from nearby states to wait outside, hoping to gain entrance should someone leave the event early. Roland found a seat in the balcony. From the stage, Kathryn said, "I have been visiting

Concordia today, and I understand my childhood friend Roland Petering is here. Now where are you?" Embarrassed, Roland looked up to
see two ushers who led him to the stage. The two friends recalled
happy days when they would play in the apple orchard adjoining the
property and stir up some good old-fashioned mud pies. Mama would
bring them fresh baked cookies. Roland was quite impressed with his
little playmate that evening. "She has such a tremendous ability to
project herself to her audience." Many wept as the Holy Spirit filled
the auditorium.

Roland never dreamed his flaming red-headed friend would
become respected around the world, but early on, there were signs.
Kathryn would take him to King's Heralds at the Methodist church on
Sunday afternoons. There she would effortlessly deliver monologues
at a young age. Even then, her dramatic style was in development.
Kathryn also excelled in the contest to be the fastest at looking up
Bible verses.

She was a born leader, no doubt, very eloquent and not at all shy,
attractive with long curls, and a fine personality. Kathryn was always
vivacious and in the middle of everything going on. The other children
liked her. Roland, however, thought some of the girls were perhaps
envious. On one occasion, Kathryn was transported to Concordia in
a black stretch limousine. Her chauffeur escorted her to her mother's
door and in one hour returned to take her away.

Roland remembers when Kathryn was in her twenties and a boy
from Kansas City, Edward Hickman, was in Los Angeles. He murdered
a girl and put her body inside a trunk. There was nationwide coverage
portraying the young man as a cold-blooded killer. Kathryn went to

visit him in jail and preached to him before he was hung. She had a burden for souls and did not want him to perish.

Kathryn never forgot her childhood friend, Roland Petering; she sent him signed copies of every book she wrote. Roland's memories of Kathryn have always been good ones.

Another childhood friend, Ora Blackwell, remembers when Kathryn was the talk of the town. *Redbook* magazine did a very complimentary feature article on Kathryn in 1950. Everyone in town had to have a copy. They just could not believe the same mischievous little redhead was now a famous faith healer of national recognition. Most of Concordia didn't believe in such things. They were staunch Lutheran conservatives. Frankly, they felt the whole family was a little strange. Kathryn was affectionate in public, and Geneva wore trousers instead of skirts. Mr. Kuhlman was too quiet. It seemed that Kathryn was almost too much for them to handle.

The Missouri Pacific rail brought salesman to Concordia, eager to sell their merchandise. Papa would meet the train with his dray wagon to take them into town to sell their wares. Kathryn and her friends loved the train. They would walk the train tracks to the next town four miles away. They were careful to arrive back in time to catch a ride home in style on the Missouri Pacific line. Mama probably didn't know about these little escapades.

Erma Freese has lived in Concordia for eighty-three years. She remembers Kathryn as a neat little girl, always nice, walking around town with her little sister Geneva, whom the family all called "pet." The two sisters were close, and like their mother, were always impeccably dressed.

Joe Kuhlman was a robust, rugged man that everyone liked for his down-to-earth attitude despite being one of the wealthiest men in town. Erma had a relative whose son was dying of cancer. Kathryn came to pray for him, and although he later died, they never forgot how Kathryn prayed. "Her prayers were like thunder."

The Kuhlmans were active and well respected in the community. In those days, it was reputation, not education, that garnered respect. Papa was a peaceful man who was never involved in controversy. His reputation was one of honesty and hard work. One time, he walked five miles to pay back a nickel he had accidentally overcharged a customer. Mama was a fine Christian woman and a meticulous homemaker who had the biggest and most beautiful flower gardens in Concordia.

Fannie Lee Campbell managed a bed and breakfast across the street from the beautiful little Methodist church where Kathryn's radical conversion took place. Kathryn last saw Fannie when she visited the church in 1972. The minister was a young woman who happened to be singing *He Touched Me,* Kathryn's theme song. To her surprise, the pews, pulpit, and piano were the originals. Nothing had changed.

Kathryn was not well thought of by the congregation. Fannie said, "She is too religious. She used to dance and shake around like the rest of us when she was young." Perhaps, they remembered her as a prankster. Or, as Roland Petering suggests, they were envious.

According to Kathryn, she was expelled from school several times for trying to make people happy. She was always motivated by good. One day, she noticed a funeral with just a few people paying their respects. When you heard the church bells ringing and it was not Sunday, this meant someone had passed away. Mama would stop at the church and listen by the door. The ringing of the bell told you two things; you could determine by the sound of the bell which church it was, and the number of rings gave you an indication of the deceased's age. One ring was for a young person, two rings were for a middle-aged person, and three rings were for an elderly person. Naturally, the talk of the town was who died. This particular time, it was an elderly person. Upon hearing the bells, Kathryn told the students, "Let's go. We will make the dead happy and contribute to humanity." Kathryn was a born leader who found school to be confining. She assumed the other students felt the same way.

Emma's parents and Kathryn's grandparents, Grandpa and Grandma Walkenhorst, lived close by. Colonel Walkenhorst fought in the Civil War; he was well-educated and had a school named in his honor. Although he didn't need to work, he would travel occasionally selling encyclopedias. Kathryn's grandmother and mother visited each other frequently, which contributed to Kathryn's intellect, perhaps as much as the school where her grades sometimes faltered.

Once, Grandpa Walkenhorst asked Kathryn to pick out the ripest, reddest watermelon in the garden. Kathryn plugged every melon on every row and, after some time, proudly ran to announce the winner. She even talked her way out of her well-deserved punishment. Papa would say, "Don't accept something just because someone says so. You just have to find out for yourself and see if it is really like that."

At times, Kathryn's abundant energy and radiant health must have worn her poor mother out. Kathryn was rarely sick. Mama would bundle her up in a big coat, hat, and scarf before sending her off to school. She did not allow Kathryn to bring lunch like the other children. Mama had her come home because if she was gone all day, Kathryn became too wild to do anything with.

HARMONY, USA

In Concordia, Missouri, the Fair has always been the event of the year. Main Street is blocked off and transformed into a magical playground with carnival rides lining one side of the street and games played for prizes on the other. It is open twenty-four hours and provides food and entertainment for all ages. The biggest attraction is the parade. Some parades feature local dignitaries and beauty queens riding in convertibles, followed by homemade floats. It is wholesome entertainment that leaves you feeling like the good ole days in Concordia—referred to by many as Harmony, USA.

Naturally, this was one of Kathryn's favorite events of the year. She had a special friend, which allowed her to ride the merry-go-round and ferris wheel free of charge. Kathryn took full advantage, riding as much as she could between thirty-minute intervals where she checked in with Mama. Often, she would become dizzy or sick and would need to be lifted off the ride.

Mama entered the contests for flowers, baking, and fancy work. Many times, she won the blue ribbon, but she brought home the red ribbon on occasion. Almost everyone had something to enter. Kathryn had none of Mama's talents, but she did have her prized possessions: a banty rooster and a hen. Eager to participate, she ran home and carefully tucked them in a box, placed the box in her wagon, and made her way to Main Street. "Of course, they will win a blue ribbon, or at least a red. They're beautiful. Papa will be so proud." As she was pulling the wagon along, skipping and singing, a farmer hauling produce came out of nowhere and crossed the street in front of her. She screamed and spooked his horses. Kathryn ran out of the way, but the wagon and her prized possessions never made it to the fair.

Concordia was a perfect place to grow up. It offered security, freedom, community, and an outlet for a precocious young lady who might not have fared as well in the big city. Kathryn often told of her childhood, acknowledging the debt of gratitude she owed to her "wonderful big world" in Concordia, Missouri.

"I have always been proud of the fact that I was born in Concordia, where the people are still the best in the world, and they remain the very salt of the earth, with sound principles and morals that have remained unchanged with time. My early training did much to influence my life."

Harmony in the home, with loved ones, and in the community enhances one's natural gifts and allows the recipient to become all God intended. Kathryn was proud of her heritage. Papa and Mama both came from people of substance and dignity. She never wanted for anything and was given the freedom to follow her heart wherever it led.

In 1976, a monument honoring Kathryn was erected in the heart of town. It read:

KATHRYN KUHLMAN

Birthplace - Concordia, Missouri

Member of Baptist Church

Ordained Minister of the Evangelical Church Alliance

Known for Belief in the Holy Spirit

MYRTLE AND
MR. PARROTT

*M*yrtle promised Mama and Papa that she would send Kathryn back in time for school in the fall. They boarded the train and headed for the West Coast. Myrtle kept a close eye on her little sister; after all, she was only sixteen, and she had never been away from home.

Kathryn was glued to the window, taking in everything in this brand-new world. On a stop in Kansas City, Missouri, Kathryn spotted a red patent leather purse. Myrtle could tell she loved it and could not resist buying it for her. Just like Papa, Myrtle wanted to please her little sister. Before Myrtle married Mr. Parrott, it was Myrtle, not Mama, that Kathryn went to when she needed help. Myrtle missed her lively personality. She had prayed all night that God would touch Mama and Papa and allow Kathryn to go with them for the summer. Kathryn stayed close to Myrtle all summer; she worked hard at every task she was given. She was happy, very happy.

Found among her belongings was the journal Kathryn kept, telling of those days:

"I think if we go on with God and live the Christian life, then our school friends and all with whom we come in contact with will know that we are children of the King. God will reward us.

"One evening at a church service, so many people were hungry for the Word of God, but they hadn't had the chance to hear God's Word as we had. I remember so well one Sunday in a very small mining town in the state of Idaho when they asked us to sing and play to the people of that deserted-looking place. They didn't even have a church or a schoolhouse.

"At an evangelistic service in Wenatchee, Washington, the crowds were lining and relining the altar, crying for mercy. I noticed, from where I was sitting, a young man to whom my attention was drawn because of the wicked look upon his face. Later, in a testimony meeting, after he was saved, he said that he and two others were coming that night to steal.

"It is a wonderful sight to see the sick being prayed for and seeing them healed. I remember one especially. It was a crippled young man who walked. Jesus is the same yesterday, today, and forever. He is still healing the sick and making the blind see today. God is going on; let's go with Him.

"While traveling, I noticed everyone was thoughtful of the other person. They were not selfish; they worked together for the benefit of all. 'Thou hast been faithful over a few things, I will make thee ruler over many things' (Matthew 25:21)."

MYRTLE AND MR. PARROTT

God's blessing was molding and shaping Kathryn. The Parrotts had an extremely successful ministry. Myrtle was like Mama, strict and big on theology. Their meetings ran for several weeks with services each night. One six-week meeting in Atlanta was so successful that they had to bring in three or four trucks to carry away the wheelchairs and crutches that were no longer needed. Numerous people were slain in the Spirit.

Everett Parrott attended Moody Bible College in Chicago and sat under Dr. Charles Price, who had a well-known healing ministry at the time. Myrtle helped write the sermons that had heavy messages full of Bible language. Everett used her notes, and if he ran too long, Myrtle would pull on his coattail.

Healings were done at the end of the sermon. Attendees wrote and handed in three-by-five cards with their name, address, and need. They never knew when their names might be called, so attendance was guaranteed night after night. The Parrotts reached nondenominational people, not just backsliders. At each meeting, many were born again and healed.

At summer's end, Kathryn was to return to Concordia. She sat in a cold room with a steam heater crying. Her bags were packed, and Papa had sent her ticket. She sat, looking at her suitcase sitting in the entranceway, haunted by the nightmare of leaving this new life she dearly loved.

Mr. Parrott had taken to bringing Kathryn before the people to give her testimony. The crowds loved her, and she loved them back. He asked, "Kate, what is the matter?" He was the first one to ever call her Kate and only one other of the two who would get away with it. "Don't you want to go home?" he asked.

Without hesitation, she answered, "No! I want to be in the ministry."

Myrtle was relieved when Mr. Parrott replied, "Well, you don't have to." She was crazy about Kathryn and enjoyed the companionship. Kathryn was full of love, and it was a wonderful time for the two sisters who remained close for the rest of their lives.

Kathryn sent an anonymous friend a letter from Seattle, Washington, in 1924. She was in boarding school and wanted to hear all the latest happenings in Concordia. The letter told of her pranks—like climbing out the window with her roommate to roam around a little when the rules ordered them to remain in their rooms and study. Kathryn signed the letter, "your ole tormentor and tease, Katie." This was likely one of the two Bible schools where Kathryn was thrown out for sneaking out and meeting boys. Her behavior also caused her to fail a class in preaching.

Kathryn's estate contains an amazing study of the Parrott's ministry on the sawdust trail. Myrtle sent dozens of postcards and photos home to Mama. The sawdust trail was a literal term in those days of evangelism—describing the sawdust floors of the tents. Early photos Myrtle sent to Concordia show them traveling in a black Model T with running boards, spoke wheels, and a canvas top. Four large suitcases were strapped to the back. They would park in a scenic location in the countryside near a river or a lake. A "tent sheet" was stretched over the canvas top past the side of the car to form a protected area. That was the extent of their living quarters. There they would unload the supplies and cook over an open flame. If they were lucky, they would catch some fish for dinner. Mr. Parrott and Myrtle bathed in the river, but somehow they always looked well put together. They were a couple—attractive, young, and on fire for the Lord.

When they went into town, down came the canvas top. The luggage was stacked in the back seat to form a tall block. The block was covered by the tent sheet, so banners proclaiming "Jesus Saves, Baptizes with the Holy Spirit, and is Coming Again" acted as a moving billboard. And finally, an American flag hung on the rear of the vehicle. They worked hard, so it is no surprise their ministry had a special anointing.

By the time Kathryn joined them, they had moved on to bigger cities and were staying in hotels. Myrtle sent photographs from churches they ministered in, including Minnesota, Missouri, South Dakota, and Iowa. Eventually, Portland, Oregon became their headquarters, and although they still traveled a great deal, they had a place to call home.

The Parrotts adopted their daughter, Virginia, in 1942. In Myrtle's Will, dated 1958, she claimed her now ex-husband was spreading vicious lies about her, especially to her daughter.

Myrtle continued to be the only person Kathryn allowed to critique her preaching. And Myrtle never got over the fear that Kathryn might do something to embarrass the family. Still, Kathryn was loyal to the sister who helped lead her in the calling of her life. Kathryn looked after Myrtle from then until the day she died. Mr. Parrott never lost his desire to preach the Gospel. Decades later, in a nursing home in Santa Ana, California, he disappeared. They found him next door, in a shopping center, standing on top of a car and preaching with two suitcases open for the offering.

Showing his overly-driven nature, an elderly Everett Parrott entered the Department of Motor Vehicle Office (DMV) in Portland, Oregon, to take the driving test from hell. The DMV officer jumped out of the car and ran into the office, screaming, "My God! He is trying to kill me!"

When Kathryn was just sixteen, she became very distressed after one of their services, in which only a few came forward for salvation. Heading towards the car, Kathryn dropped her head on Myrtle's arm and broke down. She cried out, "I can't stand it. I just can't stand it. I can't stand it. Why didn't more people come?" She clung to Myrtle's arm as though she would never let go. Myrtle had not fully recognized the call of God on Kathryn's life until that night. By 1943, Kathryn's photo appeared in the Portland newspaper announcing her Sunday afternoon meeting. It was held at Norse Han, overshadowing that of Everett Parrott, who announced his Sunday morning radio broadcast.

The five years she spent with the Parrott's had a profound influence on Kathryn's future. She believed in miracles. She had witnessed the lame walk, the blind see, the deaf hear, and the greatest miracle of all, the salvation of lost souls that transforms lives forever.

GOD'S GIRLS

*W*omen have always been attracted to men of power, especially one on a stage or platform. Myrtle suspected some of the ladies were a little too enamored with Mr. Parrott. This distrust brought havoc to their ministry and separation to their marriage. Myrtle, Kathryn, and Helen Gulliford, their pianist, were left in Boise, Idaho, while Mr. Parrott went on to South Dakota. When Myrtle's somber preaching fell short, she decided to return to Mr. Parrott.

That is when providence stepped in. Kathryn's message of grace and love impressed a local Nazarene pastor who invited her and Helen to stay. Kathryn's call to the ministry was as definite as her conversion. The door was wide open for the two friends to step out in faith and begin their ministry.

They called themselves God's Girls, and for the next five years, Idaho became their frontier. They evangelized Emmett, Caldwell, Pocatello, and every small town in need of a spiritual revival. Many of the churches were closed. Kathryn was never shy about assuring them they had nothing to lose and everything to gain. Helen Gulliford was one of the best evangelistic pianists in the United States. Together, they were a powerful team, with Kathryn's dynamic preaching style and Helen's beautiful music. The two were inseparable. They slept anywhere there was a room, including a scrubbed-out turkey house. They were young and viewed no obstacle too great. Building their ministry was all that mattered.

Helen wrote the Parrotts, keeping them informed of their progress. She bragged that Kathryn preached like she was preaching to thousands. The Parrotts decided to surprise them. They drove up to find the church completely packed. Farmers were standing in the vestibule, engrossed in Kathryn's message of salvation. Helen was right.

Kathryn's face glowed as she looked to heaven with all the love her heart could hold—then she looked to the people. She spoke in long, husky syllables, the only woman who could make God a four-syllable word.

"Oh, just give your hearts to Jesus. He will set you free, take away your sin. Come into His glorious presence. Oh, God loves you so much. You will never be alone again. Come, Jesus says come."

As the farmers came forward, they crowded around the altar— heads bowed, hats in hand, weeping and repenting; the glory of God filled the place. Both Myrtle's and Mr. Parrott's eyes filled with tears as they exchanged knowing glances. "Look what God has done with little Kate." Kathryn had become more like their biological child. They had contributed to and encouraged her talents, so they took great pride and joy in witnessing the fruition.

Myrtle's only concern was that Kathryn would not get her theology straight. Kathryn didn't know what theology was, but she knew about salvation. People responded to her love.

"My first sermon was on Zacchaeus up a tree, and if anyone was up a tree, it was me. After about six sermons, I thought I had exhausted the entire Bible," Kathryn said.

When God calls you to do something, He gives you the way. Helen was a tremendous help and a mentor now that the Parrotts were not around. She was experienced, having previously worked in several large successful ministries. Kathryn trusted and respected Helen's opinion. It was a team effort. Kathryn developed a real hunger for the Word of God. She searched the Bible day and night. There was more than she could preach in a lifetime.

Kathryn's tenacity was unending. Twin Falls, Idaho, greeted God's Girls with open arms. The second evening, Kathryn slipped and fell on the ice, fracturing her leg. The incredulous physician told her not to stand on the weakened leg. Her perseverance to preach the Gospel never heeded his advice, fractured leg or not. She didn't miss a service. Every night, she would arrive smiling on crutches, her leg firmly held in place with a heavy cast.

A member of the congregation had been a nurse in World War I; she wrote, "I have seen courage and determination on the battlefields of France. I saw that same courage and determination last night in a young lady who stood on the platform preaching salvation." Photographs Kathryn kept of those days are like a replay of *It's a Wonderful Life*. Stamped "Rupert, Idaho, 1931," the photos show Kathryn and Helen sitting side by side under a big oak tree, petting a brown and white dog. Their similar stylish waves with a side part and matching white dresses almost make you wonder if they are sisters. Helen was only four years older than Kathryn but looked much more mature. Kathryn's handwritten memories on the photo express it best "Tender years notice our dresses are alike—ha."

It must have been part of the package early on. Another photo shows a Union Pacific train with Kathryn leaning out the window of the engineer booth. Helen stands on the top step just outside. Once again, they had on the same dress, a fitted sleeveless knit. Kathryn added a white hat, pearls, and gloves. It could double as a promotional picture of a singing duo. Young and fresh-faced with sweet, wholesome smiles and a friendly wave—anyone would feel pleased to have them visit their town.

And visit they did. For five years, God's Girls worked the Blazing Trail in Idaho for Christ. They had no staff, janitors, or prayer partners. They walked or rode buses, survived on day-old rolls, and lived by faith. They had the blessing of God, each other, and the love and respect of the many they helped along the way.

The two of them were as close as any friends could be. Both dedicated, talented young women united in the pursuit of the rarest of treasures—the human soul. Its value can be measured only by eternity. No gain is as great as a soul eternally saved. No loss is as sad as a soul eternally doomed. No joy so exquisite as to witness a soul's conversion.

By 1933, God's Girls had become a finely tuned evangelistic team. Their style and confidence were fully developed. Kathryn incorporated all her talent with Papa's business ability to bypass every norm in the ministry at the time.

It probably worked for her, not against her, that she was extremely attractive, tall, and thin, with sparkling blue eyes and naturally curly hair. Kathryn always looked even younger than she was. Her age was always one of her best-kept secrets.

Kathryn knew how to capitalize on it too. Her handbills featured a pretty, coquettish picture and the moniker, "Girl Evangelist." It certainly got the attention that drew them in.

Kathryn, in all her success, never changed. In her last years, an older gentleman came to Pittsburgh to photograph her going up the stairs to the pulpit. She didn't use the pulpit. She changed into a long, flowing gown like she wore in the California miracle services. She lifted her skirt as she took the steps. "That is it, Miss Kuhlman; lift your skirt a little higher. That is it." Kathryn stopped, turned her chin over her shoulder, and suddenly looked years younger, glowing and vibrant. She snapped her fingers, "Gotcha!" she said as she lifted her dress to show her still shapely legs. Kathryn looked over at her friend and winked. This could be quite effective.

Kathryn knew that once she got people in the door, it only took that one service to get them hooked. She maintained the same style in her preaching throughout her life. There was no hellfire and brimstone and no condemnation. Kathryn's concern was much like Christ's was when He walked the earth. Neither one was focused on punishing sinners, believing their lives of misery were punishment enough. Christ came to see that they had love, care, help, sympathy, and healing. Therein was the hope to draw them away from their sin, even if it took praying at the altar until the wee hours when the last person left.

Kathryn spoke with authority from a heart that was always full of love. She captured the hearts and touched the spirit of men and women.

Preparation is an important part of any undertaking—timing is another. The cities in nearby Colorado were beckoning God's Girls to the southwest. Kathryn was respectful of the money received during the difficult days of the depression. She was so conscientious that she was afraid of being criticized for having more than one dress. So, she had three dresses cut out of the same bolt of yellow material. At the last service in Pueblo, heads were bent in silent prayer. Suddenly, the stillness was broken by a drunken voice bellowing, "My God! Can't I ever get away from that yellow dress? I see it when I sleep at night. I see it all day long. It haunts me!" The service barely survived the unscheduled interruption.

By August, God's Girls had worked their way to Denver. Their first revival campaign was in a warehouse at 1733 Champa Street. The blessings of God were upon them from the beginning. All of Denver were noting and observing the results.

December brought a wonderful white Christmas. Unfortunately, Kathryn didn't make it home to Concordia. Denver had embraced them, and the New Year was full of promise.

THE FIRST SORROW

*K*athryn's greatest desire was for Papa to hear her preach. She looked forward to that day with great anticipation. Papa was still the greatest man in the world. "Oh, my Papa will be so proud of his little girl. It will be like when he would come to my recitations at church. Papa's big, sweet, adoring smile was all I could see."

Kathryn's ministry in Denver was growing, requiring any extra money she had for handbills and newspaper space. So, for the second time in her life, she did not make it home for Christmas.

Kathryn's home, for the time being, was at the St. Francis Hotel, room 416. The telephone rang at 4:30 p.m. on Tuesday, December 28, 1934. Kathryn recognized the voice on the other end. "Kathryn, your father has been hurt. There has been an accident."

"Is he badly hurt?"

"Yes."

"Tell Papa I am coming. I am leaving right now."

In a matter of minutes, Kathryn was blindly guiding her old maroon Ford V8 through the snow and ice in shock at what she had just heard. She didn't even feel the cold. She didn't feel anything. "I am on my way, Papa. I am on my way. I love you, Papa." Kathryn drove out of Colorado and into Kansas, where the weather got worse. She drove even faster, barely able to see through the drifting snow. There was very little traffic on I-40. The windshield wipers were like a clock, counting down every minute Papa had to wait for her. "I am coming, Papa. I am coming. Oh God, I feel so alone, so alone."

Kathryn looked at the gas gauge pointing to empty just as she saw the sign, "Kansas City, 100 miles." Concordia was only sixty miles past Kansas City. She had nothing to eat or drink since she left Denver and had only stopped for gas. "Yes, yes! I will be there in just a few hours now."

She found a telephone and called home. Aunt Bell answered. "Tell Papa I am almost home. I will be there as quick as I can."

Bell replied, "But Kathryn, didn't they tell you?"

"Tell me what?"

"Your father was killed. He was hit by a car, and he died almost instantly." Receiver in hand, almost frozen in body and mind, no words or emotion would come. Kathryn dropped the phone and slowly walked to the car. It was almost midnight, and her whole world had come to an end. Tears started to run down her face. Not Papa, not my Papa. She never dreamed anything could ever happen to Papa. Hadn't he always been there? When the kids were sick, he could not bear to go to work. He would stick his head in every few minutes and check on them, but Papa was never sick. He was the strongest, health-iest man in all of Concordia. Not Papa. No, it must be a mistake. Papa cannot be dead. It is just a dream, a bad dream. Driving was a nightmare. The white, icy roads were blinding as the headlights reflected the glare in her tear-filled eyes. Her body trembled as she struggled to keep the car on the road.

The moment she arrived, all her hopes were shattered. Her first love became her very first sorrow. Right there in the living room, where she and Papa had shared so many happy times, lay his body in a casket. Kathryn had to face something she had never faced before, but it would take time. The next two days, she hid away from the world all alone in her room. She never went in the living room to look, not once. She had never known sorrow. The funeral in the Baptist church was well attended. Joseph Adolf Kuhlman was well-known as a three-term mayor, but more so, he had the respect of the entire town from his life of integrity. Kathryn remembered not one word or song from the service. The only thing she heard after they cleared the church was, "Let's leave the family alone." One by one, Mama, Myrtle, Earl, and Geneva went forward to say goodbye. Only Kathryn was left. She stood up, walked to the casket, and laid her hand on Papa's shoulder; not his hand or his face, but the shoulder that had always been such a comfort. Their last real conversation had been the past summer in the backyard, standing by the clothesline: "Baby, remember when you were a little girl, and you would lay your head on my shoulder? You'd look up at me and ask, 'Papa, can I have a nickel?'"

"Yes, Papa, and you always did."

"Because that was what you asked for. If you had asked for my last dollar, I would have given you that too."

She laid her hand on his shoulder one last time, and at that moment, she knew beyond a shadow of a doubt that Papa was not there. It was only a black wool coat. This was her first real spiritual experience since her new birth at fourteen.

As they lowered his body into the grave, she came face to face with the reality of death; Papa was not there. It was only cold flesh. She knew the meaning of going beyond the grave. She was not looking into the ground but up to a Savior. She knew the meaning of, "if there be no resurrection of the dead, then is Christ not risen?" (1 Corinthians 15:13). With Papa's last heartbeat was the hope of the hereafter with Jesus Christ.

The power of the resurrected Christ was real to Kathryn. There were no more tears or heartache. Papa was still with her. In moments of weariness, alone in the dressing room, she would sense his presence, knowing he was proud of his little girl, proud of what she was doing, and she knew that she could always lay her head on the shoulder of her heavenly Father.

Whenever Kathryn came to Concordia, she would visit Papa's grave in the beautifully manicured old cemetery, where many of the Kuhlman family are laid to rest. It was never sorrow, but a joy that filled her heart; for she knew what an incredible gift she had been given, and that one day they would be together again. Kathryn seldom mentioned Papa's financial demise in the last few years of his life. She chose to remember happier times. The great depression had all but wiped him out. It was never clear just how the accident that killed him happened, whether or not the automobile hit him at all. Papa had walked into town to get Emma some eggs and slipped on the icy street as he headed home. The eggs broke, so rather than upsetting his wife, he turned around and went back for more. He had become hard of hearing, and his cap covered his ears to protect them from the cold.

Things were not the same. All he had worked for was just about gone. Emma was unhappy, Kathryn was long gone, and it must have seemed like there was not much to live for. Papa was a proud, strong-willed German who had lost his will to live.

Did he see the car, hear the car? Did he just want it all to end? Was he like so many others who had lost it all in the great depression? Joe Kuhlman was out of hope. He must have known something. He had written the will that likely left him defeated after a lifetime of hard work. He could only offer his four children one dollar each.

In Emma Kuhlman's journal, dated January 11, 1935, five dollars were paid to Dr. Shrasman, two dollars and fifty cents to Dr. Lissack, two dollars for the recording of a will that only left one dollar each to Myrtle, Earl, Kathryn, and Geneva. It appears that Mama immediately began renting rooms in the house to get by. The following year, her son, Earl, moved home and began paying rent and fixing up the house with his money. Earl probably missed Papa as much as Kathryn. Papa supported his love for the race cars he built in front of the garage. Earl raced at the State Fair. One car was so fast that it took two people— one to drive and one to pump the oil to keep the engine from burning up. No one would go along. Everyone was too scared, so guess who went. His elderly Papa—he was a man who had always given his all for his children.

A year-and-a-half later, not much had improved. Emma made out her will, directing her executor to purchase two separate grave markers—one for her late husband and one for herself. Papa didn't even have a marker. In a few years, Emma would have to sell the house and move. She lived in Concordia for the rest of her life. Emma died in 1958. Kathryn buried her next to Papa. The two markers Mama had requested were joined by a large one from Kathryn, reading "KUHLMAN."

Kathryn must have wondered about Papa's accident too. On rare occasions, and only with her closest friends, Kathryn confessed her fear that she was not sure if Papa was in heaven. She knew he was saved and baptized in the Baptist church of Concordia. What was it that made her wonder?

DENVER & DESIRE

*B*y 1935, in less than two years, the culmination of Kathryn's efforts brought a great reward. The lease was up on their temporary space, and God's Girls announced they would be moving on. They had made their mark on Denver, Colorado, in a campaign that attracted city-wide interest, backed by the Gideon organization and several city officials. Among them was Edmond Young, captain of the Denver Police Force. Captain Young personally endorsed their campaign, declaring it one of the greatest things to come to the city, especially for the youth. In Kathryn, they had found a real pastor—one full of love, whose dedication to God and the people touched even the hard-hearted.

A man in the congregation stood up and declared, "Young lady, you've been running long enough! We need you here. I will personally guarantee you a permanent location if you will stay." At twenty-eight years old, maybe it was time she settled down. It was rewarding to be a part of the community—see the families change, the babies born, and to go home to your bed. Kathryn prayed and agreed to stay.

The congregation went to work and built a new brick building called the Denver Revival Tabernacle, located at nineth and Acoma. Below the name on the side of the building read, "Kathryn Kuhlman, Evangelist." The real sign was the seventy-foot neon one on the roof, which read, "Prayer Changes Things." It certainly had for the city of Denver.

Opening services were a repeat of what became the standard anywhere Kathryn preached. The Denver Revival Tabernacle opened for the first time on May 30, 1935. The event was a glorious success; the two-thousand-seat space was filled. Several hundred people stood in the aisles and foyer. An additional one thousand people were turned away from the event. Their newsletter, Tabernacle Joy Bells, wrote the following about their founder: "Unusual ability, utter consecration to the cause of Jesus Christ, a love for God and souls, dogged determination, and an attractive personality."

Sentiments were high. The governor of Colorado, Ed Johnson, declared that her ministry did more for the youth in Denver than any one individual. His speech ended with a powerful endorsement that would come to life in the days ahead. "All power to the fine ladies who are carrying on the work here. I know their influence is growing, and as their influence grows and increases, this city, this state, and this nation—even this entire world—is going to gain advantage from their fine work."

Kathryn's sermon titles on world concerns drew the people out. "Is Hitler the Prophesied Antichrist?" "Ethiopia and Mussolini—What Does It Mean?" "When Will Russia Attack Japan?"

Kathryn's daily radio broadcast, *Smiling Through,* became a regular part of her ministry. Her radio show was what introduced many of her followers to her ministry. Later, she used her trademark opening line, like a warm friend in your living room; she asked, "Hello there, and have you been waiting for me?"

Kathryn's last choir director, Paul Ferrin, is married to the granddaughter of A. C. Anderson. During her five years in Denver, the A.C. Anderson family became Kathryn's family. They had never seen anyone like the founder of the Denver Revival Tabernacle. She had the greatest compassion of any human being; whether Mayor or derelict, Kathryn never left the altar until the last person was finished praying.

Mrs. Ferrin sang in Kathryn's services as a small child. "My parents thought those five years or so she spent in Denver were some of the happiest of her life. She had a great love for other people's children, and she would often take me by the hand, get my parents' permission, and take me places."

Kathryn didn't think she could preach unless the Anderson sisters sang. The youngest was Marjorie Ferrin's mother, and Kathryn made such an impact on the family that Marjorie named their first girl, Kathryn. Strangely enough, she was even born with red hair, unlike the rest of the family.

Neither Kathryn nor Helen was married, so Kathryn liked to refer to Mr. Anderson by saying to Thelma, "Could you tell our husband to go get the car." They traveled, worked, ate, and played together. Mrs. Anderson was a terrific cook who loved to share her gift with ministries. One night after the service, they set out for a picnic in the park. A police officer came and asked, "Miss Kuhlman, don't you know that the park is closed? It is late to be having a picnic." Kathryn smiled, and licking her lips, replied, "Oh, yes, officer, but these Swedish meatballs are the best you have ever had. Why don't you sit down and join us?" It was an officer who prayed, "Dear Lord, you know that we are thankful for this food just by the way we are going to dig into it and eat it!"

One day, Kathryn was running late, and in her rearview mirror, she saw flashing lights and a motion to pull over. She rolled down her window and said, "I am sorry, officer, but I am late for the radio station, and if you want to give me that ticket, you will have to go to the radio station too." The officer sat outside listening to her program. By the end, he was weeping. Kathryn did not receive a ticket that day. One family in Denver were notorious money-grubbers. When Kathryn saw them coming, she would grab little Marge Anderson and head for the backdoor, where they would skip down the alley and giggle at the great escape. For Marge's graduation, Kathryn brought her to Pittsburgh and offered to pay her way to Wheaton College. She stayed with Kathryn at her Fox Chapel home and is quite possibly the only person to ever tell Kathryn no. Marge opted to go to Central College instead.

Kathryn came to Memphis when Paul and Marjorie Ferrin's daughter was twelve years old. Kathryn skipped a whole generation when she announced to the people, "I have a namesake here today, and I'd like you to come up. You have such a heritage. I can still remember those steaming vegetables and that Swedish chocolate cake your grandmother made for me in Denver." To say it was really little Kathryn's great grandmother may have stirred calculations about Kathryn's true age.

Kathryn's estate includes numerous mementos from the days in Denver that she held so dearly. The Tabernacle Joy Bells newsletters are held together with brass brads, and the photographs of the Anderson family have handwritten sentiments. The original corporation papers for the Denver Revival Tabernacle list Myrtle and Everett Parrott as Kathryn's partners, and a contract for an Everett grand piano for Helen is signed by Kathryn. By far, the greatest memento is her original Certificate of Ordination from 1936. After years of preaching, Kathryn Kuhlman was an ordained minister.

Evangelists from around the country put the Denver Revival Tabernacle on their schedules. One day, a tall, dark, and handsome preacher came to town. With deep, soulful eyes, a chiseled jawline, and a dimpled smile, he had the looks of a leading man. Burroughs A. Waltrip was a nice enough package to make the ladies swoon, young and old alike. He was slick, a sharp-dressed man with an eye for the best.

Kathryn might have been able to resist for she had seen handsome men before, but this fiery southerner was a charismatic charmer with all the right words and moves. She was naive. He was convincing. Burroughs played on her sympathy with his story of an abandoning wife who refused to live with him or support his call. In truth, his marriage was a bit rocky.

Jessie Johnson met Burroughs Waltrip in Louisiana at a Baptist youth revival when he was only seventeen. They were married seven years later. She was a dutiful preacher's wife who never complained about the six-nights-a-week services. She worked days to help out and uprooted her family several times to follow him. By 1936, Burroughs Jr. was eight, and Billy was six. The children needed a solid foundation, and Jessie decided to settle down in Austin, Texas, in the home of her parents. She could not travel with him any longer. Jessie was weary of the never-ending financial crisis and distrustful of Burroughs's roving eye, but she had no intention of ending their marriage. It is a shame that Jessie and Kathryn never spoke. Even if they had, nothing Jessie could have said would hold a candle to a master of seduction like Burroughs A. Waltrip.

Burroughs Waltrip Jr. had two letters to remember his father by. One from Denver is dated October 19, 1936. It starts with "My Dear Son" and is full of loving, encouraging words, ending with "lots and lots of love, Daddy." The younger son, Billy, was with his father at the time this letter was written, and in the letter, Daddy was also bragging about his well-mannered and helpful child. Billy was to start school the first of the year, so Jessie and Burroughs Jr. took the train to Denver and picked up Billy. Jessie knew something was wrong. Burroughs never touched her. Burroughs Jr. and Billy never saw their father again.

It is no wonder his son, Burroughs Jr., "never took any of his protestations of love and caring seriously. Even at the tender age of eight and earlier, I could see the hypocrisy in the man. I never felt he even liked me, let alone loved me. I think he did care for Billy, not enough to be a decent man and stay with and support his family, of course. Fame, and hopefully attendant riches, was more important to him than anything else."

That very month, Burroughs Waltrip was smiling on the front cover of the Tabernacle Joy Bells with the lead article *"Victory."* "How much needed, how much desired? The enemy of our souls is powerful beyond our knowledge." How profound!

Helen fell for him first, but Burroughs Waltrip had his eye on Kathryn, the star of the show—the young, beautiful, and vibrant founder of the Denver Revival Tabernacle. His wheels were probably spinning at the very thought of what they could do as a team. Kathryn was resistant. She was as protective of her ministry as people were of her. She never dated or spent time alone with men, but she was like many women. Love is a powerful motivator. People in love do crazy things; reason flies out the window, and emotion steps in.

Your first kiss, the first time you hold hands, the first embrace, the moment when you look in each other's eyes and know that you have never known love like this before—this is what Kathryn was up against. So, he had been married; he was getting a divorce. Every human being makes mistakes. He was a fabulous preacher and a wonderful guy, always with a great story and a greater dream. Kathryn related to him on so many levels. Why would God deny her love? Of course, it was right. Then, why did it feel so wrong? Kathryn had never been exposed to the likes of Burroughs Waltrip. Love is blind, and she only saw a wonderful man of God—with a ministry larger than hers. His church was in Mason City, Iowa. Unlike the conservative Denver Revival Tabernacle, Burroughs' congregation worshipped at Radio Chapel, a unique church in America. The magnificent art deco structure was built for seventy thousand dollars, an amazing amount for the 1930s. Radio Chapel seated seven hundred in upholstered opera-type chairs designed by the "Louisiana Pulpiter" himself. The stage looked more like a high-tech set. The pulpit disappeared with the touch of a button. Blinking lights across the ceiling resembled the stars in heaven. Music was provided on a grand piano or organ with an automatic screen that dropped down to project the words of the songs. It was pure Hollywood, and so was the dashing Burroughs A. Waltrip. Today the building is a television studio.

He was quite adept and far ahead of his time when it came to raising money. He was a smooth manipulator. Today, Burroughs Waltrip would probably have his own television network. Even the sharpest businessmen were no competition. If Burroughs Waltrip went after your money, life, or wife, you would have to watch out.

Kathryn and Burroughs frequently ministered in each other's churches. By 1938, they were so in love the inevitable became the course of discussion. Kathryn kept the Western Union telegrams Burroughs sent her to the Louis Joliet Hotel. At the time, Kathryn and Helen were leading a revival at the People's Tabernacle in Joliet, Illinois. Kathryn's program from that meeting described it: "The Tabernacle auditorium is now being crowded in these nightly services, where music, song, and sermon blend in the getting of the Gospel to the hearts of men. Over thirty converts have been won to Christ, and the campaign has just started. Miss Kuhlman, who has attracted widespread attention in various cities in the west, is the sole winner of tremendous merit. Miss Helen Gulliford has no peer as an evangelistic pianist. We are highly fortunate to have them with us for this campaign. The nightly ovations that frequently break into cheers to greet Miss Kathryn Kuhlman, noted girl evangelist, at the nonde-nominational revival, where enthusiasm and increased spiritual inter-est are running high."

Burroughs was in Mason City, reveling in his success. Life could only get better if he could close Kathryn on marriage. By now, Kathryn had taken to calling him Mr. This was what Myrtle called Mr. Parrott. Its significance can only be that she looked upon him as the love of her life, the one she would be joined to in holy matrimony forevermore. Even so, she had reservations.

8 September 1938 4:12 p.m.

Ordered tux for 18th. Am marrying heathen in
blue, Mr.

The subtext would be Kathryn as the heathen in blue. It does not
sound too good. Divorce was not looked upon as it is today, especially
for a minister. Most likely, Kathryn was afraid she would always be
seen as the heathen who broke up his marriage.

9 September 1938 9:44 a.m.

Darling, put our love first. Please, I want
you to.

Mr.

Again, Kathryn had reservations. There was something else
she wanted to put first: God, the church, her faithful followers, and
her conscience.

9 September 1938 10:25 a.m.

Arrive in Joliet tonight. Discuss plans if
you wire yes immediately.

Mr.

Kathryn had not said yes. All the pursuit was on Mr.'s end. Could
it be that the suave and confident Burroughs A. Waltrip had made a
fatal mistake, and something he hadn't counted on had taken place?
Maybe for the first time in his life, he was actually in love. And how

could he resist? Kathryn was an excellent catch. She was independent, strong, savvy, successful, and delightfully engaging. Together they looked like the ultimate couple.

```
10 September 1938 10:41 a.m.

Very enthusiastic. Am planning first wedding
shower.

Must have you.

Mr.
```

It appeared his dream had come true. She had not said yes, yet he had ordered a tux and was planning his first wedding shower. You can see the pattern: he pursues, she resists.

```
10 September 1938 4:01 p.m.

Decision unanimously rejected. Stop Advice
wiring affirmative by Western Union at once.

Love, Mr.
```

His earlier telegram was not in response to an affirmative from Kathryn. Her telegram said no. Unfortunately, no was a word that Mr. did not understand. It is doubtful he had heard it very many times. The chase was on.

Kathryn had a heart for children her entire life. She met Burroughs' children. Had she known the truth regarding him filing for divorce, not paying child support, never seeing his children, and leaving Jessie holding the bag with the bills he had run up, there was no way he would have gotten this far. She had not saved her heart to give to one without conscience.

Against the advice of absolutely everyone, including her Denver family, the A. G. Andersons, on October 18, 1938, Kathryn, Helen, and her closest friends, Lottie Anthony and Ina Fooks, headed for Mason City. On the way, Helen decided she could not be a party to this union. She and Lottie stayed behind in Des Moines at the Brown Hotel. Kathryn and Ina went on to Mason City.

Mr. was waiting with bells on. On the marriage license, Kathryn's age was stated as twenty-five, six years below her actual age, thirty-one. His mother, Mrs. Lila Waltrip, or "Mumsy," was to be his witness. Even his mother was trying to stop this travesty. Everything was wrong. Kathryn was sick to her stomach. She knew to be in God's will is to be in peace. That little voice turned into a bigger one, and during the wedding, she was overcome and passed out. It was almost midnight before they left Radio Chapel. With only a few presents, the celebration was more like a wake.

Kathryn gave the telegrams, marriage license, and certificate of divorce, along with other critical pieces that accounted for in those days, to her trusted, extended family, Gene and Ruth Martin. She sent Gene to Denver to interview Lottie Anthony and Ina Fooks on tape. These tapes were kept in a safety deposit box in both of their names.

What Kathryn avoided in life, she wanted to be told in death. She was a master at getting around the issue of her marriage and divorce. She didn't believe it should make any difference if she was married or not. Still, she knew many of her followers might object. When pressed with dates obtained from legal evidence, she would simply defend herself by saying, "I never took my marriage vows. Do you know what happened? I will tell my vows. That is the truth, so help me, God. If I signed an application for a marriage license, it was brought to me for my signature. I do not remember signing any such thing. He changed, and I refused to live with him. I haven't seen him since."

In her later years, she frequently reflected on her past. Kathryn had three big loves in her life. They were the ones who shaped her into a woman of extreme complexities and enormous endurance. No one was ever able to keep up with Kathryn regardless of age or sex. She never felt she was God's first choice. He called many men, but few answered the call.

She had sacrificed the one thing most women aspire for: the pursuit of love. She had never had a boyfriend. Her dedication to her call left no room for personal relationships. To be a woman in ministry during her lifetime was a rarity. To lead large congregations in your twenties was almost unheard of, regardless of sex. What most would consider a sacrifice, Kathryn aspired for.

We must be careful what we say and use wisdom before we speak. Words are like seeds; you put them in the universe, and they grow. At the little Methodist church in Concordia, when Kathryn announced that she was going to find a good-looking preacher and marry him, the seeds were planted.

She was exhausted, and her head was spinning. "I knew better. What have I done? I should never have married a divorced man." They left the church, and Mr. drove Kathryn to the elaborate newlywed suite he had carefully chosen. He parked in front and went inside to check in. Kathryn slid over and quickly sped away. When Mr. came out to carry his bride over the threshold, his bride and Buick were gone. Mr. panicked. What could have happened? He called the police.

"No, we cannot take a missing person's report this soon." Finally, he hired the Pinkerton Detective Agency to find her.

Kathryn had driven back to Helen and Lottie at the Brown Hotel in Des Moines. She knew she had made a mistake and asked for their support in explaining to the Denver congregation that she would get an annulment. Pinkerton tracked Kathryn to the Muleback Hotel in Kansas City. Mr. wasted no time in getting there. Once again, he charmed his way back into Kathryn's heart. They drove to Denver, hoping and praying that together they could resolve the adamant refusal of the congregation to accept their marriage. What they faced was a grave disappointment. The Denver Revival Tabernacle was in a terrible uproar and would not accept their founder marrying a divorced man. Kathryn had no choice but to give up the church she had worked so hard for. The congregation she had taught the power of love and forgiveness to had none for her. They were too caught up in legalism and judgment. Instead, they essentially drove her right into the arms and control of Burroughs A. Waltrip.

Kathryn was devastated and heartbroken. "I cannot take the blame. It was a shaky situation anyway, but I should not have gotten involved with a man getting a divorce. I knew better than that, but I've been loved by the greatest, and I've loved back in return. What more can you expect?"

Yes, they had all tried to talk her out of it, but wasn't she entitled to love? At first, people blamed her for breaking up his marriage, but Mr. told them repeatedly that it was already on the rocks. Marrying a divorced man was a stigma beyond what she was prepared to face.

The newlyweds returned to Radio Chapel, where Mr. announced that Kathryn would be preaching on Friday nights. Much of the congregation were women. The news of their handsome pastor's marriage was not exactly greeted with warm wishes. In one fell swoop, Kathryn had gone from leading her church to being a Friday night attraction in his. Many times, she would sit behind him on the stage and weep. It was his pulpit, and all too soon, she realized he didn't plan to share it much. She felt embarrassed over the difficulty she had accepting her new role as a wife.

Burroughs may have been trying to protect Radio Chapel by keeping Kathryn in the background. Too much change too soon might bring about the same result as in Denver. He encouraged her to enjoy being a housewife for a while. She could cook and clean, shop, and take care of him. It was only temporary, and she could catch up on some much-needed rest.

As a couple, they were doomed from day one. Anytime you consciously go against God's will, it is only a matter of time until it all comes tumbling down. Six months later, after a long struggle to keep up with the finances of Radio Chapel, Mr. lost his church. Two well-known, talented ministers, each with their successful churches, decided to go against all they knew to be right.

Although their closest friends and family members tried to warn them, they didn't listen. They charted their course into the desert. What must they have felt when they had to leave Mason City, Iowa, with only their two new automobiles and suitcases? Embarrassment, shame, defeat, loss, regrets? When it seemed nothing could get worse, it did. Meetings they booked, together or separately, were never a for sure event and, on some occasions, were canceled when they arrived. Nothing travels faster than bad news. Sometimes, one would hide out in the hotel room while the other ministered. Mr.'s reputation of mishandling finances had finally caught up with him. Kathryn had her cross to bear as the wife of a divorced man—one who left his first wife and children to marry her.

There were good times. Despite it all, they loved each other. The lack of work and money gave them the free time neither had much of in the past. They were able to enjoy the simple things: picnics by the lake, walks in the park, holding hands as they window-shopped, and breakfast in bed. Love is supposed to be a splendid thing; unfortunately, Kathryn felt a heavy weight on her heart, and tears were ever so near.

She loved Mr. more than anything in the world, even more than God. She worshipped and adored him despite all she knew to be true. He was the love of her life, and deep down, she knew it was mutual, but God had never released her from her original call. Mr. seemed threatened by her need to preach, while Kathryn grieved by her need to do so.

After only three years, Kathryn began spending time in Portland with Myrtle, in Denver with friends, and anywhere she could to escape the control he inflicted against her preaching. In answer to the probable biblical examples that he gave her against women in the pulpit, she wrote a book titled, *To Speak or Not to Speak* by Kathryn Kuhlman Waltrip. It is a passionate plea, thoroughly researched, listing every example in the Bible to dispute his claim. You sense this is something she had been working on for quite a while. Here is a verse she uses, followed by a short excerpt from the book:

"And it shall come to pass in the last days, saith God, I will pour out my Spirit upon all flesh: and your sons and your daughters shall prophesy...and on my servants and on my handmaidens I will pour out in those days of my Spirit; and they shall prophesy" (Acts 2:17–18).

"God is to call whom He chooses, man or woman, to "tell forth" the message of salvation to a lost and sin-cursed world. And with that world reeling and rocking in the throes of violent death, it would seem that all who loved God and loved souls would rejoice in the fact that anyone, even if it be a woman, is lifting up the Christ under the blessed inspiration of the Holy Spirit, and, like her sister of a bygone dispensation, is being heard because of the power of her utterances; and priceless souls are being won to a saving knowledge of the Lamb of God."

In her despair, Kathryn formulated a secret of her success, which set her apart: "Since by her very nature, her message should be tender, compassionate, and appealing, a woman preacher must be specially anointed of the Holy Spirit to bring her message. It is a marked prerequisite for the woman who would obey the Lord in her ministry. Every message must be saturated with prayer."

DEATH, RESURRECTION, & ACCEPTANCE

*M*any have run away to Los Angeles, California. It is an easy place to get lost. Mostly everyone is from somewhere else, and there is little of the accountability one faces in his or her hometown. You can be whoever you want to be in Los Angeles, and nobody cares. They are in their little world, and neighbors rarely speak to one another.

The Waltrips rented an apartment in Los Angeles in 1946. Mr. was out of town preaching one weekend when Kathryn had an experience that returned her to the hands of God. There was no sleep that Friday night, only sweat and tears from the worst struggle Kathryn had ever faced—that of releasing the man she had loved. In her darkest hour, she cried out, "My God, I have failed you. I have lost my way. Forgive me, Lord, and forgive my Mr. Keep him in the shadow of your wings. Heavenly Father, you have lifted your anointing off of me, and I cannot bear it anymore. I must have it. Take not thy Holy Spirit from me." The following day her confirmation came:

"I remember walking down a dead-end street and realized my life was a dead-end street. It was four o'clock on a Saturday afternoon. It was at that time and in that place that I surrendered myself to the Holy Spirit. There are some things too sacred to talk about, but I said it out loud. 'Dear Jesus, I surrender all. I give it all to you. Take my body. Take my heart. All I am is yours. I place it in your hands.'

I will only say that at that moment, with tears streaming down my face, God and I made each other promises. He knows that I will be true to Him, and I know that I will be true to Him. At that moment, I yielded to God in body, soul, and spirit. I gave Him everything. Then I knew what the Scripture meant about taking up your cross. A cross is a symbol of death. That afternoon, Kathryn Kuhlman died, and when I died, God came in—the Holy Spirit came in. That was the first time I realized what it meant to have power."

Kathryn had struggled for years, trying to rationalize what she knew all along. She was not able to be the wife he needed. She was never meant to be. She felt deep guilt over her rebellion against God and all those who loved her. She was tired of trying to justify herself. Burroughs returned home to the worst news of his life. Kathryn had come to the place where she had to make a choice. By remaining with him, she would only hurt both of them. They talked at length. "It is not for lack of love. It is consecration. You know how much I love you, but we were wrong, and I have to make it right." Finally, he agreed. "Okay, Kathryn, if that is the way you want it, I am not going to fight you. I won't force you to be my wife. I love you, and I promise to leave you alone." Somehow, in all the uncertainty of the last few years,

Kathryn was the solid rock he could count on. He begged her not to go, but there was no turning back. They held each other tight that night, both knowing it was their last night together.

At the Los Angeles train terminal, Mr. tearfully appealed to her one last time. "Kate, you get on that train, and you will never see me again. I promise you." In a daze, they gazed into each other's eyes. There were no words left to say, no tears left to cry—only the hard, cold truth that it was never meant to be. As the train pulled away, Mr. blew the last kiss she would ever receive from the only man she was ever in love with. It was the hardest thing Kathryn had ever done, for she loved him more than life itself and, for a time, even more than she loved God. Once again, Kathryn was leaving town with only her suitcase and a one-way ticket to Franklin, Pennsylvania. In Franklin, she would again have the opportunity to preach on her own. She was back on track.

Kathryn made her greatest decision, her greatest consecration. She had loved deeply, but now she made a choice for the Master, a life of service, vowing to put Him first. She spoke of her death-to-self experience in many of her messages. "No one in the Bible was perfect either. From just stupid enough to believe the Holy Spirit is the greatest power in the world. It is not by might or power but by His Spirit; He has to choose the most unlikely things in the world, those of the foolish to confound the wise and the weak to confound the mighty. No flesh should glory in His presence. The Holy Spirit will not share His glory with any person. The minute a man or woman wants to share the glory, the power is lifted off that ministry.

To be in the perfect will of God costs much, but it is worth the cost. The true cost is everything. That is the price you pay. Kathryn

Kuhlman died a long time ago. I can tell you the day, the hour; I can take you to the spot. But you see, for me, it was easy. I had never forgotten from whence I came—a little crossroads town in Missouri with a population of 1,200. I was born without talent, unattractive, with no hair, only red fuzz. One day I just said, "Wonderful Jesus, I have nothing, nothing but my love. That is all, but I love you with all my heart, and I offer you my body as a living sacrifice. Jesus, I don't have a thing. If you can take nothing and use it, I offer you that nothing. All I can give you is my love. I give you every ounce of strength in my body. If any man loveth me, let him take up his cross. In a real sense, Kathryn Kuhlman died that day."

All she had was the suit she wore, her pulpit dress, and her Bible. Kathryn's memory of the ride to Franklin, Pennsylvania, was a blank. She sat, staring out the window, lost in the dichotomy of the transition—sorrow and heartbreak to peace and purpose. Haunted by the pleading look in Mr.'s eyes when he said, "You will never see me again," she could not help but wonder if he was planning to do away with himself.

It would all be so much easier had she not finally faced the truth. The truth was that both could not have ministries and that she would never realize her power. Mr. was like most men in the 1930s and 1940s. The man was the boss, and the little woman took a back seat. Mr. ran the show, and Kathryn could not handle it. She never had plans to be a homemaker.

Kathryn had seen the women hanging all over him. She came to understand what Myrtle had been through all those years with Mr. Parrott. He was married when he chased her. Who is to say he might not do the same again? There were no certainties with Mr. and every certainty in God's Wsord. She had made a grave mistake, but God never makes mistakes. "He does not need golden vessels; He does not need silver vessels. All He asked for is a yielded vessel." She was poured once again into another vessel.

Waltrip v. Waltrip, correspondence from Dr. Waltrip's attorneys Taylor and Gubler of Las Vegas, Nevada, dated January 27, 1947, charged that "Mrs. Waltrip commenced proceedings for divorce against him approximately five years ago. Since that time, he had been extremely upset because of the marital situation of the parties, and his earnings had reduced to a negligible amount. During this period, his wife was continuously active in her profession as an evangelist.

The present divorce proceedings were motivated entirely by the fact that Mrs. Waltrip, because of her career, refused to live with Dr. Waltrip and that, consequently, there is no possibility of the two of them living together as husband and wife. Dr. Waltrip was willing to secure a divorce and thereby make it so that there would never be any occasion for Mrs. Waltrip to be embarrassed by marriage. This seemed to be Mrs. Waltrip's desire at all times for the reason that she constantly has, since the marriage, insisted on carrying all of her work under her maiden name."

To protect her, the divorce was filed in the name Johanna Kathryn Waltrip. On April 3, 1947, the divorce was final, and Kathryn's maiden name was restored. Leaving Mr. behind, divorce in hand, Kathryn wept for the pain she had brought to his life. She had forgiven him completely and held only herself accountable. She loved the unlovely, with a gift not only to bring out the best in others, but she also thought the best of them. For a time, Burroughs A. Waltrip was a bright star in the Kingdom. For the rest of her life, she would wonder if he was okay. Had he gone overseas to teach? Why did she never hear of him preaching anywhere? Was he alive?

Whenever Kathryn heard the whistle of a train or the clacking on the track, she remembered that ride from Los Angeles to Franklin always—what flashed before her eyes was the look on his face. She was haunted by the memory that would bring her to her knees, tearfully praying for his safety. "No one will ever know the price I paid for this ministry. It cost me everything." He was the one and only man she ever loved. There were many opportunities to date as her fame and success grew. There were wonderful close friends who knew the great loss she felt. She would cry soft tears—sometimes even for hours—lamenting, never regretting the love of her life.

Twenty years later, she was known around the world. The Kathryn Kuhlman Foundation was buzzing in February of 1970 with the usual stacks of mail. Maggie Hartner was at her desk when Kathryn happened to walk behind her. She glanced down at a pretty pink Hallmark Valentine card with two hearts sitting in purple flowers. As Maggie opened the card, she realized the moment of truth she so desperately needed had finally arrived. All she saw was the signature "All my love, always. Mr." No valentine in the entire world could have meant as much.

Kathryn asked, "Where's the envelope?" Maggie had already thrown it in the trash. Kathryn dropped to her knees and dumped the trash can on the floor, scrambling for an address. Trash was flying as she searched for the one with the handwriting only she would recognize. "Yes, oh God, here it is." She turned it back and forth, not willing to accept that there was no return address, but there was a postmark. "Loesch, come quick. I want you to do something for me. Go here immediately and find him!" Loesch was a devoted employee who had a miraculous healing in one of Kathryn's meetings. There was nothing he would not do for Kathryn.

On a plane to Hawaii, Kathryn started crying and, with trembling hands, pulled the card out of her purse. She handed it to Ruth Martin, her confidant. "All these years, you just don't know. God has answered my prayers. What if I hadn't happened to walk around at that very moment? Oh, thank you, thank you, Lord. I've been vindicated. When Loesch finds him, you and I are going to fly there. I don't want to speak to him. I just want to see him walking down the street and see if he still walks tall and straight and handsome as he did before. We will make it an overnight trip. I am not going to tell you where it is, but we are going to do it."

Ruth was always able to make Kathryn laugh. She could see now was a good time to lighten things up, and Ruth and Kathryn started in. "You know, Ruth, I can see why Gene loves you so much. You're exasperating, but I was loved by the best."

Ruth grinned as she said, "Oh, so now you are an authority on marriage?" Kathryn had nicknames for her favorite people.

"Oh, squirt, you cannot picture me with an apron and kids? I am married to the Lord. I just never wanted another man. He was the best. I am satisfied in my mind and heart with all of it. The two ministries just would not work."

Ruth opened the valentine; Kathryn later gave it to her to help tell this story. The inscription on it, still in perfect condition today, reads:

THE HANDMAIDEN

This valentine is bringing
My warmest thoughts your way

Along with special wishes
For a very happy day
For at "remembering" times
like Valentine's Day
And through the whole year, too,
I spend some very pleasant hours
Just "remembering" you.
All my love, always, Mr.

All of Loesch's efforts were in vain. By now, Mr. was an expert in obscurity. The postmark was not from the town where he lived. Kathryn and Ruth never got to take that trip. Knowing Kathryn's heart, Ruth saw it as a blessing. That love, that old feeling, would have been rekindled.

Burroughs Allen Waltrip seemed to have disappeared off the face of the earth. The few known details are as follows:

Although his children, Burroughs Jr. and Bill, never saw or heard from him again after their trip to Denver in 1936, Jessie Waltrip saw him in 1945 for the last time at his mother's funeral in Louisiana. His brother, with a background of ill will, told Jessie that Burroughs had died in prison in California for embezzling money from a woman. She finally told his sons in the late eighties. Jessie was a real Christian and an outstanding mother who raised two fine sons. She never remarried, and it is a tragedy that she went to her grave not knowing the truth. Nobody bothered to check the archives of the California prison systems. Burroughs Allen Waltrip was never in prison in California, not the state or the federal.

The same year Kathryn received the valentine, which shows promise that Mr. did get back on track. A family friend told his younger son that they had seen a billboard in Los Angeles for a revival held by Burroughs A. Waltrip—so close, yet so far. He probably sat incognito at the Shrine Auditorium, proud of his precious Kate. Now it was he who sat in the background, understanding how she must have felt.

Numerous hours of research have been spent trying to find out what did happen to the once-promising evangelist. There seems to be no trace of him. Maybe that is just what he wanted. Some never recover from a great loss. He had the world in his hands and let it slip right through his fingers. In his possible shame and embarrassment, he gave up so much—his family, friends, and purpose.

Still, his contribution lives on. Kathryn Kuhlman's only love was a great gift. Burroughs Allen Waltrip was the catalyst of Kathryn's death to self experience. That one act led her to her third and final love—the one in which she would become the vessel used to save and miraculously heal thousands: the Holy Spirit.

FRESH ANOINTING

*F*ranklin, Pennsylvania, was the beginning of the ministry that made Kathryn Kuhlman unique. In her time in the desert, her surrender, and hours on her knees in prayer, she came into the greatest revelation of her life. It would change her relationship to God, the church, and legions of followers who were searching for a closer relationship with God. Kathryn Kuhlman deserves a tremendous amount of credit for bringing the Holy Spirit to the forefront. No longer was she a minister with a message of salvation and healing. She was a yielded vessel to the person of the Holy Spirit, an oracle of God through the miracles in the ministry of Jesus—who would visit this earth again. Yes, there have been others with tremendous healing ministries, but in time, Kathryn alone operated in the unique gift of the word of knowledge.

When Kathryn Kuhlman died to herself, she was baptized in the Holy Spirit. It was an electrifying experience, impossible to explain—a touch from the hand of God that led to an unquenchable desire to know Him more. Shortly after she arrived in Franklin, Pennsylvania, Kathryn began teaching a series on the Holy Spirit when the first miracle occurred. No one was more surprised than Kathryn. The following evening, a woman in the congregation stood up. "Pardon me, Miss Kuhlman, please. May I give a word of testimony regarding something that happened last evening when you were preaching? While you were preaching on the Holy Ghost, telling us that in Him lay the resurrection, I felt the power of God flow through my body. I knew instantly and definitely that I had been healed. So sure was I of this that I went to the doctor today, and he confirmed that I was healed." The tumor was gone.

Kathryn could relive that which was especially meaningful, as though it were happening for the first time. This first miracle never failed to amaze her, just as the thousands that followed. For the rest of her life, people from around the world flocked to her services. Her level of surrender in her relationship to the Holy Spirit has not been seen since.

Kathryn didn't call out generic healings. The Holy Spirit called them specifically through her. "There's a woman in the second balcony. You have a heart condition. God is healing you now. Come claim your healing." She could describe the person and the physical need, sometimes even down to their clothing. The people of Franklin fell in love with Kathryn just as they had in Denver, and a two-week engagement turned into four years. After two years, a dispute over Kathryn's right to the Tabernacle's use left M.J. Mahoney with an empty building. Kathryn's congregation found a new location for their preacher lady. The new place of worship was an abandoned roller rink in nearby Sugar Creek. Her faithful followers saw their reward in the renovated facility that seated two thousand. Within six months, the $30,000 mortgage was paid off, and the people owned the building.

Her radio program became a favorite of the locals and those in nearby Pittsburgh. People were encouraging her to move to Pittsburgh, but Kathryn would tell them, "These people took me in and loved me. There is no way I could leave them. The roof would have to cave in before I left."

Pittsburgh must have been her destiny. On Thanksgiving Day in 1950, under the accumulation of a massive snowfall of forty inches in three days, the roof of Faith Tabernacle caved in.

Kathryn arrived in Franklin; she rented a little room in the attic of the Businesswoman's Club with one window. A photo of her standing in front shows a happy, relaxed, and lovely Kathryn. It is very hard to believe, but she is thirty-nine years old. She met two women God would use to bless her life. Both were wealthy widows. They were Jessie Vincent and Eve Conley. Jessie worked at the bank. Eve's husband, a successful businessman and a gambler, had recently died. After his death, Eve stayed with Jessie. The three of them became friends. Eve was an excellent cook. The two women invited Kathryn to join them for Thanksgiving dinner. Kathryn loved their company, but they were not Christians in the full sense. They were very earthly.

After dinner, Kathryn seized the opportunity and told them she was on a higher mission than turkey and dressing. She shared her testimony and her Bible, pointing out Scriptures proving Jesus Christ was the promised Messiah, the Son of God. Before Kathryn left that evening, all three women got on their knees, and Kathryn led them into the Kingdom of heaven.

Kathryn moved into Jessie's big house shortly thereafter. She found a home and a family in Franklin. The people embraced her.

Jessie and Eve treated her as though she were their very own. Jessie died shortly thereafter and left everything to her dear friend, Eve.

Eve had bought a smaller house near the Tabernacle. She was a refined woman who had traveled extensively in the circles Kathryn hadn't yet dreamed of. She became Kathryn's mentor in the finer things of life. Up to this point, much of Kathryn's adult life had been spent scrimping and saving just to get by. Even in the good times, her existence would not be considered a lifestyle of the rich and famous.

Eve provided a home with elegant table settings, fine food, and complete adoration for her protege, Kathryn. Eve inherited Jessie's large jewelry collection; however, Eve owned an even larger one from her husband's investment in a jewelry store and gambling days. She shared it all with Kathryn, who was like a little girl walking into material heaven on earth.

Eve fashioned the image that promoted Kathryn in Los Angeles, California, and on television. She taught her the style, the elegance, the way to hold your posture and head high as you enter the room, and the mystique that never lets others know too much.

At an exclusive restaurant, Kathryn whispered to a friend which fork to use. "I would never have known how to set this if it hadn't been for Eve. Eve taught me so much. She is more responsible for who I am today than any other friend I've ever had. She's gone now, but I still miss our dear Eve so much." Everything about Eve was first class—from the classic black dresses that she wore to her fine diamonds and jewels. She taught Kathryn how to dress, how to wear clothes that complimented her, and what things to look for in fine jewelry. From Eve, Kathryn learned how to make a first visual impression, one that people would remember.

Together, they traveled to the theatre in New York, to the Bel Air Hotel in Beverly Hills for shopping and dining, and abroad to develop Kathryn's appreciation of other cultures. Eve Conley was Kathryn's true mentor and best friend. A friend with faith to gain by being a part of Kathryn's life. The women could talk openly about anything, and Kathryn never had to worry about being judged for what someone else might perceive as bad for a lady preacher.

Eve was a wise businesswoman. She had assisted her husband in building lucrative businesses, and she passed all this on to Kathryn. Eve had an amazing talent for details that Kathryn picked up and used in her ministry for the rest of her life. They lived and worked together for seventeen years. Eve instituted many of the standards that became an integral part of Kathryn's services. She was as much family, probably more so, as anyone could be. She took incredible care of Kathryn and was the one Kathryn went to for advice. They lived together at the Fox Chapel home that Eve purchased when they moved to Pittsburgh. Kathryn came home one day and found Eve lying dead on the floor.

Kathryn faced her Pittsburgh congregation with a broken heart, one that can only be understood by another who has suffered the great loss of someone they held so dear. The people poured out their love and tried to console her that Sunday. One of them wrote Kathryn a letter the following day:

Dearest Kathryn,

There are times when one should take the time and sit down and properly express one's appreciation and love for one who has helped by teaching and showing their love and by being so patient, loving, and kind to us—who not one of us are worthy.

THE HANDMAIDEN

One thing I am sure of, and that is the love you have for your people, the way you have shown it by everything you have done, and by the way you stick with us.

Sunday was a day that surely expressed all of the people's love that they have for their preacher lady, and I know you would not exchange that love; it is just a small reward you have received. One day you will receive that beautiful "Plum of Glory" for the work you have done and for the love you have expressed in so many ways.

Miss Eve's work is finished here on earth, and what a beautiful job she has done. God gave her to you to attend to your needs, and now her work is finished, but there is still more for you to do. Whatever it might be, our preacher lady will be as near perfect as possible and will do a great job.

Hope this letter expresses just a little bit of the people's love for you, and maybe it will help the big hurt you have.

If any of us could remove the hurt from you that you have, you know we would bear it for you in exchange for what you have done for us.

From then on, Kathryn was lonely for Eve. Jessie Vincent, Eve's husband, and her sister-in-law's estates had been inherited by Eve. Eve left everything to Kathryn, who now owned one of the finest personal jewelry collections in America. Those were not the things that made

Kathryn truly happy, though. Life was not the same after Eve's death. Kathryn dropped dress sizes that she never regained.

On a trip to Palm Springs, Kathryn and Ruth Martin were sitting around the pool wearing fur coats when two men asked them to dinner. Kathryn wasted no time in telling them: "No! We enjoy each other's company." She immediately suggested they go to the Bel Air Hotel in Beverly Hills for a couple of nights. "Eve and I stayed there," she said. Kathryn was looking for the same dining experiences she had shared with Eve for so many years. She cried, "I miss Eve at dinner. I am so lonely for Eve." Ruth knew she could never fill Eve's shoes; upon check-out, Ruth suggested that they not stay there again, and Kathryn wisely agreed.

Kathryn continued to eat at the Bel Air Hotel. The staff knew her favorite table, her favorite things on the menu, and as they do with all celebrities, they gave her the star treatment. Try as they may, no one on earth ever gave her any treatment to equal that of Eve Conley's.

Kathryn's black alligator briefcase held all the paperwork from those she considered her family, whether by blood or love. There were her family's wills, the papers showing Kathryn as the executrix of Eve's estate, and a file of correspondence between her and the Martin's when they dissolved their business partnership. These were the documents she held dear.

In her Louis Vuitton handbag was a small black wallet with Eve Conley's driver's license, social security card, and other identification. Kathryn would use the ID to check into hotels and hospitals anonymously. She always carried a piece of Eve with her—in her heart and her handbag.

For almost thirty years, Pittsburgh, Pennsylvania, was a Mecca of healing for thousands. Everyone knew where its favorite daughter lived. Her home at 350 Fox Chapel was a rambling four-bedroom ranch-style house in one of the nicer areas of town with beautiful grounds that backed up to a park-like setting. Kathryn loved the wildlife that came out each night. She lived just a little above middle class, taking lunch at the counter of Stouffer's, where she knew all the girls' names. As she left the office each night at five or six, the policemen on the street tipped their hats and said, "Good night, Miss K."

The police loved her. Since she came to town, crime was down, and picking up alcoholics on the streets or brawling in bars had significantly decreased. The department installed a special buzzer at Fox Chapel that went directly into the police department. Kathryn bumped into it a few times, causing unnecessary alarm. They followed her home from late meetings and waited until the garage door closed and the lights came on before leaving.

Once inside, Kathryn could relax, watch a little television, or read. In her hours of solitude, she received her best Bible training on her knees in prayer with her favorite companion, the Holy Spirit. The revelation of those hours was shared in her "Heart to Heart" talks on radio stations that eventually covered most of the United States. They were right on track. She stayed in the middle of the road but called black, black and white, white. She admired Billy Graham and his plain descriptions of faith and of being born again. Her favorite greeting when on the radio was one of a faithful friend who called up to encourage you every day. Kathryn would say, "Hello, there. And have you been waiting for me? It's so nice of you. I just knew you'd be there." The people of Pittsburgh knew Kathryn from "Heart to Heart," her radio talk show. She also preached at Faith Temple near Franklin.

Her supporters encouraged her to move her ministry to Pittsburgh, where her headquarters were located and the talk show was taped.

It did not take Kathryn long to make her mark on the city. *The Pittsburgh Sun Telegram* headline for Saturday, August 15, 1953, read: "Kathryn Kuhlman celebrates 5th Anniversary Communion at Syria Mosque." Below the headline was a beautiful shot of Kathryn. To commemorate the event, an all-day Sunday service, including communion for the six thousand attendees, was planned.

It had only been five years since Kathryn preached for the first time at Pittsburgh's Carnegie Hall on July 4. The fireworks from her dynamic preaching style had attracted overflowing audiences several times a week. Ever since, crowds have come from all over the tristate district: Pennsylvania, Ohio, and West Virginia.

The mammoth stage of Syria Mosque where the foremost artists had appeared was filled with two hundred ushers serving the Lord's table which contained six thousand individual communion glasses. The bread and wine were served to those representing all faiths, nationalities, and colors. Hundreds arrived the night before, and many slept on the steps and sidewalk. The doors opened at 8 a.m., long before the starting time of 10 a.m., and police had to close the doors because too many people were blocking the aisles and hallways.

In the front hall was a five-foot anniversary cake that would be cut after the service because so many of those attending were fasting for communion. The inspiring service was filled with testimonies of God's amazing grace. A young Russian woman who had fled her native country found salvation through attending, as well as a Polish immigrant who knew his life was in God's hands because he survived several of the worst Nazi concentration camps.

THE HANDMAIDEN

"It is through the power of God, the great Healer, who makes these people whole again," Kathryn said as she handed out more than one thousand roses to men who declared they had given up alcohol with the help of Kathryn's prayers. One was a man who said he had tried to kill his family with a shotgun. Three times he was committed to institutions for his abuse and addiction to alcohol.

A "Holy Hush" fell all over Syria Mosque as Kathryn asked all six thousand to turn around and kneel on their seats and pray for forgiveness of their sins. The windows of heaven opened up as six thousand prayers went up to the Father.

Kathryn was presented with a gold badge from the Pittsburgh Police Department for "rescuing many derelicts who haunted the lower north side." The badge meant more to Kathryn than they would ever realize. It was among her precious jewels in her Louis Vuitton jewelry box; next to her diamonds and pearls sat a treasure of her heart—lives restored, families made whole, and the promise of faith for generations to come. What the world says is earthly trash are made into treasures with heavenly rewards.

Mildred Moran was one of those treasures. She was known to everyone on the north side, spending more time in the police department's number 12 station than anybody in Pittsburgh.

"I started taking dope and ended up in the penitentiary. Then one night, I went to hear Kathryn Kuhlman. From that day on, I was a new person. I found Jesus. Living now is beautiful. I can face the world, and I no longer have to hide my face," said Mildred. No sickness, disease, addiction, haunting present or past was beyond the healing power and restoration of God through His simple handmaiden. "All can be healed spiritually, and that is the greatest miracle of all."

By 1955, four thousand letters a week came from around the country requesting literature on the ministry of Kathryn Kuhlman. One was from a California man who became so enamored with Kathryn's striking signed photograph that he moved to Pittsburgh to follow her, and follow her he did.

Harold Pressler was a good-looking "Romeo," who at twenty-nine was smitten with Kathryn—now forty-eight years old and looking like thirty. He called her at home, followed her around like a doting puppy, and attended all her meetings. Harold said, "Once I was in the third row, and she smiled at me, out of the 1,500 people there."

The ardent follower disturbed her, and she placed a call to the Pittsburgh Police Department. They arrested Pressler on a charge of molesting. Kathryn was reluctant to prosecute at his hearing and suggested instead that he be treated as a social case. Pittsburgh Press ran a photograph taken in the courtroom showing Pressler, attorney Louis Little, and a sweet, head-cocked Kathryn. Kathryn stated, "There was never anything indecent in Mr. Pressler's behavior."

The 1950s were a return to the good life, bringing many people back to God. In Howard Whitman's book, *A Reporter in Search of God,* he describes the condition of the world.

"Churches are dusting off pews they haven't used in years. Memberships are booming. Evangelists from Billy Graham to Kathryn Kuhlman are packing them in. People are gobbling up religious books as if they are spiritual headache tablets. One metropolitan newspaper featured the story of Jesus in the same big black type it customarily reserved for drug rings, murderers, and Hollywood divorces." Almost half a century later, history is repeating itself. Spiritual quests have once again become a priority for the masses—only this time, the new age gurus have slipped, leaving much emptier and more confused than when they started.

Facilities providing relief from the addictions of alcohol and drugs offer no better odds than repeat offenders of the criminal world. Both mainly serve as a financial drain of the citizens and families who are programmed to turn to man for outward healing instead of God for the true healing that comes from within.

One needs only to look at the bottom line of such programs against those liked by the ministry of Kathryn Kuhlman. Love of God and man working together for the good of all. It is never the effort of one human being but of many that enable a ministry to bring forth a community that supports and prepares its members to exhibit the faith that finds peace in the storm.

By 1957, the ministry had grown into a religious, charitable, non-profit corporation called the Kathryn Kuhlman Foundation. The foundation financed all public meetings, sixty television stations, and fifty radio stations—as well as funding a variety of humanitarian causes.

From her early days in Idaho, Kathryn became and remained conscious of the hunger present in her own backyard. Needy families were provided with food and assistance to help them get through difficult periods. Scholarship programs and student loans insured the future of young men and women—not only in preparation for ministry at schools like Wheaton College in Illinois (where Kathryn's television and radio programs are available for public viewing) but also in fine arts programs such as the Cincinnati Conservatory of Music, as well as programs offered at the Carnegie Institute of Technology.

The diversity of the foundation went well beyond the normal Christian boundaries. It was a humanitarian effort, not one based on your religious affiliation but rather in the belief that showing support and love opens all doors. Hundreds of thousands of dollars were given to support Teen Challenge—an outreach ministry for teens involved in drugs, crime, and gang warfare. Support was provided for a rehabilitation farm in rural Pennsylvania that helped teenaged drug addicts find themselves and the purpose of a meaningful life again.

The Western School for the Blind received $40,000 in assistance after Kathryn happened by one day and watched as the precious children played outside. She was compelled to help those less fortunate. Instead of putting fortunes into building physical monuments of concrete and brick, she invested in monuments of flesh and blood. Her ministry made a huge difference in Pittsburgh and carried the full support of civil as well as religious leaders.

There was no scandal, no manipulations, and no gossip among the congregation for money or selfish gain. Members of the Pittsburgh and Youngstown congregations could only rejoice in the visible returns of their giving—all over the city and all over the world.

The assemblies of God missionaries, Gene and Ruth Martin, were two people in Kathryn's life everyone loved and respected. Deeply passionate about their work, with good looks and charm on their side, the two made a dynamic soul-winning team. Gene and Ruth traveled the world for the sake of evangelism, spending weeks at a time in undeveloped areas. Their approach was clever and creative. An illustrated children's story time ran until dark, so when parents picked them up, they too heard the Gospel, many for the first time. Innovative musical productions included Gene playing three instruments at once and Ruth on the accordion, piano, and organ. They were perfectly prepared to be part of Kathryn Kuhlman's team.

The Martins had traveled with Kathryn's sister Myrtle and her evangelist husband, Everett Parrott, whom they had met at a revival in Dallas, Texas. Myrtle always encouraged them to attend one of Kathryn's services; she told them, "You need Kathryn, and she needs you."

In 1961, Gene and Ruth were ministering nearby and drove to Pittsburgh to attend their first Kathryn Kuhlman service. They dined with Kathryn afterwards at the Fox Chapel home, where she and her dear friend Eve Conley lived. During the delicious dinner Eve prepared, Kathryn spotted Ruth admiring a huge diamond ring Eve had given her. She slipped it off her finger and had Ruth try it on. "Now, don't you feel a lot better wearing that?" Eve said, shaking her head, "You girls are all alike." Ruth left wearing the ring and with an invitation to spend the night on her next visit. It was the first of many times when Kathryn entrusted fine pieces of jewelry to Ruth for her enjoyment.

After dinner, Kathryn inquired about the missionary work that Myrtle spoke of. They explained their philosophy of building churches for the nation that already spoke the language, understood the culture, and was already an active part of the community. This approach had proven to be more successful and long-lasting than traditional missionary work.

Kathryn got excited when she saw the tremendous passion for their work. She exclaimed, "Now that is something I could believe in!" She then took them on a tour of the Kathryn Kuhlman Foundation offices located nearby in the Carlton House Hotel.

The following morning, one of Kathryn's secretaries called to let them know that Kathryn was working on her radio program in the recording studio of the foundation offices. Kathryn extended her apologies. She would not be able to join them for breakfast. As they were eating, a secretary delivered an envelope and expressed Kathryn's appreciation for their visit. She grinned and said the envelope was for their overseas work and that there would probably be more to come. The envelope held a check for $1,000. They were thrilled and immediately delivered it to the Assemblies of God Foreign Missions Department. To their delight, Gene was named their exclusive liaison with the Kathryn Kuhlman Foundation.

Kathryn had a standard of excellence. Money was not the issue. A few months later, they received an additional check for $5,000 along with a letter:

"God has spoken to me, you know the place, so take the thousand dollars along with the $5,000 check enclosed, and if you need more, just telephone me. Build me a church where people can be born again. Let us not limit God in anything, for I am firmly convinced the only limit of the power of God lies within the individual."

The $6,000 total was exactly what was needed to complete a church in Nicaragua. Gene sent Kathryn photos of the completed building. "The photos speak for themselves. This is the kind of missionary work I believe in. Not only will I think of you as our friends, but also as our missionaries. You will always be a part of this ministry too."

Kathryn invited them to come to Pittsburgh and speak in her Sunday service in Youngstown, Ohio, as well as her Bible study service in Pittsburgh. Gene called to explain that they had taken some wonderful 16mm color movies, but they would need a powerful projector to show them in an auditorium that seated several thousand. It was no problem. Kathryn had the best one available, along with its operator.

Before the service, they were surprised to hear Kathryn ask, "What is next?" Gene happened to have a list of missionaries that had requested assistance. He began reading from the list of the missionaries in need along with their potential. Kathryn bowed her head and closed her eyes as she listened to the names. When Gene said, "Macau," Kathryn suddenly proclaimed, "That is it! That is our next place!"

Gene was a little confused at her hasty decision. Gene said, "But you don't know anything about the potential. It is located at the Pearl River where refugees flee in the middle of the night from communism."

Kathryn didn't need to know. She pointed upward. "He knows, and I know what He wants me to do. After your presentation today, we'll ask the people for $40,000 to build a church in Macau."

Kathryn's worship service was very impressive. She now had a beautiful choir under the direction of Dr. Arthur Metcalf, a well-known, sophisticated man of classical training. Dr. Metcalf was with Kathryn until the day he died on February 20, 1975—exactly one year to the day before Kathryn left this earth.

Kathryn walked up to the podium and said, "We welcome our missionaries, Gene and Ruth Martin. We are anxious to see the color film they have brought of the church we helped to build. They are also here to tell us of their next project, which God has laid on my heart as well as theirs."

She took a seat on the front row and watched the presentation. Her heart was fixed as she recognized the value of reaching those the world had forgotten. She wept for their future without the outreach and love from foreign missions.

Gene was just about to close with prayer and ask for their help when he sensed someone standing behind him. Kathryn came forward, under the conviction of the Holy Spirit, and poured her heart out to the people. The $40,000 was raised within one week. It was a gratifying and wonderful experience for everyone involved. Before her death, nineteen other churches were built from donations to the Kathryn Kuhlman Foundation. Two memorials were erected in Kenya and Vietnam. In their careers, Gene and Ruth Martin built 120 churches. Those now have satellite churches, bringing the total near 200.

Twenty-three churches were built and subsidized by the Kathryn Kuhlman Foundation all over the globe; some were in places we've heard of—India, China, Costa Rica, West Africa, Indonesia, Malaysia, South Vietnam—and others less familiar—like Thakurpukur, Cotonou, Dahomey, Kuala Lumpur, and Corn Islands. Kathryn was generous and provided funding where needed and at the request of her trusted director of Foreign Missions, Gene Martin.

Section One
OF KATHRYN KUHLMAN'S PHOTOGRAPHS

1. *Kathryn Johanna Kuhlman*

2. *Joseph and Emma Kuhlman with Myrtle, Kathryn, and Earl Kuhlman*

3. *Kuhlman family home in Concordia, Missouri*

3A. *Methodist Church in Concordia, MO*

4. *Kathryn Kuhlman and her mother, Emma*

5. *Kathryn Kuhlman with her baby carriage*

6. *Kathryn Kuhlman and family*

7. *Kathryn Kuhlman with childhood friend*

8. *Kathryn Kuhlman on the back porch of her home*

9. *Kathryn Kuhlman and friend*

10. *Three-year-old Kathryn Kuhlman in watermelon patch*

11. *Kathryn Kuhlman with car*

12. *Kathryn Kuhlman at waterfalls*

13. *Kathryn Kuhlman with friend*

14. *Kathryn Kuhlman sitting at waterfalls*

15. *Everett and Myrtle Parrott*

16. *Evangelists Everett and Myrtle Parrott on the road*

17. *God's Girls*

18. *Burroughs Allen Waltrip Sr. aka "Mister"*

PITTSBURGH

The Kathryn Kuhlman Foundation was located on the sixth floor of the Carlton House Hotel in a suite with a string of adjoining rooms that included a recording studio for her radio program. The offices were a reflection of their founder, with soft feminine decor accented by the floral arrangements that were present throughout Kathryn's life. It started with Mama's beautiful gardens, then her homes, offices, and the set of the *I Believe in Miracles* television program. Fans and supporters were always sending handmade gifts, and most of them landed here—paintings, dolls, and kitsch included. The environment was cluttered but cozy and homey.

Kathryn made the place come alive—strutting in, barking orders, and laughing like a schoolgirl. She was tall, slim, loud, and confident. Her energy was electric and exuberant. She would be tugging at her auburn curls, scratching her thigh, holding your gaze with her glittering blue eyes, poking you in the ribs with a chuckle, or grabbing your arm tight with her bony fingers.

The girls called Kathryn "pastor" and worked under the direction of "Maggie," the name Kathryn dubbed Marguerite Hartner. The two of them had met in 1943 when Kathryn had a six-week preaching engagement at Jack Munyon's Peoples Church on the north side of Pittsburgh. It was one of those times when Burroughs Waltrip had to hide out in the hotel to avoid any threat of scandal and cancellation.

They struck up a friendship right away. Maggie recalls, "I liked her so much." Kathryn returned to Los Angeles to make one of the most important decisions of her life. She kept in touch with Maggie by letter, and now she needed a friend. Maggie joined her in 1948, the beginning of her first visit to Pittsburgh, and stayed to the end and then some. She became Kathryn's "alter ego," the voice on the phone you had to go through to get to Kathryn—the one who was responsible for delivering the bad news that Kathryn herself found impossible to do. Maggie Hartner completely devoted her life to the work of the Kathryn Kuhlman Foundation. From 1950 until she died in the early nineties, her job was probably the most difficult and the most rewarding. Maggie was attractive, quiet, stern, dignified, and standing tall with fun concentration on the job at hand. She controlled the count of all monies received after almost every meeting—a testimony of the trust Kathryn placed in her.

Margaret Dillion was one of the "girls" at the Kathryn Kuhlman Foundation. "We were all friends in the busy office, dedicated to one cause—one goal. Kathryn was demanding in a wonderful way. She expected everyone to be in unity with the vision. Souls, souls—it is all about souls!"

Kathryn was a businesswoman in the office and a real lady—one who would tell you exactly what was on her mind. She worked seven days a week, twenty-four hours a day, in her sincere dedication to the cause. She was prudent but kind. There was a fine line you knew not to step over. Kathryn was very much in the know and knew how to manage and remember the important things. She gave her staff specific instructions on how to properly manage the incoming mail. They were to open and read each piece and underline the important items in colored pens, which allowed her to view the items of interest and save time.

The staff knew it was such a different world now. When Kathryn was on the platform, there was a "Holy Hush." Such a transformation when the Holy Spirit came on her. They all recognized the Holy Spirit working through her, and she never took the credit. "Do not look at me, honey," she would say. She would rebuke bad things in the name of Jesus, and that would be the end of it. Kathryn knew who she could trust; Eve, Maggie, and Maryon were those closest to her. I do not think she would change a thing if her ministry were here today—not one thing.

Maryon Marsh was Kathryn's secretary. She and her sister, Ruth Fisher, joined the Kathryn Kuhlman Foundation in 1951 and stayed for twenty-six years. Like so many others, it was after a spiritual experience that involved physical healing for Ruth. In those days, it was only the four of them in two rooms. Kathryn and Maryon shared a desk, and Maggie and Ruth worked off a small table.

"She was flamboyant, a natural showman," says Ruth Fisher, who became a minister and had a television program for thirteen years. "She had that electric personality that just lit up a room. But she was a real, caring person too, and obedient to the Lord. She's just what is needed today." She hand-signed and read the important parts of every letter. When Ruth Martin was in Pittsburgh, she typed fifty to one hundred letters a day, and the other girls did twice that many.

Millie Heldman described the blast of energy when Kathryn walked into the office. "Kathryn was just one of the girls, a tremendous worker, so full of life and love. She knew God, and the energy from her dedication to Him was contagious. Most of the girls were still there seven years after Kathryn went home. We all loved her."

Millie devoted thirty years to Kathryn's ministry. Her mother would listen to Kathryn on the radio. Millie could not stand Kathryn's theatrical voice. One day, she saw a sign being put up at Carnegie Hall, announcing a two-week meeting featuring Kathryn Kuhlman. She could not wait to tell her mother, "Well, your girlfriend is coming to town."

Millie decided to see for herself what all the fuss was about. She was a strong Christian but considered herself conservative, even skeptical of faith healers. Millie attended the meeting and recognized the presence of the Holy Spirit. She came back for more. One night, she sat near a woman with a humongous goiter on her neck. Near the end of the service, the woman gasped, and Millie watched as it completely disappeared.

Along with her office work, Millie sang in the choir. Kathryn's choir traveled on the bus to other meetings. They stood on stage, feeling the cool breeze right behind them, watching as twenty years disappeared from her face. They watched as the nuns and priests at Notre Dame fell under the power. The pivotal viewpoint was a highlight for the choir; they often stood for hours with no relief as God sent His Holy Spirit to touch and change lives forever.

When people around the office would ask Kathryn for advice, she answered, "I do not know why you ask me. You are going to do what you want anyway. It is not what happens; it is how you handle it."

On the platform, she was a spiritual giant. In the office, she was a businesswoman who counted on the total dedication of every member of her staff. The standards Kathryn lived by were expected of one and all. No gray areas or special treatment existed; either it is or it is not.

Personal lives were left at home. The employees of the Kathryn Kuhlman Foundation worked full-time and attended or assisted in several services each week. Some of the women never married, choosing instead to follow their leader's sold-out lifestyle. Those that were married had handsome husbands who were involved as ushers and catchers.

One cannot forget Loesch. Charles Loesch was Kathryn's handyman, driver, protector, and faithful, dedicated follower. He, like so many others who devoted their lives to this ministry, was miraculously healed in one of Kathryn's services. He was healed from both an alcohol and a cigarette addiction. Four months later, a bent-over hunchback with one leg that was four inches shorter was made whole. His leg started "vibrating" like a jackhammer during the service. Kathryn asked, "What is this? You've been healed, sir!" He stood up straight for the first time in many years to find both legs were the same length.

A bit like "Max" in the movie *Sunset Boulevard,* Loesch drove Kathryn to the airport or anywhere else she needed his assistance, and he took care of her Fox Chapel home as well. He abandoned all to serve Miss Kuhlman in any way, including repairing antiques Kathryn bought at a bargain, entertaining Kathryn's nephew Paul Crane, or waiting for hours in the cold. Kathryn was in Youngstown during a terrible snow and ice storm. She knew if she made it home, she would not be able to make it up the steep driveway. When she arrived, Loesch was waiting at the bottom of the hill to help her up.

Loesch knew, just as all those who worked closely with Kathryn, that her heart problem was escalating. At the end of a long day, Kathryn sat back in her chair and sighed, "Look, girls, you can see my heart beating." The entire side of her chest was moving with each beat, but she would not slow down.

Another time, before the Youngstown service, Kathryn was feeling sick. Her abdomen and ankles were swollen. She was in extreme pain and thought nobody was watching. For her birthday, the "girls" had bought her a new dress. They peaked in to surprise her, and when she realized it, she jumped up, full of life, and went on the platform to hold a great service.

Yes, Kathryn was a trooper, and all good entertainers know the show must go on. Kathryn's trust in God was definitive, but not in man. Even the best members of her team could be frustrated when she double-checked something or asked two people to do the same thing. This would occasionally create mass confusion. Delegating responsibility and leaving the matter alone once she did was not easy. The overall effort was so important to her because everything had to be perfect for God.

As with most perfectionist employers, someone would inevitably end up in the doghouse. Just as Kathryn let you know when you had done a good job, she didn't fail to let you know if she was displeased. There was equality, however, and everyone was fair game. The staff would joke, "We'll be the one next week." Kathryn was not perfect, but she had one vision, and she stuck to it to the very end. Kathryn had near impeccable taste in choosing key staff members. Everyone wanted to please and protect her, and their level of devotion to the ministry was overwhelming. Even her choir director, the distinguished Dr. Arthur Metcalf, would stop by and help out, sitting on the floor, putting stamps on envelopes.

Kathryn loved Christmas—huge trees with lavish decorations, parties for the staff and choir, and buying presents. No matter where she was in the world, she would come home to Pittsburgh for Christmas.

Elaborate programs with twenty-foot Christmas trees were only a small part of the celebration. The Christmas party that Kathryn treasured the most was the one for the needy children. Most parents will tell you they never really knew love until they looked into the face of their child. Kathryn saw love in every child; each one was her own. She saw the hope and promise in their innocence. She took delight in personally shopping for the toys, dolls, and clothing the congregation passed out at the gigantic party about the birth and the love of another child, Jesus Christ.

Of course, Kathryn herself was showered with expressions of love during the holiday season. Ruth Martin received an envelope from the Kathryn Kuhlman Foundation dated January 3, 1972 with "personal" typed on the front. Inside was one of Kathryn's business cards with a handwritten note on the back. "Save these two personal notes from these two employees for the book to be published!"

She could have chosen many. There were approximately twenty people in the office then. She chose only two. One is from a young lady who worked in the back—a quiet, unassuming, relatively new but dedicated employee. Somehow, Kathryn knew, as she did in many other things about this project, that God's timing surpasses any plan of man. Carol Gray was that employee, who today almost single-handedly carries on the Kathryn Kuhlman Foundation. She develops and sends out the treasures Kathryn left to both the faithful followers who are still around today and to a new generation of followers who have never heard of the woman who became the foremost female evangelist of the century.

NEW YEAR'S EVE

*I*t was the afternoon of New Year's Eve, and Kathryn decided to take time to go through some of her mail. She knew that later in the evening she would be spending time with friends, and then come the next few days, it was back to scheduled services. As she looked at the envelopes, it filled her heart to see that there were cards from her staff.

"Dear pastor,

I could not have this year pass, and another begins without expressing to you for your many kindnesses during the holiday season and throughout the entire year, and I am so glad for the opportunity to write this note here, in the place that has meant so much to me the past year.

While looking back on 1971, which is soon to end, I believe the words most appropriate for myself and my family are 'Hitherto hath the Lord helped us.' And I don't know what we would have done without that help.

Thank you for my best and happiest year, and if I never have the opportunity to tell you so, please know how much I love working here.

I HOPE AND PRAY THAT YOUR YEAR HAS BEEN AS WONDERFUL AS YOU HAVE MADE IT FOR EVERYONE ELSE!

My love and devotion,
Carol

AND A HAPPY NEW YEAR!!!"

The second is from her trusted personal secretary, Maryon Marsh.

"Dear pastor,

In the midst of thank you notes to others, I feel that I am the MOST BLESSED PERSON in the whole world and most inept in expressing that gratitude. I have been privileged to be a part of this ministry, and I admit that what I am today—if anything of credit—is a result of your faithfulness to the Lord and your example. I am so proud of you always!

Our Christmas party was lovely, and I was so happy to be a part of it, but I still contend that the top of the triangle 'ran second' to the entertainment on the bill ... IT WAS JUST FUN!

Christmas afternoon, I was alone in the bedroom when I opened your envelopes, but I didn't feel alone—in fact, the presence of someone else would have been a 'trespass' of sorts. How can I say thank you for something that is beyond thanking for—what is there to say, except to give you my best in return even though I shall never attain the summit or fully measure up to the highest pinnacle that I have set.

Thanks for everything ... the material, the spiritual; thank you for being you, so human and natural and warm, yet far more!

Always my love, Maryon"

It has been written about Kathryn that she was difficult to work with, demanding, and frugal with her salaries. Those who were there have said in over forty interviews that any of the above difficulties were worth it. They understood the reward was worth the price. The benefits were without measure, the blessings beyond compare.

A spirit of integrity and honor surrounded the people and the ministry. Kathryn refused to build a mailing list from churches. The only time you were placed on a list was if you sent a prayer request to the Kathryn Kuhlman Foundation. However, solicitation mail was never discussed. When a family sent an offering, a file was created and kept correct with all the family members' information. Every few weeks, a letter was sent, thanking them for the offering and asking how their loved ones were doing.

This personal touch that is so lost today was the backbone of a ministry whose congregation never listened to pleas of the church's financial crisis and never squirmed during lengthy manipulations to sow seed or save the television ministry. Kathryn's ministry left it to God to handle. In 1970, the television and radio expenses alone were already close to $1 million.

Members grew so confident in this integrity that they began changing their wills. Almost everyone wanted to leave something to the Kathryn Kuhlman Foundation—so many, that Kathryn sent Gene Martin to college for estate planning courses.

Gene began keeping a list of people to contact. He would interview them and give the attorneys the appropriate paragraph numbers to draw up the documents. People left their property, financial holdings, and bank accounts—confident in knowing their investments were in the salvation of mankind. One left $60,000 after Kathryn died. Gene used it to build a church as a memorial in Africa. That investment is still paying off today.

The congregations were not especially wealthy; they reflected this country ethnically, financially, and intellectually. Kathryn loved them all. A two-dollar donation from an aging widow meant just as much as the thousand-dollar donation from the president of the bank, perhaps more. It showed obedience and sacrifice.

One day, Gene arrived at the home of a Hungarian widow. Her old two-story wooden home was in the ghetto of Pittsburgh. With her husband gone, she needed assistance with her will. She was now responsible for all they had accumulated from a life of hard work since immigrating to the United States. At first, they had menial jobs, but in the land of opportunity, her husband landed a good one.

The woman was so gracious. She said, "My husband did not trust banks, and I need you to help me. You represent Miss Kuhlman to me. Oh, thank you for coming. I want you to help me count it."

Gene was confused, "You mean it is in this house?" She nodded, "Oh, yes, my husband said never trust a bank." Concerned, Gene tried to explain, "In this neighborhood, these people would kill you in a second if they knew you had a lot of cash in here."

She saw no need to worry. "Look at me; they don't think I have anything. Come, come. I will show you." She led Gene to the bedroom, closed the curtains, and lifted the mattress. There were large bills everywhere. Gene began to count as she organized stacks of money.

"Yes, ma'am, there are almost seven thousand dollars here."

"I have more," she said, "can you come back tomorrow?"

Gene took her hands, "Please, listen to me. You must go to the bank and rent a safety deposit box to put all this money in."

She was scared, "Oh no, I don't know if I can."

"Yes, you must," Gene said firmly. "Take your grocery cart. Put all the money in paper bags, put them in the cart, and go right past the store into the bank. You and your husband have worked all your lives for this money. It could burn up in this old house when you're not home, and all you've saved would be gone."

The widow started crying, "Oh, you don't know how we've been saved. You don't know!"

Gene was pleading, and he could see she was beginning to under-stand. "Now, you must do this. Do it first thing tomorrow. Please." And she replied, "Well, alright then. I will go tomorrow just as you have said."

Gene saw her a few days later at church. "Did you go?" Standing proudly, she said, "Oh yes, they were very nice. Thank you."

Such were the people and the workings of an organization that took care of each other, rather than taking advantage of each other. There was so much love, and it flowed from the top down. The ushers would have laid down their lives for their pastor. It was a two-way street. They were a large extended family, unified in purpose.

The Pittsburgh and Youngstown ushers always tried to outdo each other on Kathryn's birthday. Every year, a large brown paper sack was filled with cards and checks. That way, Kathryn could buy one nice present instead of receiving a lot of little ones she didn't need. One year in the seventies, her birthday monies totaled $20,000. She went to the bank, deposited the checks, and asked the teller for cash. The bank manager returned. "Miss Kuhlman, why do you want this much cash?" Kathryn told the simple truth. "You see, it is my birthday. Haven't you ever wanted to have a lot of cash to buy just exactly what you wanted to? Well, that is why. Now, may I please have my money?"

Kathryn left with the cash, and she and Maggie went shopping. They were walking past an antique store when Kathryn spotted it in the window—a seven-carat, beautiful pavé diamond heart necklace. The gift from her ushers became her favorite piece of jewelry. She almost always wore it. When Kathryn died, it was the only thing Maggie wanted. Maggie pleaded with Tink Wilkerson, and finally, he agreed to let her have it in exchange for Kathryn's Bible. Maggie agreed, knowing Kathryn had several Bibles. There was a great deal of conflict, and the exchange never took place. The heart necklace remained with the rest of Kathryn Kuhlman's estate in Tink Wilkerson's attic for twenty-two years. It is a spectacular piece of the collection. This collection is helpful in understanding and bringing forth Kathryn's character, similar to her own heart being so delightful, pure, and engaging. She became a force of love whose life exemplified, "Well done, my good and faithful servant."

After twenty-five years of ministry in Pittsburgh and the tristate area, the world's most unique minister was given the gala event of her life. A black-tie event at the Hilton Hotel was held with 2,500 of her favorite people.

Gene Martin emceed the evening, reading congratulatory telegrams from around the world, including New Zealand, Africa, Vietnam, and CBS, where *I Believe in Miracles* numbered four hundred shows. There was a special presentation from Washington, DC. Carl Albert, the Speaker of the House of Representatives, sent his endorsement along with a United States flag that had flown over the Capitol the previous day.

Dr. Robert Lamont, the pastor of Pittsburgh's ultra-respectable First Presbyterian Church, had given his stamp of approval in 1967. When Carnegie Hall was no longer available due to renovations, he invited Kathryn to hold her Friday morning miracle services in the neo-Gothic landmark free of charge. She stayed for nine years.

The evening began on a light note with Dr. Lamont's declaration of approval because "Whether she knew it or not, her theology was Presbyterian!" Before he agreed to Kathryn's use of their facility, he asked to examine her financial records.

"I've been doing this for years and can report that her finances are cleaner than the United Presbyterian Church." Dan Malachuk, the publisher of Logos International, presented her with a plaque. "He giveth without measure." An exquisite gold medallion was sculpted, depicting Jesus on the front and Kathryn with hands of healing extended on the back. For a contribution of $10 to the worldwide mission fund, guests could have one of their very own.

Dr. Arthur Metcalf, Kathryn's choir director for eighteen years, directed the interracial concert choir, dressed in formal attire. Kathryn came to the stage and called the people who had been with her the entire twenty-five years to the stage. Her assistant, Maggie Hartner; her accountant, Walter Adamack; organist Charles BeeBee; and pianist Jimmy Miller. Kathryn stood to the side as the crowd gave them a standing ovation.

Kathryn was radiant in a long aqua and silver evening gown. The spotlight and entertainment were on Kathryn at her best—joking, reminiscing, laughing, crying, and ad-libbing twenty-five years' worth of material that kept the 2,500 laughing, applauding, and weeping far into the night. It is impossible to tell who appreciated whom the most. Suffice to say, it was a mutual admiration—a society of people who loved Kathryn and the woman who could not have done it without their confidence in her and her ministry for twenty-five years.

LIFE IN THE CITY
OF ANGELS

The Golden State of California is known for being open to new ideas or new ways of presenting old ones. In Los Angeles especially, nothing brings the people out like a good show.

The Los Angeles Times wrote, "Kathryn Kuhlman is a great showman. She is vibrantly alive and seems to be an unending series of motions and facial contortions. She waves her arms, throws her head back, and laughs heartily; she clasps her hands to her face and titters girlishly; she goes from one emotional extreme to another in seconds. She would be at home at any stage under any circumstances." A series of invitations were arriving at the Kathryn Kuhlman Foundation from pastors across the Golden State, encouraging Kathryn of the tremendous work she could offer their state. One year later, a spirit-filled Lutheran revealed God's plan to her, and she agreed to come to California.

THE HANDMAIDEN

One day, Kathryn asked Ruth and Gene to meet her in Los Angeles. She believed it was time to hold some meetings there, and she showed them letters from The Four Square, Assemblies of God, and some independent Pentecostals. She told Ruth she would like to start in Pasadena because she would not be sponsored by one pastor or one church; no one but God could take the credit for her coming.

Ruth became her representative in the planning. A small number of pastors were enlisted to enroll singers for the choir, directed by Kathryn's own Dr. Metcalf, and ushers for the monthly meeting on Sunday. Kathryn agreed to come to their church once a year in response.

The first meeting at the Pasadena Civic Auditorium was overflowing. Three thousand seats were not nearly enough. At the third meeting, Kathryn announced they were going to the Shrine Auditorium.

Los Angeles, California, played an important role in the life of Kathryn Kuhlman. There, as a teenager, she sat on the balcony of Angelus Temple, watching Aimee Semple McPherson—another flamboyant evangelist that Hollywood embraced. They were completely different, but had she not personally witnessed Aimee, her path may not have been as clear.

On a dead-end street in Los Angeles, California, she gave up the man she loved and charted the course God had intended for her until the day she died on earth. Now, Los Angeles was calling again, and Kathryn was ready. She had achieved a level of success in her ministry equivalent to the leading men of her time, and she had done it without intentionally intimidating any of them. In some ways, she was one of the boys. She looked like a woman, but she thought like a man—tough in business, accustomed to running the show and making all the decisions. She was unstoppable once she put her mind to something, and California became her next conquest.

California became the place Kathryn was happiest. She held a monthly miracle service at the Shrine Auditorium and filmed her *I Believe in Miracles* television show at CBS Studios. The Century Plaza Hotel acted as her home away from home, but it was her rented apartment in Newport Beach that she loved.

Sunny skies, beautiful weather, the Pacific Ocean, and an abundance of flowers and foliage everywhere were perfect settings for her new life. She was away from the daily responsibilities of the Kathryn Kuhlman Foundation, away from the cold weather in Pittsburgh, and suddenly everything became more beautiful and glamorous, even Kathryn.

It was when the Shrine meetings were so well received that Kathryn felt the call to hold one or two-day miracle services in cities across the United States. She asked Gene Martin if he would be her advance man. Since he was an evangelist, he already knew many pastors that he could easily gain their assistance for the meetings. The two agreed that Kathryn would help fund the church buildings Gene built overseas, and in exchange, Gene would devote nine months of the year to her miracle services.

It was an awesome undertaking. The dates and locations were selected. Gene met with local pastors, arranged for auditoriums, and established a local Kathryn Kuhlman office with a secretary to handle the details—like registering the busloads of people that came from various churches, cities, and states nearby. The phone numbers and dates for each city were announced on Kathryn's radio program. Sometimes there would be two or three services in two or three cities in one week. The pastors organized volunteer ushers, choir members, and the music director.

Gene would arrive the night before with Kathryn's choir director, Dr. Metcalf; her organist, Charles Beebee; and her pianist, Jimmy Miller. Sometimes the choirs were made up of one thousand voices. The meetings were open to anyone—any denomination, believer, or heathen. They were all welcomed, and they all came: Protestant, Catholic, Jewish, Orthodox, or nonbelievers.

Kathryn believed in order, and that noise was not a sign of power. She ran her services, never allowing anyone or anything to interrupt, especially when the Spirit was moving. She didn't want anyone to be turned off by outbursts of speaking in tongues, words of prophecy, or dancing. She was completely aware of how the masses viewed that kind of behavior and wanted everyone to worship with a spirit of unity.

Kathryn called Gene Martin "the solid rock." He was extremely technical and itemized every single aspect to ensure a perfect event. It was one of the secrets that ensured each meeting would be full. He developed a foolproof system for all Kathryn's meetings. Each meeting was planned out months ahead of time, sometimes even a year in advance. Like a well-laid out military operation, the troops had to be assembled and trained. Kathryn was the first to establish an organized bus ministry from all over the United States as well as Canada. There were always large numbers of reserved seats taken long before the public even knew she was coming.

Each usher was responsible for a section of twenty people. Every usher and choir member was allowed two to three guests. That count, plus the buses, gave Gene an actual number of seats available to the public.

Gene laid out the groundwork ahead of time with all the ushers. A lot of ushers were Pentecostal, so it was hard to explain that there could be no getting out of order. "God wants everyone to hear. If ten thousand people are in the auditorium and someone starts speaking in tongues, only those near them can hear. Everyone else is disturbed. You must go to them and say, 'Don't do this now. You're disturbing a lot of people. They are trying to get something from God. You have something to say, but not now. Can you be quiet, or do I need to take you out?'"

He prayed to God, "Help me to know I am not offending someone. But know that I am defending your Holy Spirit and the service." It was the only way he could get by with his conscience.

Gene had to work out an explanation, touching on every situation that could go wrong. "Look over your section. Can you see any babies? Go to the parents before the service, and explain that if the baby cries, it distracts the people. Take the baby out to the hallway, and bring them back in when they are quiet. Miss Kuhlman cannot tolerate noise during the healing service. We cannot allow disturbances in the service; we do not know who God will choose to heal—a cancer patient sitting next to you, or it could be your baby that needs to be healed. We must be quiet to respect the miracle."

Gene used to tease her because "she went on so long talking." Kathryn would say, "Gene, do you think I can make God start healing people. I'm just waiting until He's ready."

Gene asked her, "Kathryn, can't you just take a little longer on the offering?" She would spend a minute or two. Her faith functioned in every way. Sometimes she even forgot to take the offering. She would just shake her head and ask him, "How can I ask them when I am trusting God for a miracle? How can I show them I don't trust God for money?"

To say his job was difficult would be a gross understatement, but to this day, Gene Martin "has never seen any ministry with the power of Kathryn Kuhlman's. I was never in a meeting that wasn't amazing. Kathryn never had to work the people up. The Holy Spirit was there before she came on."

The Shrine Auditorium in downtown Los Angeles was the home of Kathryn's miracle services from 1966 to 1976. The historic seven-thousand-seat venue has been home to the Academy and Emmy Awards. How symbolic for the evangelist that took Hollywood by storm!

The nature of the entertainment industry can lead to the opposite effect of glitz and glamour; long hours on the set, studios run by money-driven executives, and the loss of privacy and control sooner or later create a desire for more meaningful things in life. For ten years, there was not an empty seat in the house, and people happily waited for hours just to have theirs.

Ron Hudson was in charge of the celebrity door. Ruth and Gene Martin were dear friends and knew he had the finesse and class to handle VIPs. When they asked him to help out, he was pleased to do so. Some celebrities would request front-row seats, but Kathryn never lost her heart for the people. Celebrities and VIPs were seated upstairs in the first balcony. Many of them appreciated the sanctuary of not being on display near the front. Kathryn's dramatic presentation made them feel at home rather than at church. She didn't preach at them; she talked to them. Many of them watched her weekly television series *I Believe in Miracles* on Channel 13. Filmed on a beautiful set at CBS, Kathryn represented the quality they related to. Everything that Kathryn did was first class. "God deserves the best," she would say, "He is a big God, so why limit Him?" Kathryn always made it fun, and no one was ever bored by Kathryn's presentation of the Gospel.

Many of the old stars from the 30s and 40s were regulars. One night, Ron Hudson was sound asleep when at 4 a.m., the telephone rang. It was the star of the classic film *Sunset Boulevard.* "This is Gloria Swanson."

Ron thought it must be a joke. "Sure it is. Goodbye."

Again, the phone rang. "This is Gloria Swanson."

Ron began to wake up. "Is this Gloria Swanson? Do you know what time it is?"

Gloria replied, "Oh dear, I'm in Rio on holiday, and I just want to make sure we have seats for the Shrine. I'll be arriving with Ray and Francis Holmes, the Learjet people."

Celebrities and people in high places attended regularly; Robert Young of *Father Knows Best* was healed. Lucille Ball's mother, DeDe, was healed of cancer, and Ma Kettle was an usher. Jimmy Durante, who was Jewish, accepted Jesus Christ, Pat and Shirley Boone were regulars, and George Hamilton came with his mother. Hernando Courtright, the owner of the Beverly Wilshire Hotel, and his beautiful wife had a short commute, compared to the owner of Trader Vic's in Hawaii, who flew in for each service. General Bradley wanted to meet Kathryn Kuhlman. Kathryn appealed to all of them. They laughed, and they cried. In Hollywood, that spells success.

Ron Hudson was one of the few Kathryn could lean on. Ron shared that Kathryn was very human:

"She would fly into town, check into the hotel, go to CBS for tapings, and then do the Shrine. It was nonstop. I would run into her at Bullocks, where she had her hair done and could relax over lunch or while shopping. Kathryn would drive up in that golden-greenish Cadillac convertible carrying her Louis Vuitton feedbag purse. She was always friendly and down-to-earth.

"One day, we drove up to the Shrine at the same time. I looked over, and she looked so tired. She was fighting a cold, and soon, everyone wondered how she would find the energy for the hours long service. Ruth stayed with her as she walked back and forth behind the curtain, praying for the power to be. Suddenly, she came on stage, transformed and glowing. Heaven's door opened for four hours nonstop. We will never see another one like her in our lifetime. She wanted everything perfect for the Kingdom, always keeping God at the forefront. In a split second, she would come down on you with a vengeance if she felt anything was being compromised and not even know that she had done it.

"She was visually impeccable. Kathryn was first class and sophisticated. She loved clothes and jewelry. Eve taught her all about them. She was a stunning woman. Hers was a unique ministry in a man's world. Kathryn was very private. She would never do anything to embarrass herself or her ministry. Everyone was protective of her. Ruth and Maggie were true to her. They did not want anyone to hurt her and knew her likes and dislikes. Many have copied her over the years, but no one will ever replace Kathryn Kuhlman; she was real."

Kathryn would arrive between 8:30 a.m. and 9:00 a.m. and leave the building around 5:30 p.m. or 6:00 p.m. Upon her arrival at the Shrine Auditorium, the ushers were gathered for Kathryn's inspection. One usher was provided for every twenty people, a completely unheard of ratio today. Kathryn insisted they look their best head-to-toe. One time, she sent an usher home because his shoes needed polish. She gave her best and never understood how anyone could do any less. Every section of the auditorium was prayed over. The service began at one o'clock. By noon, as the choir practiced, the anointing was so strong everyone was weeping.

It was paramount to Kathryn that every detail was covered. She couldn't stand coffee breath or bad breath of any kind. She sent Ruth and Maggie with bags of mints to pass out to everyone working. Should they decline, the girls would simply say, "Well, you had better have one anyway." Her dedication was unbelievable. Think what would happen if her standards were apparent in more of the ministries today. Spirituality was not at a peak as it is now with fifty and sixty thousand filling stadiums.

The staff would try to limit the guests in the dressing room afterward to give Kathryn time to have some orange juice and rest from the four intense hours on her feet. As she left the building and looked across the parking lot, she would see those who had not been healed, and her heart would break. Sometimes, she would go to them and try to explain, saying, "I couldn't heal you if I wanted to. Only God can." That's what made her stand out. She cared about everyone, and she took no glory.

Ruth said Kathryn was always good to the people she thought she could trust. "She had little life outside the ministry. There were some who weaseled their way in to further their career or finances, then moved on. They know who they are. We all resented them and saw what Kathryn didn't until it was too late, and they hurt her greatly with their vicious lies."

After it was all over, Kathryn would leave with Gene and Ruth Martin to go somewhere and relax for a nice dinner. Gene especially would build her up for two to three hours, telling her all the things that went on while she was on stage. He always told her the good things and skipped over the bad. She never had an ego, but she needed to hear that she had done a good job. Those who loved her wanted to please and protect her. It is not unusual, as many stars have to be lifted and bragged on. Kathryn was happiest spiritually when there was a big response from people who wanted to be born again. That is what she would meditate on after each service; it gave her peace in knowing that she had done her job.

The Shrine stage is reflective of the larger-than-life way of thinking that permeates the entertainment industry of Los Angeles. It is reminiscent of those in grand opera houses, beautifully lit with spotlights from every direction to assure a great seat for every person in the building.

Every new age guru, spiritual purveyor, fortune teller, or astrological mystic has a chance to find followers in a city with an abundance of lost people searching for a deeper truth. They walked away from traditional beliefs simply because tradition itself is a boring conception in a city that seeks and endorses whatever is on the cutting edge. It has always been a trademark of the exciting city where "characters" are the norm, not the exception.

Kathryn Kuhlman was a perfect blend of character and mysticism. If she were alive today, her following would be even bigger. Her reputation in Los Angeles exploded overnight. Where else could they go and see miracles right before their very eyes? Where else could they go, in a city of millions where many feel so alone, and feel the love of God and man on a Sunday afternoon? There were no freaks in her services, just camaraderie among the 7,000 who transcended age, style, position, or spiritual affiliation. Everyone was in it together, and when it was over, they left not only with hope in Christ, but hope in man.

Love is the answer. Love heals all wounds, quiets all fears, and Kathryn believed love is something you do. It is active, not passive, not a feeling but an act. When you love, you reach outside of yourself and affect others. Self-love is destructive. If there be no love for one another, what is the meaning of life? Left to our own fleshly devices, as Kathryn said of herself, we stink.

It is when we give without expectations of getting that our lives make a difference. Karl Roebling is a Princeton Copyright and promotion man who adopted California and the lifestyle that accompanies it. He attended Kathryn's meeting at the Shrine Auditorium in 1971, which led to a 10,000-mile journey that asked the question in his book, "Is There Healing Power?" Karl ranks Kathryn Kuhlman—who he described as quick as a small bird, effortless, no shrinking violet—as number one. "One thing I had to get used to. Miss Kuhlman often lies on her hands before healing or when she feels it is not quite complete or to impart a blessing. When she does, the effect is often a stunning knockout. People fall over in a faint or slump, or in the case of the ex-addict, nearly loop-the-loop. He had flipped onto the floor at an accidental touch by Miss Kuhlman. After about three such falls, she laughingly warned him, "Stay away from me!"

Seeing those slain in the Spirit was guaranteed. Kathryn did not understand it and said that was one of the questions she wanted to ask when she got to heaven. The only biblical explanation was that it was like when Paul was slain on the road to Damascus. Kathryn never witnessed it until she became a part of Parrott's ministry. Pentecostal and Charismatic believers have accepted it for many years, but the more traditional were shocked and amazed when they witnessed priests, nuns, and other denominational representatives go down on the stage of the Shrine. Sometimes, she would touch them, and other times she would not.

Gene Martin remembers one day when Kathryn simply gestured with her hand as she turned and faced the 300-member choir. Immediately thereafter, a mass of peach and raspberry robes standing nine rows deep crumbled to the floor. Nobody was hurt when they fell. The ushers caught people when they could, but they were not always aware of who would go down. Many who were determined not to be slain in the Spirit, were. It's like 10,000 volts of electricity from God showing you who is in control.

Legendary Gospel songwriter and artist, Andraé Crouch, will never forget the Kathryn Kuhlman meeting he attended. "She had a powerful ministry. We have never seen anything like it since. One Sunday, in the parking lot of my dad's church, a familiar voice came on the radio. She reminded me of my mother, with her slow speech and over-emphasizing of words. She would laugh and giggle. Kathryn worked a lot with Teen Challenge, and she was interviewing Nicky Cruz. I was blessed by his testimony. He was an ex-gang leader. I later met Nicky Cruz, and three months after that, I moved to the Teen Challenge premises. I worked with the choir, and they put me in charge of the van going to the Shrine Auditorium. My bedroom at Teen Challenge had a eucalyptus tree just outside the window. I was allergic to everything. My eyes would swell, my nose was always stopped up, and I was taking a lot of medication that left me lethargic. Any breeze affected my singing.

My Church of God in Christ was seated in the second balcony of Kathryn Kuhlman's service at the Shrine Auditorium. It was the early 1970s, and I was in my twenties. Before the service started, I remembered how I started to cry when I heard Kathryn on the radio.

Kathryn came out with earrings, red lipstick, fingernail polish, and a fancy gown. She was everything but what my church preached about. As Kathryn sang *He Touched Me,* I wondered, 'Where am I?' There was an extreme presence of the Holy Spirit. It was so powerful, and I was amazed at the way it was moving. I was asking myself all these questions. Is she for real? Her dynamics and uniqueness intrigued me. She was like some flamboyant Broadway actress speaking in long, slow phrases. As she pointed a finger to the second balcony, she said, 'Wait a minute. Someone in the second balcony, you're seated with a group, and you are trying to figure out if I'm real or not. You are about the third row up. You have bad allergies. If you inhale right now, you are healed.'

I inhaled deeply. Both my nostrils and my throat were clear. I told the guy next to me, 'That's me.' He looked at me and said, 'Me too.' We were healed at the same time. I wept uncontrollably. I could cry right now just talking about it. God's timing was perfect. I had not even made a record yet, and now I could sing freely. It was a revelation of God's power and the Holy Spirit. God wants us to be delivered and healed more than we want to be. We need it. He showed me He was real and that He could work through anyone in a split second."

Kathryn's prayer life wasn't following anyone else. In her meetings, she was a real worshipper and praiser. She used her uniqueness for the glory of God. She had her style. There are people used of God, in which you can see other people's influences, which isn't bad, but she followed what she heard the Spirit tell her to do. It was not to be like anyone else or to sound like anyone else. Nobody had ever seen anyone like her. She was unique.

Andrae continued by saying:

"I praised her and told people about her. Her clothing style and her inability to sound or be like others didn't matter. When we love God, He works through us. She had a passion for God. She never took any of the credit; all the glory went to God. People need to know that they can be used of God and affect other people for the rest of their lives.

"You saw the character and personalities of God, Jesus, and the Holy Spirit. Kathryn showed you that the Holy Spirit is a real person; His unique personality flowing in a person, causing them to recognize His voice, speaking what He wanted them to speak, to get the results through the blood and stripes of Jesus Christ. I saw the uniqueness of the personalities of God. If you had any questions about the Holy Spirit, she could bring them out."

Kathryn paid the price for her gifts from God. Those uniquely designed by God with a specific anointing pay for it. The gift is free, but to know the cost.

Andraé knows the cost. He gave up the glamour and hoopla of the LA entertainment world to be the down-to-earth pastor of the Pentecostal Church that his father and mother founded. With his ordained twin sister, Sandra, by his side, they devoted their lives to the troubled area of the San Fernando Valley where they grew up.

Andraé Crouch was always a pioneer, and it was nowhere more evident than at the New Christ Memorial Church of God in Christ. Women played a very important and active role. It was not unusual for the women of the church to stay shut in, fasting for seven days at a time. Andraé once said, "Go forth in whom God has created. God is not interested in gender; He is interested in the agenda."

Andraé's testimony expresses the true wisdom, shown from one having nothing to prove of himself. Kathryn would love and appreciate the ministry of Andraé and Sandra Crouch.

Karl Roebling observed some classic Kathryn moments that day at the Shrine. A couple on the stage was telling their story. One month ago, at a meeting in Portland, he had been healed of multiple sclerosis. The wheelchair that had been his companion for nine years was no longer needed, and the medical professionals were without explanation. He was full of life, praising God, and Kathryn touched him with a double dose of the Holy Spirit. His wife was jubilant and asked Kathryn for a favor. When they were married, he was in his wheelchair, but now she wanted to marry him again while he stood. She wondered if Kathryn would do the honors and marry them a second time.

Of course, she would. Right now! It is doubtful there was a dry eye in the house while the husband and wife stood side by side to renew their marriage vows. Kathryn was overwhelmed. She was laughing and crying as she told the audience, "This is what I live for, friends. This is what I live for." She looked up and added, "I just want to be so very careful to give you the praise." The music played softly as the simple wedding vows began. "Do you take this man?" It was more than Kathryn could bear. Surely, each time she heard those words, she recalled when she was on the other side of the preacher. Her sense of humor and quick wit were her natural ways to pull herself together. "Which one of us is taking these vows?"

It was one of those true to nature, real moments in life when we are lost inside the lives of someone else. No one was able to draw you in, to lose yourself like Kathryn Kuhlman. Her audience connected with her on a deeply spiritual but human level and felt the emotions she felt. Her love for others was at the very core of her being, and she made you realize just how good it feels to care. As the happy couple walked down the center ramp into the audience to the wedding march, you too understood what she meant by, "This is what I live for."

Kathryn operated moment by moment. She didn't need notes or outlines. She didn't deliver sermons. Her show, if you want to perceive it as such, was akin to being an actress whose lines were so well delivered, you believed they were her own. Kathryn's only writer was the Holy Spirit, and she had never seen the script. It was this spontaneous quality that kept each meeting fresh.

The dynamics were compelling as she would whisper and step back deep in thought, then the driving words of knowledge that she could not contain exploded from her lips with an intensity that could not be questioned. You knew she was for real, and everything she felt came out of her deep love for God and man.

Kathryn had been warned for years to slow down. Her heart condition demanded it, but she loved what she did more than she loved herself. In that same meeting in 1971, after scores were healed of devastating disease and injury, she cried out in an earnest plea to her heavenly Father. She stepped back and lifted her hands to Him, "Please, don't take my life from me. Please, don't take my life from me. I want to see it through to the finish. Trust me, please. I will never betray the trust You put in me. I can't do anything. I am completely dependent on Your Holy Spirit." She was so modest, giving all the credit to whom it belonged. She knew her role was only that of an intermediary. "I have a recurring nightmare that one day my gift will be gone. I step onto the stage, but there are no people. If I ever walk on that stage and the Holy Spirit is not there, that will be the last time."

It was what she lived for. Her number one goal was to do her best to be like Jesus on this earth. One of the last healings that day was the perfect finale to the greatest show on earth: the show of God's amazing power through one who completely died to self, so others could be blessed and healed, so they too would become living examples of amazing grace.

There was a loud, primal scream like that of a devil who didn't want to come out. Kathryn was speaking to an adorable little boy about four years old who was dressed as a cowboy. "Come on. Come on. Walk." They had just removed his brace. He screamed again, not even wanting to try. She moved in closer and commanded him to walk. He still wouldn't budge.

The house was dead silent. All eyes, all hearts, were deadlocked into the fate of this precious child. Again, Kathryn commanded him to walk. She spoke with love and authority, never wavering. "Come on! Walk! Come on! Walk!"

Maybe he would be one of those who were not healed. The audience began to accept it.

They felt sorry for Kathryn as well as the little boy. However, she was determined, for she knew what was holding him, and she wasn't going to let go.

With more love than ever, as she looked at his father on the opposite side of the stage, she said, "Go to Daddy. Run! Run to Daddy! Run! Run!" He took off like a rocket. The building rocked in every direction as every seat in the house went crazy with joy. More than a child was set free that day at the Shrine Auditorium.

I BELIEVE IN
MIRACLES

*C*BS Studios was home to Carol Burnett, Red Skelton, Jack Benny, Sonny and Cher, and Dinah Shore, but they had never met anyone quite like Kathryn Kuhlman. At the time, women preachers were not on television. Kathryn wanted the best of everything for the Lord, which led to her choosing CBS Television City to produce her *I Believe in Miracles* program. The network was not accustomed to producing religious programs and requested the payment of $200,000 for 83-minute shows in advance. That was fine with Kathryn. She had never been limited in her faith, and God had never failed her.

CBS provided top-notch professionals. In true Hollywood style, they changed her gowns, softened her 1940s hairdo, and taught her to speak to the one person watching instead of the thousands to whom she was accustomed to speaking. Her wardrobe was magnificent. Some were so glamorous that she wasn't sure if they were preacher material. Those she trusted would assure her that God gave her the body to wear them. Embarrassed and delighted at the same time, she usually gave in to the glamorous image the designers at CBS created. She had a star on her dressing room, her name on a director's chair, and her hair and makeup people. They treated her better than their stars.

After viewing the first show, Kathryn changed two things. The first one was easy. On the suggestion of her head usher's wife, who had worked with Aimee Semple McPherson, she would not cross her long legs. It looked too suggestive. The next thing was a bit more complicated. She showed Ruth Martin the tape, "Check it out. Look at my neck and jowls. See what we can do." Ruth researched plastic surgeons in the area and made an appointment.

Kathryn listened as the doctor described the procedure, the follow-up, and possible complications. She looked at Ruth. "So, when can you do it?"

Ruth was confused. "Me? I don't even need it."

Kathryn replied in all seriousness, "Well, how will you know to take care of me if you don't?" Kathryn had a way with everyone. No one ever said no to her.

Ruth had her face done at her own expense and looked even better than ever. She could not wait to show Kathryn the results. The next time Kathryn saw Ruth was at a meeting in Tulsa. Ruth was waiting patiently for Kathryn to say something. But Kathryn said nothing. Finally, Ruth blurted out, "Thanks a lot, Kathryn. You put me through all that hurt, and you haven't even said a word!" It was a game the friends played fully to get to one another.

Kathryn was next and was one terrible patient. She had never stayed overnight in the hospital. All night she tossed and turned, making her already swollen face and neck worse. In those days, you wore a "helmet" until the swelling went down, and Kathryn looked like something out of a horror film. Showing her sense of humor, she let herself be photographed. Gene and Ruth stayed with her in Newport Beach until she healed. She looked great. She looked ten years younger, a very important value when you are on television and in the public eye. You see, no one realized she was already fifty-eight years old when she came back to LA. Early on, she began avoiding her true age. It was easy to get away with since she looked so much younger. Once, she jokingly told a reporter she was eighty years old, and they printed it. A reader wrote in, "If Kathryn were eighty and looked that great, that would be the greatest miracle of them all!" Confident in her appearance, she was now ready to roll the cameras.

Once a month, for two consecutive days, stages 33 and 43 belonged to *I Believe in Miracles.* CBS shot 83-minute programs. They had one chance to get it right. There were no retakes. Ruth interviewed and scheduled the guests ahead of time. Kathryn never spoke to the guests before taping. She wanted to keep everything fresh. After taping, they would view the tapes and call it a day. As usual, the crew had a difficult time keeping up with Kathryn. She was raring to go when the power came on her. *I Believe in Miracles* was the longest-running show produced at CBS at the time.

Kathryn was an approachable star. The crew was not uncomfortable seeking her prayers in their personal lives or those of their loved ones. She graciously gave of herself to all of them. She was treated with the respect she deserved—from the studio head to the janitor. Her effect at CBS penetrated every level.

Charles Cappleman, affectionately known as "Cappy," had been with CBS for forty-four years. He even became the senior vice president of west coast operations and engineering. Mr. Cappleman sold Kathryn her time slot. "She changed CBS forever and changed the way I thought. The entire mood changed when she walked into the building. She made a difference. Everyone at CBS loved her and wondered if she was for real. Later, they realized she was. She would pray for anyone, anywhere. Even the crew became fascinated with her, and many went to her services at the Shrine Auditorium and volunteered."

Jim Hesson was his boss at the time. Jim had almost drunk himself to death. Kathryn went to see him twice to pray for his healing. It looked pretty bleak. The X-rays showed no trace of a liver. Within nine months, he completely recovered and miraculously grew a new liver. The doctors called it Kathryn Kuhlman's liver. Jim Hesson was so taken with Kathryn Kuhlman; he was willing to leave CBS and go to work for her. Sadly, Jim Hesson put his faith in the servant, not the Master. Nine months after Kathryn died, so did he.

Willie Dahl was her stage manager. Willie and Cappy worked together on the Carol Burnett and Red Skelton shows, so he called Willie about an all-new show with a religious lady. On the first day, Willie walked onto a beautiful set with flowers, chandeliers, and a grand piano. Kathryn came out and graciously introduced herself to everyone on the crew. Anything you wanted from her was no problem. The director was extremely quiet, as was Kathryn while she tested her microphone. The time cue was given. Willie took a prop vodka bottle and filled it with water. He positioned it where Kathryn could see the bottle, and on her cue, took a big gulp, wiped his mouth, and said, "I'm going to need a big drink to get through this." Kathryn lost it completely. She was howling with laughter. From then on, she only wanted Willie to do her show.

Willie and Art Gilmore, her announcer, shared the same sentiments. "The show ran like a top. It was a piece of cake. She was a joy to work with. She welcomed anyone new and noticed if anyone was missing. She was a great lady with a terrific sense of humor who we all loved and respected."

The set was so quiet that Willie had to send the stagehands outside to open a pack of cigarettes. The normal sequence at the close of the show was the time cues being counted down, and then the director called, "Bring up the music and fade to black," as Kathryn was still praying.

Willie would lightly tap her on the shoulder and whisper, "Lunch, one hour." Willie was unable to make it on one occasion, and another rather inexperienced stage manager filled in. Instead of the light tap on the shoulder and whisper announcing lunch, he did what was normal on any set; at the top of his lungs, he called out, "Lunch, one hour!" This was not the kind of thing you did when you had a preacher deep in prayer. Kathryn came out of her chair like she had been shot out of a cannon. She told Cappy from then on if Willie couldn't make it, neither could she.

The quiet set was disturbed one other time when they were on a soundstage next to the *Sonny and Cher* show. The loud music was banging through the walls, and every pause had to be edited out at the expense of CBS. Occasionally, the shows shared dressing room space. Can't you just see Kathryn in Cher's decked-out American Indian decor dressing room, complete with totem pole?

A few times, Kathryn delighted everyone in her handling of a difficult situation. One day, an obnoxious actor, who was on everyone's nerves, loudly complained they were running behind, and he needed to finish on time. Frustrated, he said loudly, "Yeah, lady, if we finish on time, that would be a miracle!" Never one to lose out on an opportunity, Kathryn came back with, "If I do, will you believe?" She did, and pointing her finger at him, she smiled and asked, "Now, do you believe?" The crew was delighted.

Kathryn noticed many of the crew wearing embroidered jackets from the other shows. She asked Willie where she could get some. The next thing he knew, she presented everyone on the crew with a spiffy "Kathryn Kuhlman and The Boys" jacket.

At the end of a long day, when they were finished, Kathryn would go up to Cappy's office, open her briefcase, and ask how much? Right then and there, she counted it out. She was the only person who ever paid CBS in cash.

Dino Kartsonakis was Kathryn's pianist for seven years. Ruth Martin first heard him play in one of Ralph Wilkerson's services at Melodyland in Anaheim, California. Also featured were Pat Boone and Andraé Crouch. She came up to him afterward, complimented his talent, and told him she would like for Kathryn to meet him.

Shortly thereafter, Kathryn and Ruth were in Paul Webb's office on Sunset Drive. Dino had stopped by to see if they had any booking engagements for him. He had just got out of the Army, where he played mostly for the officers' wives. Ruth thought he might fill a place for the youth and told Kathryn. Dino looked up to see Ruth and a woman who looked like a 1930s fashion model coming toward him. "So, you're Deeno," she said, in her own special way, pointing the longest index finger he had ever seen. Kathryn looked right through him as though this were some great revelation. "You're Deeno," she said again. He looked to Ruth, thinking this lady was from another planet. Kathryn trusted Ruth's judgment concerning his talent. She was more interested in the person and asked Dino about his family, a subject he delighted in sharing. She liked what she heard and invited him to join her and play at CBS. Dino wisely rented a tuxedo, which Kathryn thought was great. When he played for her, she was sold. Ruth was right. He would be a great addition to the show and draw a younger audience. For the next seven years, he held court on almost every stage with Kathryn.

Dino was just a little Greek kid who grew up living over a fish market in New York City. His gift was in his hands. He worked hard and practiced enough to go to Julliard, and now, like so many others, he moved to Hollywood seeking fame and fortune. But for right now, he was driving an old car and living in Los Feliz, California. It was a long way from the glamour of the CBS studios and the stage at the Shrine before an audience of 7,000.

Kathryn could sell anyone. She consistently sold Dino, so he always had an instant audience. It took a while for him to grow on Kathryn personally, but once he did, he became her pet project. Soon he was a slick, manicured package with custom-made tuxedos, diamond jewelry, and a redefined nose. Just as Eve had mentored Kathryn, teaching her about the finer things in life, Kathryn loved and treated Dino like a son. She taught him about nice things: art, jewelry, furniture, restaurants, and hotels.

It was platonic. She respected his talent. He was fun to be with, and who wouldn't enjoy a handsome young man on their arm for dinner? Together they were the kind of eye candy that created whispers from one end of the room to the other. She did not enjoy eating alone in her hotel room. Dino provided the companionship she needed to share in those wonderful years.

Kathryn exuded power and presence. Even those who worked beside her for years were intimidated, but not Dino. He was funny. Kathryn loved his grandmother, Yaya—so much so that she eventually helped move his parents to California.

Dino knew how to get what he wanted out of Kathryn. Dino worked Kathryn like a child works his wealthy parents. In the beginning, he managed to play on Ruth, inviting himself to go to eat after the Shrine or taping at CBS, telling her, "I'm alone, why can't I go?" Kathryn gave him too much, too soon, and consequently, he became like a spoiled child. One day, he was a struggling young man, and almost overnight, he was a star. It was, for him, a difficult transition. Kathryn took him on trips around the world, made him a star, beautifully furnished his home, and dressed him like royalty. Not once did she think the trust between them would be destroyed.

Kathryn never lost the childlike wonder and qualities that enabled her great faith. That childlike effervescence bubbled over into a love for the pranks that most of us outgrow. She was game for a good-hearted joke on somebody else. A crew member wanted to play a joke on Carol Burnett and asked Kathryn to help. "Why, sure, I'd be happy to," she said. There was a long-standing bet on Carol's set that no one could unexpectedly crack her up. The two great ladies were always in control of their respective shows. In the prepared scene, Carol was to say her line and open the door for one of her co-stars to come in. As Carol opens the door, the unexpected occurs. Kathryn Kuhlman walked through the door, looked Carol in the eye, and asked, "Have you been waiting for me?" Carol Burnett's longstanding professional presence was lost that day as she rolled on the floor, hysterically laughing with the woman she had imitated so many times. This time, the laugh was on her.

Carol returned the visit to Kathryn's set with a surprise walk on. Everyone at CBS admired Kathryn, including Carol Burnett. "I think this woman is incredible. Every time I hear her, I feel like a better person." Sonny and Cher dropped by to let her know they, too, were fans.

"You're the best. We laugh, but we know that you are real."

One day, Kathryn's soloist, Jimmie McDonald, noticed a diminutive figure watching quietly in the wings as Kathryn spoke of Jesus Christ and salvation. She dabbed her eyes with a handkerchief as she, too, felt the power of the Holy Spirit.

Perhaps, she would have felt uncomfortable, but she also noticed many of the burly crew members watch silently with tears in their eyes. Jimmie could hardly believe his eyes; the woman was Bette Davis, the award-winning actress whose film roles are now classics. He asked Bette if she would like to meet Ms. Kuhlman. Indeed, she would, but she didn't want to interrupt. At the next break, Jimmie told Kathryn, who, of course, was extremely happy to do so. Jimmie escorted Bette over and introduced her to Kathryn. "Hi there, Honey. I'm so honored that you would come to my taping." Bette had been a fan for years. At the time, she was filming on a nearby soundstage and could not resist the opportunity to come by and let Kathryn personally know what a blessing she had been in her life.

Kathryn was thankful; she understood the difficulties and the loneliness of being a celebrity, and she sensed a need in Bette Davis.

"Would you like for me to pray with you, dear?" Bette looked at her with those famous eyes and nodded her head. Kathryn took her hand in hers and prayed for God's blessings over her. Miss Davis dabbed her eyes one more time and thanked her for the prayer.

Many of Kathryn's *I Believe in Miracles* programs are available for viewing at the archives of the Billy Graham Center in Wheaton, Illinois. They are timeless treasures that speak to every age, denomination, and personal struggle. It is not uncommon for people to come and spend days watching one after another.

An especially tender series of interviews are those with the Jesus People. One day, on a break from taping, Kathryn was informed that a couple of hundred hippies had gathered in a nearby room and asked to meet her. She called Dino and Jimmie to go with her. As they walked in the door, the group began singing praise choruses in three-part harmony as beautifully as any she had ever heard. She was so moved by them that she never noticed their appearance that turned off most of the establishment. They were longhair hippie types, dressed in freaky clothes. She judged them not. As she listened and looked at their faces, each child became her own. One of the "wildest looking Jesus freaks" acted as the spokesman for the group. "Miss Kuhlman, we are all believers. God has rescued us from drugs, and we wondered if you would pray for us. We need a touch from God to help us continue our walk with Him." She not only prayed, but laid hands on each one as they sang the "Hallelujah" chorus over and over.

It was the one time she told her producer the previously scheduled show would have to wait. This was a divine move of God, restoring the innocence of His children, and the opportunity to impact all America was right before her. The "Hallelujah" chorus became an integral part of her services from then on, and the Jesus People came back again and again. The sheet music of the song, written by Jerry Sinclair, is among her belongings. Kathryn now stood in the forefront with a virtual army of Jesus People behind her.

Sitting in a tie-dyed granny dress, Kathryn was proud to be one of them. "You've seen them in magazines. They are the most wonderful people in the world, but have you seen their hearts?" She adores them as she takes their faces in her hands; she looks deeply into their heart. It is a beautiful picture of love touching love. There is no staging, no dramatics, only the presence of the Holy Spirit. "How old are you? Have you ever been on dope? How long? How did you know that you were hungry for Jesus? Are you happy now?" They answered openly with complete confidence. They had tasted everything the world had to offer, and nothing could meet their need or thirst. Just as Jesus said to the woman at the well, "He who drinks of this will never thirst again," they are satiated with the love of Christ in a beautiful, abundant way.

Jesus was all they needed; a constant friend, always with them, and they felt His presence. It was not an experience; it was there for life. Something immediately happened when they completely submitted, and the change put such love and peace on all their faces; you could only smile as they pointed to heaven at the end and sang Kathryn's theme song, *He Touched Me.*

Another series of interviews that are deeply moving are those with Gene Martin. Kathryn introduces him, "I count Gene and Ruth Martin as members of my own family. They are among my closest friends. We have traveled around the world together. He is the head of the mission's department of the Kathryn Kuhlman Foundation, one of the largest works of any foundation or church. Together, we have built twenty-two debt-free churches around the world. No one can surpass you. God called you, and you're the greatest."

Gene nods his head in appreciation and explains their work. "We go into the world, seek out an area, and find a native preacher who needs a place to house the congregation. It's the tool that has been so overlooked. The building gives permanency to the work of God. The Kathryn Kuhlman Foundation builds the mission stations and gives them debt-free." Kathryn laughs at the irony: "We have no church building of our own." In her ministry, Kathryn chose to put her money in people, not buildings.

Gene shows some slides. "Foremost, and one of the finest in the world, is in downtown Taipei. It's four-and-a-half stories tall, the tallest building in the area. Until our mission into Panama, they were unreached for Christ." As Gene spoke, Kathryn listened quietly and allowed him to take over. It was a rare moment of the trust Kathryn was not usually inclined toward.

As Gene gave his testimony, it was crystal clear that he had not changed one bit over the years. He was the same sensitive, spirit-filled man that day. Like Kathryn Kuhlman, Gene Martin was so touched by God's grace and the need for it that his emotions spill out of the heart like one who is sold out.

"Ruth and I visited a leper in Taiwan. We sang, and Ruth played the accordion for an hour. Everyone loved it. Then it came time to distribute the gifts that were so beautifully wrapped. His eyes filled with tears, saying, the American woman had discarded their clothing and costumed jewelry, and these people were so thrilled to receive them.

They asked us if we would like to visit a ward. We went to the lepers' area where there was a Buddhist boy, who was visited once a month by a Buddhist monk. Once or twice a week, the Christian women came to shower and clean him up. They showed him the love of Jesus. In a few months, he told the Buddhist monks not to come back.

Being a Christian is giving life, not taking. As we were leaving, there was a fresh rain with a heavy overcast. A wonderful German nurse who had volunteered there for twelve years told us, 'You said you would come back. Some of these people will not be here, but they have something they want to say to you.'

The Tai sang, "God will take care of you" in their language."

This was the work of the mission's department of the Kathryn Kuhlman Foundation, and Kathryn was touched and pleased. "The only Christ they can see is through us. The greatest achievement in the world is to win someone to the Lord Jesus Christ through love," she said.

The Kathryn Kuhlman Foundation purchased 1,000 wheelchairs and crutches to give to the Vietnamese, who had lost limbs when the enemy's mine traps exploded on them. Kathryn and the Martins personally went to Saigon to deliver them. ABC sent a film crew along in preparation for a documentary. There are several programs with excellent footage from their visit. During the Vietnam War, Gene made seven trips on behalf of the foundation to oversee the building of a Protestant chapel that was dedicated during their visit.

The sole purpose of this trip was for Kathryn to be with the Vietnamese people. They arrived at Konsanat Air Force Base in South Vietnam, the busiest military installation in the world at the time. She went with no political agenda; her purpose was to show the love of

Jesus to people all over the world. A line of government representatives, along with Major Kee, the Protestant chaplain, was waiting with the red carpet. The Missionary Alliance was there to thank her for her humanitarian work.

Kathryn, along with her trusted followers, visited an outdoor central market in Saigon as they made their way to the hospital. Their mission was to distribute the gifts of wheelchairs and crutches. The injured soldiers greeted them with big smiles and bright eyes. Since their injuries, the crippled soldiers had been unable to do anything but lay in their hospital beds. Their happiness was apparent as they wheeled around and hobbled on crutches, thanks to Kathryn's generous donations. That in itself, made the trip worth it to Kathryn.

Next, she visited the Vietnamese Rangers who had defended the capital city. They stood proudly in line as Kathryn, through an interpreter, stopped along the way to ask several of them their ages. They were only teenagers, and it was disturbing to her. A jeep arrived, and the colonel took the wheel with Kathryn in the front seat. Two soldiers with automatic weapons sat behind them, and they went to the perimeter where the fighting took place each night.

Kathryn was fearless as she was taken by helicopter up to the Cambodian border, a dangerous area in the war-torn country. Ruth remembers the warnings of the American pilot and co-pilot, "Why are you here? What are you doing? You should be home. We get paid for this. Look at all those B-36 bomber craters everywhere. One could hit us at any time. It's uncomfortable for us to have to fly you."

There was a curfew at night. The streets were dark. You had to keep your drapes pulled and the lights off. There were bombs so close that they stood on the hotel roof to watch the bombs drop. They were scared, but they had a job to do.

The first lady invited them to visit the palace. A female senator joined in for a conversation through interpreters. Kathryn was especially taken when the prime minister's wife escorted her through the city, showing tremendous concern over the poverty of the people. Before the war, Saigon was known as the Paris of the Orient.

She showed Kathryn an orphanage the American servicemen began that was surrounded by barbed wire. The Viet Cong had surrounded the village, and the old men took out their rifles to defend their homes. The men and women used bicycles and tricycles to distribute the homemade bombs they had made. They sped out into the thickets, killing many of the Viet Cong and capturing others; still, some lost their lives and left little children behind.

On a visit to a military prison in Northwest Saigon, the 2,400 inmates gave Kathryn a plaque they made from wood and tin cans of the scales of justice. They were so appreciative that somebody cared.

Kathryn sat beside Gene in a director's chair, dressed in fatigues made from the fabric the Vietnamese Rangers had sent to her. She was wearing the first skirt in the history of the Rangers.

She went to Vietnam for the value of one human life. "I remember the children looking into my face, the men, the American Soldiers, all their precious mothers loved their children, just like Mama loved me. All over the world, mothers love their children.

"There is so much sin. War is so unlovely. We must forget our differences. Come back to the one who loves you; greater than the power of all the Armies, Air Force, Parliaments, or power of government is the power of love. Get back to love.

"American men have given their lives. The least I could do was go and give them the love of God through Jesus Christ, who gave His life for them. They didn't speak the same language, but everyone speaks love."

The wisdom of her words is still applicable today. Kathryn didn't go to Vietnam for political reasons or personal gain. She went to give love, hope, and faith to those who so desperately needed a Savior. She was presented with the highest Medal of Honor the Vietnamese bestow to anyone.

CELEBRITY STATUS

"I beeeeelieeeeve in meeeericles...because I beeeelievah in Goooood." She strung out keywords, so they became four syllables. Kathryn became the subject of numerous impersonations within the entertainment industry and a favorite at private parties. You know that you have made it when Middle America knows, without being told, who's being imitated. She was larger than life in every way; her looks, her dramatic speech, and effervescent style resembled no other. It was uniquely hers.

Rowan and Martin's Laugh-In was one of the top shows of the era. For weeks, Ruth Buzzi imitated Kathryn. Of course, she never used her name. In Kathryn's favorite segment, Ruth Buzzi stands in a supermarket checkout line. She wears a red wig and a beautiful silk gown with flowing sleeves. She reaches down and picks up an orange. "Is this an orange? Oh, yesssss! It is an oooraaange! A beautifully, divinely shaped orange!" She repeats the exaggerated gestures as she examines more fruit. Kathryn's already melodramatic speech and gestures were emphasized even more. Kathryn loved it so much that she wired the comedian a dozen roses with a note saying, "No one enjoyed the satire more than I." Ruth Buzzi never imitated her again.

Others who imitated her stopped the moment they encountered her face-to-face and realized she was the real thing. Candice Bergen knew she was the real thing. When she was asked to be a guest host on *The Dick Cavett Show,* her only request before accepting the offer was to interview Kathryn Kuhlman.

ABC did a documentary in 1970, showing Kathryn at her Fox Chapel home in Pittsburgh, Pennsylvania. Kathryn, who rarely cooked at all, bought a housedress and pretended to be at home in the kitchen. It was a little staged, trying to portray someone quite human and ordinary. The camera doesn't lie, and that probably explains why it never ran.

ABC must have learned from its mistake. They later sent a camera crew with Kathryn to Vietnam. This time they captured the true mission and heart of this very extraordinary woman. That documentary was excellent in content and style, reflective of the bravery and faith innate to Kathryn.

Kathryn was at home with her celebrity status. She was born a star and destined for greatness. She loved the people, all of them, and they loved her. Johnny Carson invited her to be a guest on NBC's *The Tonight Show.*

Johnny's introduction set the stage for the powerful interview. "Along with Billy Graham, she is one of the best known for her belief in the Holy Spirit. Welcome, Kathryn Kuhlman." The audience went crazy, at once giving her a rousing standing ovation. She looked stunning as she glided to her seat like a supermodel in a long, sleek gown with a beatific smile and dancing eyes. When they finally settled down, Johnny gave a befuddled take to the camera. "Well, that's one-upmanship." The audience showed their love for Kathryn by applause that lasted much longer than the one they had given Johnny just a few minutes ago.

Johnny froze at the controls in her presence. "I'm fascinated by you. You're hypnotic, charismatic, mesmerizing." Kathryn knew the truth. It was not the flesh before him that he described. "That is just amazing to me. I am the most ordinary person in the world." No way was Johnny buying into that. "You have a great effect on people. You are very out of the ordinary. Have you ever met anyone you didn't like?" Without hesitation, looking a bit mischievous, she replied, "No, not even Dr. Nolan," who had written a book disputing some of the miracles in her services.

"No matter how unloving they are on the outside, they hide behind a mask. All have had sorrow, heartbreak, and felt sympathy." Johnny not only treated Kathryn with the utmost respect, but he brought up things on national television that showed his more serious side. He must have surprised the millions of viewers accustomed to his usual light-hearted comedy.

"You preach the Gospel of the Holy Spirit. Why don't you like being called a faith healer?" Kathryn played off Johnny Carson like they were a tag team for God. "They don't understand. I've never healed anyone. I simply stand there and tell the people how big God is. I give them hope and faith. To say there was no healing because of one's lack of faith is the cruelest thing to say." Her way with words overpowered people. Intrigued by her candor, Johnny asked, "Do you believe nothing is impossible when people with faith receive no healing, and then others with no faith are healed?"

Kathryn replied, "Yes, I have to believe God is sovereign. I've seen too many unlikely people healed."

Johnny was taken by this kind of grace. "You are a fascinating woman with no detractors." As though she never heard the compliment, Kathryn continued. "I don't understand miracles. Many cases are psychosomatic, but don't they realize that is one of the hardest patients in the world to cure? Mental illness gives them something greater than themselves. I give them God. I am not a healer. If I can give hope through Jesus Christ, the Son of God, to the most insecure generation in this poor whole world, the only security is hope, faith, and confidence in God."

"A brilliant woman, a Kansas City Reporter, brought her friend to a service. He died, but she wrote me that it was the greatest thing that he came. It prepared him to die."

"I love people. What this nation needs is a fresh baptizing of the love of God." Johnny Carson's curiosity was peaked, and the king of late-night talk shows opened the door even further. "The Holy Spirit, what is it?"

In closing, Kathryn reached millions of viewers in her biggest audience ever. "The three members of the Trinity are the Father, the Son, and the Holy Spirit. The Holy Spirit is the mighty power of the Trinity in the world today. I believe the Bible so much that I would die for what I believe. Ye shall receive power after the Holy Ghost has come upon you."

Dinah Shore was the first female to have her own daytime talk show. It was popular for many years. She introduced Kathryn as quite a woman, one of the country's leading faith healers. She didn't know how Kathryn felt about being called a faith healer. Comedian Lily

Tomlin was probably the guest that initiated Kathryn's presence. She had attended a miracle service at the Shrine Auditorium. "I went at 7 a.m. The doors did not open until one. There are 7,000 seats, and I barely got one. I was mesmerized. I saw so many miracles at the Shrine that I got bored." Lily spoke with humor and love, and Kathryn took to her.

The interview was mostly between the two of them. The wild and wonderful Lily even asked Kathryn about reincarnation. "Well, the Bible does not teach it, so I don't believe in it. I'm going to be me forever. I know absolutely nothing about psychic healing."

Charlton Heston was the next guest, and he sat down next to Kathryn. When he came on, Dinah tried to gain control of her show again by asking him about faith. With little expression, he replied, "Faith can move mountains in any direction." When you talked about faith, Kathryn had a lot to say, and even the man who played Moses couldn't get a word in.

On a station break, Charlton changed seats with Lily, who was sitting on the opposite sofa from Kathryn. Lily took Kathryn's hand and held it as though Edith Ann, her childlike character, had taken over. It was a mutual admiration experience.

Kathryn closed with some simple words that day: "It is always thrilling to see God work. So simple is the power of God. We try to bring God down to man's level of mercy and compassion. I feel sorry for those who don't believe. It is the greatest treasure, and everything else is built on it."

Kathryn's first major book was *I Believe in Miracles.* To promote her book, she was at the May Company in LA. There was a line around the second floor, down the escalator to the first floor. A working man in overalls approached the table where Kathryn was signing books. She stopped and looked up, "Oh, you have been working hard." He put out his hand, then noticing they were still greasy, rubbed them on his overalls.

She stopped him, grabbed his hand, grease and all, and said, "Oh, it's alright, sir. It doesn't matter."

He looked desperate. "I've come right from work, and I didn't have time to wash my hands. I apologize, but my wife is so sick. I wanted you to pray for her." Kathryn assured him to think nothing of it. She asked all about his wife and exactly what was wrong. She stood with that man for ten minutes, praying a very long prayer. Right behind him was a woman dripping in diamonds, with a fur stole and hat. She had Kathryn's book, and as she came up to the table, she laid the book down, expecting Kathryn to talk with her. Kathryn asked if she would like a name inscribed, which she did. Kathryn wrote the name and some short notes, handed the book back to the woman, and said, "God bless you." That was just how Kathryn was.

Her compassion toward the working people was unbelievable. Another woman approached, "I am off duty, but I clean floors here, and I'm on my break, so I am not dressed very well." Kathryn looked at her hands, seeing not only were they hardworking, but also crippled with arthritis. Kathryn took the lady's hands in hers and spent several minutes praying for God's blessings and His healing upon this woman.

Kathryn was accessible to the people: the sick, poor, hardworking, and helpless. Although she was a media superstar, her needs were very simple for her stature. She never required special attention. It was freely given to her. There was nothing to prove. She was always one of us, down-to-earth. She never considered herself high and mighty.

Kathryn came to an understanding early on that some of the others who have been in ministry for decades did not understand; it was unusual strength, quiet strength. There was no need to be demanding or domineering. The spirit of compassion she exuded made people want to please her.

Nor was she one to name-drop or try to meet and be seen with the right people. When people wanted to meet her, it was easy to be gracious. When people complimented the way she looked, she would simply say, "Oh, that's so nice." She wasn't beautiful in the traditional sense. It was good to look nice, but looks were irrelevant. Her mind was on higher things, and insecurity was not a part of it.

In 1972, Kathryn was invited to the Vatican to meet with Pope Paul VI. Ruth set it up at Kathryn's request. As they walked across the palatial courtyard, Kathryn looked at Ruth with wonder and said, "Can you believe this?"

The Pope extended his blessings over Kathryn's ministry. Catholics have long supported her. Priests and nuns sat on many stages behind Kathryn as she spoke a doctrine they also believed in, the Divinity of Jesus Christ. Despite all this, she still insisted she was just like the rest of us. "Without the Holy Spirit, I'm the most ordinary person in the world."

LAUGHTER AND TEARS

*K*athryn was extremely protective of her ministry and rarely got close to anyone. She was a loner out of choice and didn't make friends easily. Her ministry was not going to be exploited or taken advantage of. With Gene and Ruth Martin, Kathryn could be herself: vulnerable, human, difficult, needy, and frustrated. It was that element that led to the closeness they shared. Kathryn didn't have to be "on" when she was around the Martins.

The three of them were dedicated to the work, but they also knew how to have a good time. Not anything off-color, but Kathryn abhorred being with people who took life too seriously. Life was supposed to be enjoyed. Their professional and personal relationship allowed Kathryn to express both sides. They worked and traveled together as a team, traveling around the world for thirteen years.

Kathryn never talked much about religion or the ministry after work. When the discussion of business was over, she asked, "What are we going to do tomorrow? Where are we going to go? Let's go shopping and enjoy the local sights." She was a real person, too, and real people need a life. Otherwise, they burn out and lose what is left of the anointing.

The true testimony of any ministry is the leader's behavior off the pulpit. Kathryn was refreshingly the same, on or off. She was a barrel of fun to be with, not at all a pious religious figure. When interviewing someone, she would often ask if they expected to be healed today.

Many times, the answer would be something like, "No, I came to make fun of you." Kathryn simply looked at the audience and grinned like a Cheshire cat.

Kathryn believed that everything in life was a gift, and she had a great sense of humor. She always cried when she laughed; it was heartfelt. Her sense of humor was one of her most endearing qualities. The ability to laugh at herself, her idiosyncrasies and shortcomings, was a large part of the childlike quality that enabled her to handle stressful situations.

When Oral Roberts presented her with an honorary doctorate, Ruth couldn't go. Afterward, Kathryn told her, "I'm sitting on the platform with all these men. I'm thinking, I wish Ruth were here. I could look down and mouth, 'What the heck am I doing here?'"

"We would both start laughing." Ruth responded, "Well, it would have broken up the whole thing. They would have thought we were two idiots!"

Kathryn laughed and said, "What do we care?"

Ruth checked Kathryn into a hospital in Long Beach, California, for some tests. It was three o'clock in the afternoon, and by four, both were bored. Kathryn looked at the bed and rolled her eyes, and suggested, "I can't sleep on these pillows. Let's call Gene. Have him meet us at the Velvet Turtle and bring some good ones."

It was up to Ruth to convince Miss Deadpan, the all too diligent nurse on desk duty, to allow Kathryn to go out for dinner. Miss Deadpan lifted her eyebrows, raised her eyes over her half-glasses, and snapped, "Absolutely not!" Ten minutes later, Ruth wore her down. They would sign a written release guaranteeing that they would be back by 9 p.m. sharp. The test was not scheduled until the following morning anyway.

The women left, giggling and looking forward to meeting Gene for dinner. At dinner, they had a terrific time relating their escape. Now, Kathryn had a leisurely dinner and good pillows to assure a good night's rest. Like two fugitives, at ten minutes till nine, they walked into the crowded lobby; their faces were hidden by the two king-size goose-down pillows, reveling in their incognito return from their great escape. Unable to contain their composure, Kathryn laughed until she started crying. "Don't you know that they think we're crazy Squirt?" Yes, most likely, they did.

On the top floor of the Parkville Hotel in Saigon, Vietnam, Ruth prepared to take a bath. The false bottom case that held their cash was in her care. An employee in the hallway of each floor locked and unlocked the door. There was no key. Tension and security were high. Ruth carried the case with her from the living room, to the bedroom, to the bath.

Gene was visiting Kathryn in her room down the hall. They had arranged for a small refrigerator. It was difficult to eat the native food available in restaurants. For the most part, they existed on a diet of cheese, juice, and fresh fruit that only Ruth peeled because Kathryn said, "It always tastes better when you do it." In some ways, she was like a helpless child.

Ruth drew her bathwater. There was a knock at the door. *It must be Gene and Kathryn,* she thought. She opened the door in her robe, case in hand. There stood a drunken American soldier with the old pickup line, "Honey, where have you been all of my life."

"Go away; you have the wrong room," Ruth told him. Her heart raced, and she tried to shut the door. "My husband is down the hall."

A cute little American blonde was looking real good. "Oh, come on, baby. Don't give me that line."

Sensing danger, Ruth ran down the hall, case in hand, only to find Gene and Kathryn sitting in the dark, relaxing. Like a machine gun, Ruth fired off the horror of her drunken visitor. Was there comfort? Protection? None, only the laughter of Kathryn and Gene—a much-needed relief from the horrors of Vietnam.

At the Iran Airport terminal, after flying all night and desperate for caffeine, Ruth ordered coffee. "That will be eight dollars," the local said to the affluent-looking woman as she took her first sip.

"Eight dollars? That's ridiculous; it's not even fit to drink. Give me a break." Kathryn and Gene stepped back to watch the fireworks as Ruth threw a fit, creating a scene that drew the attention of everyone within earshot. Hoping to calm her down, the local reduced the price.

Kathryn was watching, taking in the entire scene. How she wished she could get away with the things Ruth did. She would love to, but she had too much to lose. She looked over to Gene. To avoid any possible confrontation, he pretended to read a newspaper. He knew not to get involved. There was only one problem; the paper was upside down. Kathryn slapped him on the back, and tears spilled down her face. It was a perfect end to an already entertaining display of Ruth's determination for a decent cup of coffee.

Kathryn enjoyed it when Ruth made a fool of herself. "I tell you, Squirt, I can see why God loves you so much. You can just take anything and laugh it off. I don't think I could."

Still exhausted and caffeine deficient, Ruth agreed. "No, you couldn't."

The flight leaving Tokyo, Japan, was off to a bad start. The three were downgraded from first-class to coach. Kathryn took the window seat, Gene sat beside her in the middle, and Ruth was left with the aisle. They hadn't eaten, and Ruth was irritable and ravenous. It was not a good combination. She stuffed her mouth full of food and began to choke. A stewardess prepared for the Heimlich but chose to stuff some bread down instead to force the culprit down. Ruth held her throat for support, and suddenly it was over. She looked over to Kathryn and Gene for the first time in minutes. Red-faced with ear-to-ear grins was their only sympathy. Each assumed it was just another of Ruth's crazy antics.

They arrived in India and were almost immediately approached by a local asking, "Would you like to exchange your money?"

"Well, what's the exchange?" they asked. The exchange rate sounded low, so Ruth and Gene suggested waiting until they got to the bank. Kathryn was too excited to wait and exchanged way too much. "It's okay; we'll spend it."

The man, believing them to be easy prey, said, "I will come to your room. I have many rubies for very good prices. I make you a special deal."

The Martins' experience in world travel caused them to decline; however, Kathryn said, "Oh, I'd just love to see them." She was like a kid in a candy store. Gene insisted that she bring the man to their room instead of hers. The Indian came to the room, opened a big bag of rubies, and Kathryn was in heaven. She bargained with him, thought she got a great deal, and he left with most of the money—the same money he had exchanged and already made a profit on. He watched closely as Kathryn removed money from the case with the false bottom.

At the airport in New Delhi, Ruth and Gene were going to Africa, and Kathryn was going home. The Martins wore money belts when they traveled, but Kathryn loved her false bottom case. All of a sudden, the lights went out. Gene grabbed the case. As they got ready to board, the lights went out again. Kathryn was unable to grab the case quick enough this time. When the case was found, the bottom had been ripped out, and the money was gone. From that day on, Kathryn wore a money belt too.

Shopping in foreign countries was so much fun for Kathryn. She loved the bargains and had a hard time resisting the sales techniques she was not accustomed to. On one trip, she bought a short fur coat. When they got back to the hotel, she modeled it for Gene and Ruth. Gene said, "I tell you, Kathryn, your legs are beautiful!"

With a big smile, Kathryn put her hands on her hips and asked, "What did you say? I can't believe Gene Martin said that. I want you to repeat it." Her long, slender legs generated a lot of compliments over the years, but the more famous she became, the less apt anyone was to express it. It was nice to hear.

From time to time, Kathryn received bad publicity indicting her of some grand lifestyle unbecoming to a preacher. Kathryn loved a nice hotel. It was just about the only home she ever had. She loved nice restaurants, don't we all? Kathryn loved shopping. She worked hard and played hard. Shopping was a part of the play, and she was especially happy when she got a great deal at an antique or estate auction. She loved to play dress-up, but she wanted bargains.

On a Hong Kong buying trip, Ruth tried to forewarn Kathryn about shoes. "Don't buy shoes. Don't get carried away when you see the shoes. They are gorgeous, but they will hurt your feet." When they arrived at the Ambassador Hotel, Kathryn was intrigued with the tiny man who sold shoes and handbags. Kathryn ordered some ostrich handbags and got carried away, saying, "Let's have the matching shoes too." Kathryn was loving life, slapping the little guy on his shoulder, excited over a great deal. On the day Kathryn came back for the fitting, they hurt her feet, but she ordered more. They looked beautiful. Ruth noticed when she visited the Kathryn Kuhlman Foundation offices in Pittsburgh; it wasn't Kathryn who was wearing the shoes.

Kathryn bought a lot of things overseas: furs, feather pieces, black alligator everything, and a lot of presents for other people. She spent money and enjoyed nice things, but material things never enslaved her. You couldn't buy her friendship with things. All of her most extravagant and beautiful possessions were inherited from Eve.

Her large, gold, signature earrings, sold at Sotheby's, were found on a shopping trip to New York City. Kathryn picked up the earrings, and Ruth said, "Oh Kathryn, those are so lightweight and tacky; they are not even real." Kathryn liked them so much she had them made in 18K gold. She wore them for her twenty-fifth-anniversary celebration in Pittsburgh. She could have worn diamonds, but Kathryn did not need to impress anyone. The original ones, from New York, were still in her Louis Vuitton jewelry case, which is included in the collection from her estate.

Kathryn's spending was not restricted to her. She was extremely generous to her family and friends. Kathryn loved projects, and Ruth remembered Kathryn moving her sister Myrtle, her daughter Virginia, her children, and her younger sister Geneva to nicer homes with new furnishings. She loved to make other people happy and never forgot a special occasion when she could express her love with a special gift.

Just as Eve had been so generous to her, she was with others. Her mind was never on earthly possessions but on the lasting, finer things in life—those in the spiritual realm.

During a trip, somewhere in a far corner of the earth, the water was unfit to drink. The hotel was out of fruit juice. Ruth purchased some wine to take on their outing. They stood at the dock, waiting for the tourists to depart so they may board; Kathryn and Ruth stood side by side. Ruth held the large bottle of wine. Suddenly, they turned to each other, both looking like the cat that ate the canary. "Can you believe this?" Kathryn asked.

"Okay, Squirt, how are you going to get out of this one? Oh, hello there, Mrs. Member of my Pittsburgh congregation; what a surprise to see you here. Isn't it just a lovely day for an outing?"

Ruth rescued Kathryn just in time. "Come on, Kathryn, we want to get a good seat. Goodbye." They could barely keep her from busting out as they rushed for cover. Once the coast was clear, all heck broke loose. You can run, but you cannot hide.

Not every trip was Kathryn's idea of fun. To dedicate the church in Macau, Kathryn was booked for five nights. Many who attended had to swim the river to get there. Kathryn had never worked with an interpreter. The first night was extremely frustrating. Every sentence had to be interpreted into Chinese. Her unique delivery was to emphasize two or three keywords of a sentence, and the interpreter said all the words the same. She couldn't get going in her usual style. It was fine when she prayed for the sick, but the rest just didn't work.

The next night, on their way to service, Kathryn said, "Gene, you're preaching."

"But Kathryn, I don't have anything prepared," Gene responded.

"Well, that's okay. I'll pray for the sick, but I cannot preach with that interpreter!" This time the meeting went well. Everyone left happy, ready for a good night's sleep.

Kathryn had sensitive skin and was not fond of air conditioning. They opened the windows to let in the fresh air. Kathryn awoke with red mosquito bites all over her delicate face. This missionary work was not quite what she expected. Macau was not equipped with screen windows. As she looked in the mirror, the irony overcame her; she had to laugh.

Laughter is good for the soul, a natural expression of the joy found in the trials of life and in the idiosyncrasies of those human beings we treasure and trust. We are the only creations born with the ability to sing the expressive song of joyous laughter. The great loss of any day is that in which you have not once laughed.

THE HANDMAIDEN

The Martins grew so close to Kathryn that they became more like family. Family members get on one another's nerves, speak without thinking, and someone gets hurt.

Ruth acted as Kathryn's representative and was her best friend on the West Coast. Without asking, she knew Kathryn's likes and dislikes. The two women had a lot in common. Each was strong, independent, charming, well-dressed, and attractive. The first thing Kathryn remembered about Ruth was on her first visit to Youngstown. They had on the same shoes. The first time Ruth stayed in the Carlton Hotel, the secretary asked Ruth if the carpet was clean. Ruth answered, "No! It was not." Kathryn knew right away that they both respected and recognized quality in belongings and order.

Ruth was responsible for handling the Shrine, CBS, and the sixty television stations that carried *I Believe in Miracles,* and she took care of Kathryn's Newport Beach apartment. Along with numerous other details, Ruth also had a husband, a life, and a home of her own to take care of.

She was the one who people addressed with questions like, "Can't you get her to do anything with her hair?" Kathryn never changed her 1940s hairstyle.

A few times, a stressed-out and exhausted Ruth lashed out. One time was in Hong Kong, a few days after their stressful ten days in Vietnam. They had barely eaten or slept the entire trip. Every day was scheduled from morning to early evening when they were confined to their hotel. With the bombings and fighting at night, rest did not come easily.

"You know, Kathryn. When you're gone, someone back home does everything for you. You get a salary while you're gone. We get nothing. I don't have someone to do everything for me. It's just not right, and I'm tired of it. I think we should just call it quits."

Kathryn was hurt and began crying violently. Gene was stuck in the middle, unable to take sides. "Well, then, I don't want to fly home with you, so I'll change my reservation."

As on most trips, Kathryn gave Ruth jewelry to wear. Ruth handed her the ruby ring and said, "Fine."

The next morning, Kathryn wore dark glasses. She had cried all night, and Ruth felt terrible. They didn't speak for several weeks. Ruth knew she had handled everything wrong. She acted out of exhaustion and fear. She had deeply hurt her best friend.

She called Kathryn at home, anxious to apologize. Without a greeting of any kind, she simply said, "I'm sorry." Then utter silence ensued.

Finally, Kathryn spoke. "It's alright. We'll just act like it never happened, but remember, the curtains are back up."

When Eve was a little girl, she had a dollhouse she shared with a friend. If they disagreed, her little friend took the curtains down and took them home. In Kathryn and Ruth's fifteen years, the curtains came down three times.

"Act like it never happened" was a built-in defense mechanism that she adopted in 1940. She was preaching in a small church in New Jersey, staying with one of the church members.

Her hostess had a wealthy friend whose chief purpose in life was making sure Theodore Roosevelt was not elected to a third term. Election night came, and Roosevelt won by a landslide. Her husband feared she might have a heart attack when she would find out and called Kathryn's hostess to be there with smelling salts when they broke the news to her. Instead of being defeated, the woman held her chin up in the air and her nose higher than ever. "We'll just act like it never happened." She never acknowledged Mr. Roosevelt's existence on this earth to her dying day.

"It's one of the greatest lessons I've ever learned." Kathryn faced upsetting situations regularly. She could have given in to fear, anger, rebuke, or a host of other ungodly responses, but Kathryn just acted like it never happened. "It's the best way in the world to accept hurt and disappointment. It's just like that." "It's just like that" was another phrase Kathryn lived by. Translated, it meant that there is no reason to doubt or question it; it is a fact of life, and there is no way to change it. So, "It's just like that." Accept it and hush up.

To act like it never happened was not some human act of denial; it was an act of forgiveness and reconciliation. Those forgiven of much have an easier understanding of the self-inflicted bondage that put a wall between man and the blessing intended for him. Kathryn had been forgiven for much. The Granville Apartments in Newport Beach, with its fountains, flowers, and balconies, was Kathryn's California home. Kathryn and Ruth chose the location to be close to Ruth and Gene, making it convenient for Ruth to do the laundry, cleaning, and cooking. She even ironed Kathryn's two hundred percale sheets. Nothing was too much for Kathryn, including her office in Newport Beach, located within Martin Advertising.

When Kathryn came in for CBS and the Shrine, Ruth would stay with her in the Century Plaza Hotel. She would drive home on Monday night and come back Tuesday morning. On this trip, she was to be back at 10 a.m. so the ladies could do some shopping. Ruth pulled up in front and saw Kathryn sitting in a chair by the desk. The time was 10 a.m. She patiently waited outside. As time passed, she was getting more and more upset. By 11:30, Ruth was fuming. "What is she waiting for? How inconsiderate. What is she doing?" At noon, Ruth jumped out of the car, walked straight up to Kathryn, and confronted her for being selfish. The employees, who loved Kathryn so dearly, looked on as though Ruth had committed a deadly sin. Kathryn cried, and Ruth went home. She had failed to recognize that Kathryn was like a child. Ruth had always cared for her like you would a child. Kathryn needed Ruth to come in and get her. They were not friendly for a week or two. Ruth called and apologized, and once again, Kathryn said, "We'll just act like it never happened."

A Christmas card Kathryn selected and sent to Ruth explains it all. "Without you at Christmas, my antlers droop, my tail isn't fluffy, and my nose gets cold. And considering I'm not even a reindeer, that's bad." Kathryn added, "And I mean bad."

The Martins understood her joys, her pain, and her sorrows. It nearly killed her when Kennedy was shot. She turned into a heartbroken, absorbed person—from tolerance to anger to tears. Kathryn loved to follow the Kennedys and people of stature. They were representatives of the dreams she believed could come true. For several days, she stayed home, allowing herself to feel the true depths of her pain, along with the pain of the Kennedy family and the nation.

Knowing great pain and great joy, she related to everyone with an understanding of their struggle. In dying to self, there comes an innate ability to mesh with each other on a level so deep that their pain becomes your pain, and their joy becomes your joy.

One day, Gene stayed in the car as the ladies ran into a shop on Wilshire Boulevard in Beverly Hills. He smiled as he watched two women he loved playfully shopping. Someone approached them, and in an instant, the smiles faded. They listened as Kathryn took the stranger by the hand; then she bowed her head and prayed. It didn't faze her for a moment that she was in a public place. To be bold is to be brave. The only one she feared was not on this earth.

Kathryn remembered Ruth before she died by leaving two beautiful bracelets for her in a safety deposit box she and Gene shared. Ruth remembered Kathryn:

"I loved her with all my heart. In all her pain and sorrow, she taught me so much. She had so much dignity.

"Each time she prayed, I felt I had touched the Holy Spirit. She would say, 'Why brag about how much you pray? Stay prayed up all the time, and pray with anyone in need.'

"I could still hear her say, 'Ruth, if you only learn one thing from being around me all these years, don't clutter your mind with all these writings. Go to the Word of God. Every answer you need is in this Bible.'"

She was still a human being, despite her tremendous anointing. She gave it all to God. Kathryn Kuhlman is a perfect example of what's available to all of us.

MINISTRY OF
MIRACLES

The defining aspect of Kathryn Kuhlman's ministry came directly from her total dependence that absolutely every Word of the Bible was a literal promise of God.

"Truly, truly I say to you, the one who believes in Me, the works that I do, he will do also; and greater works than these will he do; because I am going to the Father. And whatever you ask in My name, this I will do, so that the Father may be glorified in the Son. If you ask Me anything in My name, I will do it" (John 14:12–14 NASB).

Kathryn Kuhlman believed in miracles. *I Believe in Miracles* was the title of her first book, as well as the name of her television program. The word miracle comes from the Latin word miraculous, which comes from the verb, mirror, meaning "to wonder at." A miracle is a surprising and welcome event that is not explicable by natural or scientific laws and is therefore considered to be the work of God.

THE HANDMAIDEN

The New Testament speaks of miracles as one of the spiritual gifts in 1 Corinthians 12, verses 10, 28, and 29. This was the promise of God made manifest through one who declared, "I'm just a simple handmaiden of the Lord."

Miracles, signs, and wonders have always been a breeding ground for controversy. With the level of those present in Kathryn's ministry, it was only a matter of time. Kathryn's copy of the November 1950 issue of *Redbook* magazine was at the top of a collection of articles documenting her fifty-year ministry. The headline above *Redbook* said, "Can Faith in God Heal the Sick?" The lengthy lead article by Emily Gardner Neal asked, "What happens to the sick, halt, and blind when Kathryn Kuhlman speaks to them? This is the amazing story of an evangelist who is performing miracles of healing by invoking faith in the power of God."

On the opposite page was a captivating color headshot of Kathryn, with an ethereal blue background, looking you right in the eyes. Somehow, before you read a word, you knew this woman was real and from God.

To be fair about anything so radical in a major publication, you had to play devil's advocate. Kathryn had been accused of using manipulation as mass psychology or hypnosis to deceive the desperately ill.

From every state in the Union and Christian countries throughout the world, as many as three thousand people came to her Sunday services at Faith Temple in Franklin, Pennsylvania (population at that time: 9,948). For her three weekly services at Carnegie Hall in Pittsburgh, crowds of four thousand often began gathering the night before to be sure of hearing her speak. And for a half-hour, five mornings a week, seven radio stations of the Tri-State Network carried her voice to the farms, villages, and cities of Pennsylvania, West Virginia, and Ohio in a program whose audience was exceeded only by those of the top newscast.

Redbook's investigation spanned several months, reviewing twenty reported healings. The bottom line was in the photos and testimonies of those interviewed and verified as healed.

The article brought respectability to that which many Christians considered believable in the Bible but impossible in the real world. Traditional churches began to accept that God still heals the sick, and many sent a member of the clergy to see the miracles for themselves.

Those who attended a Kathryn Kuhlman service for the first time found a new level of faith they couldn't wait to share. Kathryn taught that faith is more than belief; it is more than confidence, more than trust, and above all, it is never boastful. If it is the pure faith of the Holy Ghost, it will never work contrary to the Word of God, to His wisdom and will. They had never seen the power of the Holy Spirit, but they knew beyond a shadow of a doubt they were standing on Holy Ground. They were warned that a little knowledge and an overabundance of zeal tend to lead to harm. In the area involving religious truths, it can be disastrous. Keep your eyes on Jesus, not on situations, circumstances, and above all, not on yourself.

The level of Kathryn's ability to feel what others felt and see what God saw explained how her astounding ministry of miracles evolved. She loved people back to health. With compassion, commitment, and love beyond measure, she poured her heart out to God, often weeping as she prayed. The elderly, those whose hands were calloused from years of hard work, and children were especially touching. When she felt that deep level of compassion, healings generally followed. None of this would have been possible had she analyzed or tried to control any aspect of the miracles. The simple, childlike faith and the ability to yield to the only one whose power is beyond definition, created an atmosphere for the Holy Spirit to work on earth. Kathryn Kuhlman had to die for Him to live through her.

The hundreds and thousands of men and women, who were fortunate to attend, had been searching to understand the Baptism of the Holy Spirit. They hungered to grow in their relationship with Jesus Christ and left with an understanding that forever transformed their walk. During that movement of the Holy Spirit, small groups crowded into homes, sat in hallways and bedrooms, and prayed—applying the teachings they had heard. They saw that God honored their prayers too. Legs were lengthened, backs were healed, and the mercy and grace of the Great Healer was before their very own eyes.

Kathryn herself was unable to explain the power of the Holy Spirit. "When it comes to me, I sometimes have a difficult time standing on my own two feet. There is a wonderful peace in having the power on you. It is very spiritual and relaxing because you are not in control. I am but a vessel He chooses to work through. How can you analyze the power of God? Who can know the mind of God?"

One miracle was so spectacular; it was the first one described by several people still living who were active in Kathryn's ministry. Kathryn never allowed newspapers or photographers to interrupt or to take pictures during her miracle services. One time she did. They lined the entire area in front of the stage.

In St. Louis, Missouri, Usher Paul Meese encouraged his lifeless neighbor to attend the miracle service. "No! I don't want to go! I don't even like women preachers, and the last thing I need is to fight with those thousands of people to see one."

Kathryn prayed, and there was a sudden uproar in the left wheelchair section. A young man screamed out as he jumped out of his wheelchair, and his body came to a natural position. The straps holding him upright in his wheelchair had snapped in two. His eyes looked over the body that used to be lifeless, from his feet, legs, chest, and arms. He lifted his arms and ran down the aisle.

Bill Spears was a veteran and a victim of Grand Mal Seizures. The once strong man weighed less than one hundred pounds and had borrowed a pair of trousers to wear under his bathrobe from a twelve-year-old neighbor. Down the aisle he came, swinging a catheter hose as he walked. The audience was no longer watching the stage.

Kathryn looked, "What's this? What's this?" He took over the stage with his testimony. "Where's your wheelchair?" Kathryn asked. The ushers brought it to the stage; it was fully equipped with a battery, straps to hold his entire body in place, and a cosmetic bag to hold the hundreds of pills he took every month. Kathryn didn't notice the catheter bag or relate the hose he was swinging as being part of it. He grabbed the battery, unclipped the post, and picked it up. Kathryn said to the usher, "You take it." The usher buckled at the knees from the weight of it, and the people went crazy.

The reporters and photographers were no longer interested in their job. Cameras sat still on the stage, mouths hung open, and heads rested in hands at the edge of the stage in utter disbelief and amazement—from an invalid to a picture of health, just like that.

Bill Spears walked out and left his wheelchair behind. When Paul took him home, his wife didn't believe it. "They have hypnotized you.

We are going to the doctor first thing in the morning!" Bill stayed up all night, rejoicing and praising God. The next morning, he told his wife, "Well, if I'm going to the doctor, I'm not wearing this. Take me to Robert Hall to buy a suit!" When they measured him for size, his waist was thirty-four inches—exactly what it had been before his illness. God had supernaturally filled him out overnight. His doctor said, "It's a miracle! You are healed!"

The army cut off his disability benefits, and nobody wanted to give him a job with his past medical problems. Kathryn asked Gene Martin to check up on him. On a layover at the St. Louis airport, Gene called; Bill answered the phone and insisted Gene come right over. He met him at the door in a beautiful uniform. "I got a job. Sit down. You won't believe it. I'm a pilot in the Civil Air Patrol. They did every test!" The healing was now complete—physically, spiritually, and financially. Within each believer is the ability to intercede in prayer on behalf of others. Paul Crane is the grandson of Myrtle and Everett Parrott's adopted daughter, Virginia. Paul called Kathryn his Aunt, skipping a generation to save the calculations of Kathryn's age.

Aunt Kathryn was a big influence on his faith. He grew up in front of people at Kathryn's meetings. When he won a trophy playing Little League Baseball, he had it engraved with "Greatest Preacher" and presented it to Kathryn on stage at the Shrine Auditorium for Christmas. "Oh, angel, that's just the sweetest thing in the world," Kathryn said as she wrapped her arms around him. She always asked how school was and how his life was, but it was the compassion and her belief in miracles that made the biggest impression. She was not like other women in the family. She loved people, all people, and was always doing something nice to help someone.

Gene and Ruth Martin paid to send him to an Assemblies of God Summer Camp. He had a terrific time making new friends, especially with a pretty little girl named Julia. Paul and Julia were supposed to have a date on the last day of camp. The director kept kidding him, "You might even get a goodnight kiss!" Paul had such a crush on her that the very thought gave him goosebumps. On their special day, Julia slipped and fell, breaking her arm on the diving board. The group gathered around to comfort her and readied her for the trip to the hospital.

Paul took charge and said to his friend, "Danny, we need to pray she gets better and ask God to heal her." Paul prayed for the healing, just as he had heard Aunt Kathryn pray. He trusted God just like Aunt Kathryn did. Snap! Crackle! Pop! The bone that was sticking out had vanished. The children got excited. "Look, we can pray for healing, and it can happen!" No counselor could have orchestrated a better closing day. Julia was the happiest of all, and Paul didn't have to forfeit that all-important kiss. The secret of miracles is not something to be analyzed. No equation or theory explained the simple faith of a child who believed he could pray to God to bring healing to a pretty little girl he had a crush on. The one certainty is that only God can perform a miracle. Only God can decide the recipient. As we grow in intellect and worldly skills, our busy lives take over. Days run into weeks, weeks into months, and months into years, before we are still enough to hear His voice.

Yet, a child who doesn't question or doubt, acts on His voice in a moment. Paul Ferrin was on stage in St. Louis when a darling little boy in braces heard God's voice. His parents were not believers, but his grandmother was and brought him to the service. It was the cutest thing. She brought him up and was telling Kathryn how her grandson had turned to her and said, "Jesus told me if you take off my braces,

I would walk." She did, and as grandma and Kathryn were talking, they realized that no one was listening. The child was standing up in his wheelchair and jumping off to the ground, over and over. Kathryn turned to him, "Come here, honey." He looked at her, then at the wheelchair. "One more time?" Kathryn nodded to the child, who jumped off one more time and ran into her arms. Can you imagine what went through the grandmother's heart?

Children were special to Kathryn. She would have traveled anywhere, to any service, just for one crippled child to be healed. She savored every moment as wheelchairs and braces were left behind—deformed feet and limbs straightened and strengthened. For the first time, a precious child could run across the platform, run up and down the aisle, and run on a playground with all the other boys and girls.

The author of *The Exorcist* had a grandson who was dying of Leukemia in a Los Angeles hospital. He called Ruth and asked if Kathryn could come and pray for him. When they arrived, the child and mother were motionless, waiting for any sign of hope. A nurse came in with food for the little boy who was withering away. "Oh, he won't eat a bite. He never does." The mother sighed. Kathryn prayed, pouring her heart and soul out for five minutes nonstop. Ruth listened with one eye open as the child ate every bite of food.

A couple of months later, Ruth paid a visit to the family's home. She looked out the window and watched a robust little boy with tousled hair playing in the yard. "Who's that?" she asked, thinking it was one of their other children. No, he was the same little dying child she had watched eating his food as Kathryn prayed for him to be healed. There was no trace of Leukemia, and his health, weight, and hair had been completely restored

DOCTORS DEFEND
THE MIRACULOUS

A group of highly respected doctors from across the country became a regular part of miracle services. Kathryn made every effort to verify the healings. She played off the distinguished physicians, who lined the front row just beautifully. In mid-sentence, she would stop, slowly look down the row, mentally noting their degrees and affiliations—John Hopkins, the Mayo Clinic, Cambridge—and with great enthusiasm ask, "What are all of you doctors doing here?" She would look away, assume her classic "look-at-God-now" stance, hands on waist with one hip out, and in perfect union, Kathryn and the audience would chuckle and grin. "Well, I just think it's marvelous! Don't you?" No applause sign was needed.

Middle America and the thousands who were a witness knew the miracles were real. Nonetheless, the analytical mind of some refused to believe, choosing instead to call them psychosomatic manipulations.

Dr. William Nolan followed up on twenty-three healings from a Minneapolis crusade and deemed them as such. His book entitled *Healing: A Doctor in Search of a Miracle* didn't bother Kathryn. It did bother H. Richard Casdorph, M.D., Ph.D., a California internist who had worked at the Mayo Clinic. Dr. Casdorph attended many of Kathryn's meetings at the Shrine Auditorium. When he had seen enough, he placed a call to Kathryn at the Century Plaza Hotel. "Miss Kuhlman, I believe we can prove them wrong." They made arrangements to meet in her Newport Beach office, where Kathryn immediately agreed to open all her records and let the chips fall where they may.

"She was so brave, opening her ministry to scrutiny, the only ministry to ever do so. She was a pioneer, a leader. There was no one else on television then. Kathryn Kuhlman was a woman of God. My patients who were ushers would do anything for her. We all would."

Dr. Casdorph researched ten cases that later became his book *The Miracles: A Medical Doctor Says Yes to Miracles!* The book is a fascinating study from a medical and spiritual perspective of documented, inexplicable cures—a must-read for the intellectual who doubts the healing hand of Almighty God.

Dr. Casdorph explains the theory he calls "full-healing syndrome." There are typically five features of healings of this sort:

1. There is usually, but not always, a friend or relative of the patient who feels a burden for their healing.

2. The second common characteristic is the correction of the physical deformity caused by the illness.

3. The next common feature of miraculous healings is spiritual healing, a change in the personality and spirit of the individual from shy to bold.

4. Typically, those who have been healed miraculously start teaching and talking about Jesus.

5. The fifth feature is that when miraculously healed people give their testimonies before groups, there are spontaneous healings in the audience, and souls are saved for the Lord Jesus Christ. Thus, it is in the lives of those touched by God. Where the Holy Spirit is, there will be gifts, including faith, healings, and miracles.

Dr. Casdorph's full-healing syndrome theory shows there are many miracles within a miracle, and the healing of one body, in turn, brings physical and spiritual healing to others. It is also reassuring that in the cases he studied, usually, those healed were not alone in their pain. Someone else loved them enough to pray, brought their loved one into the presence of Almighty God, and believed in their miracle.

The intellectual, analytical mind has trouble accepting simple truths. This is perhaps the case of the atheist, usually devoutly religious people who fight the simplicity of God's love. It isn't God but the disillusionment of the way man represents Him: the single-minded, judgmental rhetoric spewed from the lips of professed Christians, quoting the Scripture they don't honor with their lifestyle. This is the single biggest cause of atheism today. While we saw the outward appearance, God saw the heart, and nonbelievers were not exempt from the twenty years of miraculous healings that accompanied the ministry of Kathryn Kuhlman. Other brilliant physicians with multiple degrees shared in the acceptance of the Great Physician's ability to heal.

THE HANDMAIDEN

Nobel Peace Prize winner Alexis Carrel, a noted surgeon, turned from skepticism to faith after witnessing his first miracle at Lourdes. He wrote, "As a physician, I have seen men after all therapy had failed, lifted out of disease and melancholy by the serene effort of prayer. Prayer is the most powerful form of energy that one can generate, the only power in the world that seems to overcome the so-called laws of nature."

Many in the medical profession were admirers of the miracle services where the Great Physician healed as He could—healed both physically and spiritually. Kathryn received a very special Christmas present from Dr. Elizabeth Vaughan.

"Dearest Kathryn,

I am writing this before my children awake this Christmas morning because I want you to be the first person in this house to receive a present on our Lord's birthday.

Three weeks ago, I asked the Lord what you would like for Christmas that no one knew about, that would meet the desires of your heart. This 0.12 mm. toothed forceps was His answer. Let me explain what it means.

For the last four-and-a-half years, I have used this very instru-ment on every single cataract operation that the Lord and I have performed. It is indispensable to me. It has three teeth on the end that are 0.12 mm. long. You will need some means of magnifica-tion to see these teeth well. They are used to grasp tissue so that a needle can be passed through it while it is being held with firmness but gentleness. The teeth must be perfectly aligned to grasp the tissue properly. If they are misaligned one hair's breadth, they might as well be thrown away, for they will no longer grasp in an exacting manner.

The reason this instrument is so crucial is that it is used for closing the wound after the cataract has been removed. This means that the eye is wide open, and there is no margin for error in the surgeon or the instrument. If this instrument is not grasping properly, causing any pressure to be exerted on an open eye, the contents from inside the eye could be pressed out, and the patient's vision compromised, if not lost completely. All of this surgery is done through an operating microscope under high magnification. Those forceps must grab tissue 2 mm. thick and hold it firmly enough to pass a needle through it while exerting no pressure whatsoever on the eye.

I love this precision instrument. It has served me well, and been in the middle of many surgical miracles the Lord has performed. It has functioned perfectly for these four-and-a-half years of use, and now I want you to have it this Christmas morning. It is intended to serve as a reminder to you from our heavenly Father that this instrument has been in my hand as you are in His.

You are exactly what He wants you to be. He did not want you to be a pair of scissors or an instrument for extracting the cataract. He intended from the beginning of time for you to be a 0.12 mm. toothed forceps, holding the tissue so the Great Physician can do the stitching and healing.

Not many people in the world are so yielded that God can make of them exactly what He wants them to be, but you are. Our Father wants you to know, on His Son's birthday, that He loves you beyond your words and that it gives Him great pleasure to have such a precision instrument as Kathryn Kuhlman available for Him to use as He wishes.

Amen and Amen!

Dr. Vaughan."

Dr. Vaughan received an expression of Kathryn's appreciation less than a week later.

"Dear Dr. Vaughan,

The framed forceps, your gift sent on Christmas Day, is standing on my desk for everyone to see and as a continual reminder of the very precious things you wrote in your letter. I shall cherish it as long as I live!

There is no limit God can do with a person, providing that one will not touch the glory. God is still waiting for one who will be more fully devoted to Him than any who has ever lived; who will be willing to be nothing that Christ may be all; who will grasp God's purposes and will take His humility and His faith—His love and His power, without hindering, let God do great things.

MAY WE BOTH CONTINUE TO BE INSTRUMENTS IN HIS HAND!

Kathryn Kuhlman."

Today, Dr. Vaughan resides in Dallas, Texas where she is a dedicated servant whose journey has led her to assist in building Christian

Television Stations and ministry outreach in China, Russia, Israel, Mexico, and South America. The framed forceps are now in her office.

Reverend Don H. Gross, Ph.D., is an Episcopal priest with degrees in physics, theology, and psychology, including a Harvard doctorate in psychology of religion. He wrote his doctoral thesis on a Jungian analysis of New Testament exorcism. He is the founder and executive director of the Center for Pastoral Psychology in Pittsburgh, Pennsylvania, and the author of *The Case for Spiritual Healing.*

Dr. Gross was able to study Kathryn Kuhlman's ministry for many years with two personal encounters. His father-in-law, Dr. E. D. Henry, was healed in one of her services. Then, in 1965, his seventeen-year-old daughter, Elaine, died of Leukemia. Kathryn played an important part in ministering to Dr. and Mrs. Gross during that difficult time. Mrs. Gross has written of that time, including Kathryn's role.

Dr. Gross's insights were first given to biographer Allen Spragett over two decades ago. His analytical book *Kathryn Kuhlman: The Woman Who Believed in Miracles* was the first and only biography published while Kathryn was alive. Dr. Gross graciously consented to allow this interview to speak to a new generation and still agrees today with those conclusions. His insights are quite compelling, given to the following of Jung today.

"Jung has become a kind of guru for New Age religion. I take him at his word that he is a psychologist and not a theologian. Both Kathryn Kuhlman and I, however different we may be in education and style of ministry, represent Biblically oriented conservative Christianity. I say this because of a strong contemporary reaction against Jung on the part of many Evangelical and Charismatic Christians.

"I respect Jung's insights on the psychology of religion, but I disagree with his interpretation of many theological issues, especially his way of including evil in God and his objection to the Christian view of Jesus as pure light. The whole point of the Christian Gospel is that in the cross of Christ, God took upon Himself the sin, suffering, and evil of the world—not to make peace with evil but to overcome it. There, the compassionate vulnerability of God's love was the weapon that Satan could not see or understand. The resurrection was God's turning point in overwhelming the evil one. Kathryn Kuhlman would have known this at the core of her being.

"Kathryn Kuhlman is an extraordinary, creative woman to have accomplished what she has, particularly with the limitations of education and opportunity in her early life. She has unusual intensity and energy in looking forward to marriage and family life, in which a woman has a built-in normal desire in the bearing and raising of her children, but she is frustrated. There is a great and painful collapse of her hopes and of her wish to love and be loved. At this point, she turns to God as her love object. She is going to spiritualize the energy that would have gone into marriage and family life and devote herself instead to another kind of love: the love of the heavenly Father. Instead of receiving love from one person in marriage, she turns out to be the center of the adoration of many people. Mind you, this love from many is not fully satisfying. Like all public figures, Kathryn Kuhlman said, 'I live a lonely life; either I am with the crowd, or I am all alone.' But the difference was that Kathryn Kuhlman was not completely alone, but alone with God. She had found such an experience of God's love and presence that it filled the void that tempted some public figures even to suicide. And it was this experience of God's love that made her charismatic; the sense of God's love and presence radiated from her.

"Kathryn always made it clear that the absence of healing does not equal the absence of faith. This is a very great oversimplification that leaves many people feeling guilty if they are not healed. The fact that they are not healed may have nothing to do with them. It may or may not; we don't know. Such false teaching is responsible for much of the justified criticism of some of the healing ministries of today.

"Such a simplistic view isn't sound theology. Paul, the apostle, wasn't healed of his thorn in his flesh, as he called it, and he related this not to the lack of faith but to his need to be humble. He had to be reminded that he was frail and human for his good.

"If Kathryn Kuhlman were ever to get self-important, it would kill her ministry, and I'm sure she knows this. Her recurring dream of going to a service and finding only empty seats expresses her anxiety that she may lose the gift and become spiritually barren, unfruitful. Her subconscious is giving her the warning to guard against this temptation. The dream is a message to herself from herself, and she's getting the message."

Dr. Gross concluded, "I would guess that she loved her earthly father devotedly and hoped in marriage to find fulfillment of that first great love of her life. Out of her deep frustration with this hope, she turns to the heavenly Father who won't disappoint her.

"She is very hurt and looking for healing for her own heart. She found that one way of being healed is to become a channel of healings to others. Sometimes, the best way to make up for a disappointment in love is to give love. So, as Kathryn Kuhlman becomes a channel for spreading God's love to others, she receives that love herself, and her heart is healed."

Certainly, the role of women when Kathryn was growing up was vastly different than those we see in this country today; where before, they could only watch and wonder why. It was true that Kathryn considered Mr. to be one of the three loves of her life, and it broke her heart to give him up. Her love for children throughout her life is clear. It is doubtful she regretted anything, but it would be foolish to believe any human being does not delight in that perfect union when truly the two become one. Kathryn had no one to come home to, to share the little happenings of each day that makes life so precious, no one to put their arms around her weary body to give her strength.

The language of the heart was the unspoken dialogue in the life of one whose treasure was the fulfillment of God's purpose, not her own. For where your treasure is, there will be your heart also.

Kathryn's heart was fixed, on fire and flaming for God. The flaming heart is a symbol of religious fervor. When held in the hands of a saint, it symbolizes the human love of God.

Kathryn had the love of God and the love of the thousands who flocked to her meetings, the millions who watched her *I Believe in Miracles* television program, and the complete love and dedication of her entire staff, wherever she was.

In her steadfast dedication to the Word of God, Kathryn Kuhlman came to know the Holy Spirit so well that yielding to His voice, His ways, and His work became second nature. She knew how to get out of the way so He could take over. Being in His company for so many years, she became expressive of the characteristics we identify with a perfect Creator: love, peace, and radiant joy. Through her submission, complete death to self, and a pure heart—miracles and ministry became one.

1. *Kathryn Kuhlman ministering in the Pulpit*

2. *Kathryn Kuhlman service*

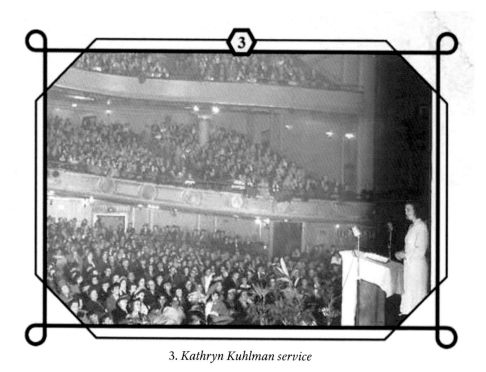

3. *Kathryn Kuhlman service*

4. *Kathryn Kuhlman with two children during a service in Pittsburgh*

5. *Kathryn Kuhlman marrying couple during a service in Pittsburgh*

6. *Kathryn Kuhlman at Pittsburgh airport*

7. *Kathryn Kuhlman in Phoenix, Arizona*

8. *Kathryn Kuhlman and Gene Martin*

9. *Kathryn Kuhlman and Ruth Martin*

10. *Kathryn Kuhlman with Maggie Hunter*

10A. *Kathryn Kuhlman and Eve Conley*

11. *Kathryn Kuhlman wearing her favorite Easter bonnet*

12. *Kathryn Kuhlman with Pope Paul – October 11, 1972*

13. *Kathryn Kuhlman and Ruth Martin in Hong Kong*

14. *Kathryn Kuhlman in Hong Kong*

15. *Ruth Martin, Kathryn Kuhlman, and Gene Martin in Hong Kong*

16. *Kathryn Kuhlman sitting for coin design*

17. *CBS Television City – I Believe in Miracles*

18. *CBS Television City – I Believe in Miracles*

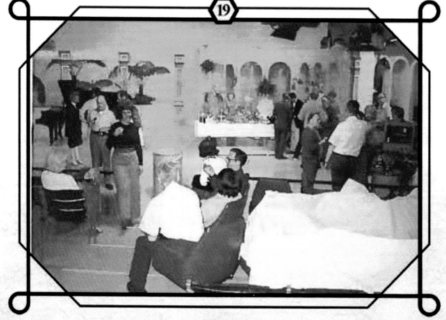

19. *CBS Television City – I Believe in Miracles*

20. CBS Television City – I Believe in Miracles

21. CBS Television City – I Believe in Miracles

22. *Portrait of Kathryn Kuhlman*

23. *CBS Television City – I Believe in Miracles*

24. *Kathryn Kuhlman and Sue Wilkerson*

24A. *Sue Wilkerson and Dino Kartsonakis*

25. *Tink and Sue Wilkerson with Kathryn Kuhlman*

25A. *Sara O'Meara, Kathryn Kuhlman and Yvonne Fedderson*

26. *Kathryn Kuhlman Funeral at Forest Lawn in Glendale, CA.*

27. *Kathryn Kuhlman Funeral at Forest Lawn in Glendale, CA.*

28. *BC Talbott wearing Kathryn Kuhlman's last pulpit gown*

BC TALBOTT

HOLY SPIRIT

To Kathryn, the Holy Spirit was a person, more than just an influence or feeling. He had a definite personality, and it was difficult to tell where he left off, and Kathryn started.

Gene Martin always said, "Her services were conducted with dignity, genuine warmth, and, of all things, a real sense of humor. There was no attempt at self-glorification, and she had a true understanding of the human nature of people's problems. This understanding I can only compare to that of Jesus; she, too, had the knack of giving simple answers to complicated questions."

If you never experienced a Kathryn Kuhlman service, come with me. If you are one of the fortunate ones who did, may you find the beautiful memories to move your spirit again as we experience the most inspiring woman of the twentieth century.

Thousands have come from near and far—Baptist, Catholic, Jew, Mormon, Hindu, Agnostic, and others searching for the presence of God. The air is electric with anticipation. They have been waiting, some for hours, expecting a miracle or to share in this glorious move of the Spirit. The doors open. People run for a seat. The choir is singing, and as you settle in, you realize there is a holy hush throughout the auditorium. It is as though the entire building is living and breathing. The lights dim, and the thousands present become one. Softly and sweetly, the mass choir and the people lift their voices in praise—singing "Hallelujah." Then begins Kathryn's trademark song, *He Touched Me.* The heavenly music continues for some time, though not a soul looks at their watch. The experience is too precious.

Kathryn is backstage, frantically pacing like a caged animal, praying and weeping, head up, head down, waiting for the Holy Spirit to come upon her. It is a conversation of dedication and cleansing with only one visible presence.

"Heavenly Father, here I stand. You know that we are helpless without your Holy Spirit. We depend on you. Without your anointing, nothing will happen. All these people have come one hundred, one thousand miles. Father, I am nothing ... but these people, they are something.

Honor your Word. Heal their bodies, their hearts, and their wounded spirits. If you don't heal them today, heal them on their way home or next Sunday in their church. Let nothing stand in the way of your Holy Spirit. Father, look upon my life. Whatever I have done this week, or in the last twenty-four hours that is not pleasing to you, I ask your forgiveness. Right now, let your presence fill my life. Above all else, may this auditorium be swept through with your Holy Spirit. We promise to give you all the glory. In Jesus' name, Amen." She then bursts from her dressing room towards the platform, each step quickening in eager anticipation of the transformation. She dies a thousand deaths before the Holy Spirit embodies her yielded vessel. She is at once radiant, glowing with God's love, arms lifted, reaching to heaven, in a flowing chiffon gown. She joins in the song, dancing back and forth across the stage on her tiptoes. She has just become the happiest girl on earth, and it is impossible not to love her back. As she looks to the crowd, there is not a sound, not even a whisper.

"The God who spoke the very world into existence, the one who said let there be light, and there was light, underneath all the uncertainties of life—He is here!

"Father God, we vow to give you the honor, the praise, and the glory for everything the Holy Spirit does in this place of worship. I pray that not one person shall see the servant—not one. We would see JESUS! Wherever one finds the presence of the Holy Spirit, one always finds Him magnifying, glorifying Jesus.

"Minister to our waiting hearts, I pray. We vow with our life to give you the glory for everything that the Holy Spirit does, for every answer to prayer. I pray that everything that happens, everything taking place in this conference, will soon be happening in every church in America, and we claim it for you. This shall be the very beginning. Father God, I pray this shall be only the beginning of that which we are seeking—this beautiful outpouring of the Holy Spirit—and soon it will be happening in every church in our land until literally, we shall shake this nation for God.

"I am going to talk to you about a person, about one on whom I am dependent. I know so well what David meant when he cried out—and oh, that cry came from the deepest recesses of his being: 'Cast me not away from thy presence, and take not thy Holy Spirit from me' (Psalm 51:11). You can strip me of everything that I have, and I vow before the visible and the invisible—before every angel in Glory, the Father, the great High Priest, and before the presence of the Holy Spirit Himself—you can take everything from me that I have and leave but the clothing on my body and shoes for my feet—and I do not even have to have those shoes—but take not thy Holy Spirit from me. So important is the mighty Third Person of the Trinity! I tell you the truth, if I knew beyond a shadow of a doubt that the Holy Spirit had been lifted, that the anointing of the Holy Ghost had been lifted, that the Holy Spirit was no longer dwelling within me, I would never again stand behind another pulpit. I would never again hold another miracle service. I would never again preach another sermon. I know wherein the secret of the success of this ministry lies. That is the reason I tell you that I am dependent on the mighty Third Person of the Trinity and have become so familiar with Him. I think the time has come when we need teaching regarding the Holy Spirit. I am so glad for those who have come forward and given real Bible teaching regarding this mighty Third Person of the Trinity, for we are living in the eleventh hour when He is pouring out His Spirit upon all flesh. But because of lack of teaching, I think that some have become too familiar with the Holy Spirit—speaking His name and using it lightly. Remember, this Third Person of the Trinity is holy—the Holy Spirit. When I speak His name, I feel like speaking it very softly. I can never tell you my relationship with the Holy Spirit, what I feel regarding this Third Person of the Trinity, and how very sacred He is to me. Remember His great importance, and do not treat Him lightly.

"Before God ever gave His only begotten Son, Jesus—before Jesus consented to come to earth in the form of human flesh, He offered Himself through the Holy Spirit. He knew He could not pay the price He would have to pay unless He had the power and the Person of the Holy Spirit within Him. Never lose sight of the holiness and power of this mighty Third Person of the Trinity, and remember something else: the sin for which there is no forgiveness, neither in this world nor the world to come, is not against Jesus Christ, the Son, but against the Holy Ghost. Be careful what you say regarding the Holy Spirit. If you do not understand miracles—if you do not understand the power of God—if you do not understand His manifestations, be big enough to admit you do not understand; but be careful lest you criticize Him. The sin for which there is NO forgiveness is against this mighty Third Person of the Trinity.

"We are living in a glorious hour! I would give anything in the world if every Christian caught the vision of this moment in which we are living. This is the church's greatest hour. God is pouring out His Spirit upon all flesh. There is a moving of the Holy Spirit that is marvelous, not only here in the United States, but in every part of the world. This great 'coming out' among the Catholics is a marvelous moving of the Holy Spirit, but we need some good biblical teaching lest we go off into fanaticism—lest we bring reproach upon this Person, the one who is the mighty power of the Trinity.

"I want to pause here and say something vitally important. No one has ever stood behind the pulpit who believes more in the fruits and gifts of the Spirit than I—who believes more in the doctrine of the Holy Spirit than the one who is bringing you this message. I believe in the Holy Spirit with every atom of my being. Call it the 'baptism of the Holy Spirit'; call it being 'filled with the Holy Spirit.' Whatever you call the experience, I believe in it—it is scriptural and biblical.

"We speak of the hour in which we are living as a time of great revival, but it is not a day of revival, but great RESTORATION. God is restoring all of the fruits and the gifts of the Spirit to the church. You may ask if I believe in speaking in an unknown tongue. I have to believe in it because it is scriptural, but I believe in the gifts only if the Holy Spirit gives the gifts, and I believe in speaking in an unknown tongue only as the Holy Spirit does the speaking. Wherever you find the genuine, you will always find the counterfeit—always remember that.

"When the Holy Spirit does the speaking, it is beautiful—one is awed by the beauty of it all. Remember, the Holy Spirit is a perfectionist, absolutely perfect in that which He does. I would give anything in the world if I had the vocabulary to let you know how wonderful this mighty Third Person of the Trinity is: so gentle, He is likened unto the gentle dove, but He is also like a consuming fire, yet a different kind of fire than we are familiar with. And when He speaks through lips of clay, it is beautiful, moving, and tender. He is love, He is gentleness, and He is forgiveness!

"Before Jesus went away, the last thing He taught was the evidence, the real true scriptural evidence, of having been filled with the Holy Ghost: 'But ye shall receive power after that the Holy Ghost is come upon you' (Acts 1:8). I am talking about an experience that enables you to say, as Paul did, 'If I must needs glory, I will glory of the things which concern mine infirmities' (2 Corinthians 11:30). I am talking about death to self. Do you want to be filled with the Holy Spirit? Do you want the baptism of the Holy Spirit? Remember, He fills what we yield unto Him. There is no vacuum in nature. If there was a vase of water here and I were to empty the water out of the vase, air would immediately rush in. There is no vacuum in nature, and this wonderful spiritual experience that I am talking about is when one empties himself and looks up and says, 'None of self, but all of you, wonderful Jesus!'

"You do not seek manifestations. You do not seek experience. That is the reason so many have received just what they have sought—a manifestation—and there is no power. If you want to be filled with the Holy Spirit, then begin to magnify and glorify Jesus. Wherever you find the Holy Spirit, you will always find Him magnifying and glorifying Jesus, and it won't be long before you are saying, 'Less of self and more of you.' It won't be long before you are saying, 'None of self, but all of you.' I am talking about an experience that means death! I am not talking about ecstasy, an experience that lasts for just a few moments. I am not speaking of something emotional. I am talking about a scriptural baptism of the Holy Spirit. 'But ye shall receive power, after that the Holy Ghost is come upon you' (Acts 1:8). There will be a death to self. That is what Paul was talking about. "I glory not in the things that I do, I glory not in these experiences. If I were to glory, I would glory in my infirmities" (See 2 Corinthians 12:9). I would glory in the death of self. That is what the Holy Spirit does through that one who has died—there is a death. We talk so much about the death of Jesus, but remember, that was His cross on which He died. That was not my cross, nor was it your cross. It was His cross. 'If any man will follow me, let him ... take up his cross'—'his' cross (Matthew 16:24). Some people do not want to talk about death—their cross, but there can never be a true baptism of the Holy Spirit until, first of all, there is a death to self. There must be.

"'Death isn't easy!' You say, 'Kathryn Kuhlman, I want power in my life. I want God to use me. I want to be filled with the Holy Ghost. I want that wonderful experience. I want everything that God has for me.' I wouldn't fool you or lie to you by telling you it is easy. It is not easy! There is a price to be paid, but it is worth the price. Hannah said, 'The Lord killeth' (1 Samuel 2:6). There goes arrogance. There goes spiritual pride. It doesn't fit in with some people's experience of what they call the baptism of the Holy Spirit. The greatest of all Christian graces is humility, and somehow, it just doesn't fit in with some of the spiritual pride and some of the arrogance that we find in some of those who profess the baptism of the Holy Spirit. 'The Lord killeth,' and it isn't easy. Death isn't easy. It depends on how much you want His Holy Spirit. How much do you want to be filled with the Holy Ghost? How much do you want to be led by the Holy Spirit? Are you willing to pay the price?

"O, there are mountain top experiences! I, too, have been there on Pisgah's lofty mountain top, so close, so near, when I have felt like saying, 'Just take me across now; take my hand and lift me over.' There are these spiritual experiences that you would never tell anyone else: they are too sacred. When you have these wonderful spiritual experiences, you cannot talk about them, for they are too wonderful and as precious as the most priceless treasure that one can possess. There are glorious experiences when the joy of the Lord fills you (and there is no joy comparable to His), and a feeling of peace and glory and happiness fills your entire being.

"'He will keep the feet of his saints, and the wicked shall be silent in darkness; for by strength shall no man prevail. The adversaries of the Lord shall be broken to pieces; out of heaven shall be thunder upon them: the Lord shall judge the ends of the earth; and he shall give strength unto his king, and exalt the horn of his anointed' 1 Samuel 2:9–10). Have you ever found that wonderful experience of being led by the Lord when the Holy Spirit touched you? Something happened the other day that I shall never forget. It was one of the most beautiful experiences that ever happened to me:

"Madame Sheikh is from one of the leading families in Pakistan. The daughter of a Nawab (Prince), the wife of a former general and Minister of the Interior, her family is traced as Muslim leaders in that country for seven hundred years. She herself organized and 'headed' the social services work for Pakistan for several years and acted as hostess while her father was a cabinet minister; and later, as the wife of the Minister of the Interior, she was known and respected by world leaders. She also holds the Order of the British Empire, awarded to her by the British Government following World War II.

"Madame Sheikh was given a Bible by a little Catholic nun and began reading it. All alone as she read, the Holy Spirit revealed to her heart her need for Jesus Christ as her Savior. It is amazing what the Holy Spirit will do in unfolding and revealing the Word of God. Madame Sheikh, in Pakistan and all alone, found Christ as her Savior and continued to read the Bible. She saw there was a baptism—she saw two baptisms. No one helped her; there was no missionary to guide her. She saw one baptism with water, and so she filled the bathtub and baptized herself. Then, she saw there was the beautiful baptism of the Holy Spirit. That is the reason, I tell you on the authority of God's Word, you do not 'teach' men and women how to receive the baptism of the Holy Spirit. The Holy Ghost will baptize you! There in Pakistan, with no help whatsoever, she received the baptism of the Holy Spirit. A doctor from Pakistan came with his son to the Shrine Auditorium in Los Angeles. The child was healed, and he told about the manifestation of the power of God, the slaying power of the Holy Spirit, and Madame Sheikh said, 'That is what I want more than anything else. If there is more to be had through the slaying power of the Holy Spirit, I want that experience.' She had no fellowship with Christians whatsoever except that close fellowship with Jesus Himself. She came to the Shrine Auditorium; it was a glorious experience for her.

"Recently, her daughter, a very brilliant doctor from Pakistan, came to visit her mother, Madame Sheikh, and she said to me, 'This is my daughter who is still a Muslim, and she just cannot quite come over to Christianity.'

"The daughter said, 'No, I cannot pay the price. I would be ostracized by my people. I cannot do it; I must go back to Pakistan.' Because I knew she would be in the United States a very few days, I said to her, 'If you feel you cannot accept Christ as your Savior now, will you promise me one thing? When you do accept Him—and you will—I want to be the one to lead you to the Lord.'

"She said, 'All right.'

"The day before she was to leave to return to Pakistan, I knew I had to phone her and ask to see her. 'You must be converted before you go back to Pakistan,' I said. She did come to see me and was beautifully converted—an experience of salvation she will never forget.

"Then, Madame Sheikh turned to me and said, 'I want to be alone with you for just a minute, Miss Kuhlman.' This marvelous lady who was once the most influential woman in the government of Pakistan did something I shall always remember: she slipped to her knees as I was standing and laid both of her hands on my feet and prayed. She stood up and quietly slipped away.

"'He will keep the feet of His saints' (1 Samuel 2:9). I want Him to not only take my tongue, take my voice, as long as there is breath in my body and as long as the old heart still beats ... but there is more than that: take my feet, lead me I pray, and when He does the leading, we follow. Do you know what it means to follow the Holy Spirit? Do you know what it means to wait when He says wait? Do you know what it means to exercise patience when you want to go forward? Do you know what it means when you want God's perfect will, and you want it more than anything else in the whole world? You want it, but remember, we were born with free moral agency, and each of us has a will that is separate and apart from the will of God. There is no person living and breathing who does not have a will separate and apart from the will of God. You and I can never know God's perfect will until the two wills become one. That is why the last thing Jesus did when He went to the cross—and I believe it was the very hardest thing for Him to do, for He was as much man as though He were not God—He looked up and prayed, 'Nevertheless not my will, but thine, be done' (Luke 22:42). Up until that hour, there were two wills, for He had a will separate and apart from the will of God.

"'And he that taketh not his cross, and followeth after me, is not worthy of me' (Matthew 10:38). Upon that cross, two wills become as one—His perfect will. Led by the Spirit, He will keep your feet, and you walk the path of His perfect will. You will only know His perfect will, however, when you get to the place where you have no will of your own. Easy? I would lie to you if I told you it is easy. I would tell you an untruth if I told you it is easy. I am talking about a spiritual experience that thousands are claiming but will never know. I am talking about the indwelling of the Holy Spirit, the Third Person of the Trinity, who will so indwell the vessel of clay, that out of your innermost being, there shall flow rivers of living waters. I am not talking about something that is emotional for just a few minutes; I am talking about life! 'But ye shall receive POWER after that the Holy Ghost is come upon you' (Acts 1:8). I am talking about a spiritual experience when you can say, 'If I wouldst need glory, I will glory in the things which concern my infirmities' (See 2 Corinthians 12:9).

"Ever since that time, I can almost feel Madame Sheikh's hands upon my feet. I can almost feel the softness of those tears. She knew because she had experienced what I am talking to you about, for if she were to go back to Pakistan today, she would be killed because of her faith in the Lord Jesus Christ.

"Not my tongue alone, but my will, my feet, for I am led of the Spirit. So led, that when I do not know how to pray, and I seek the perfect will of God, the one who knows His perfect will—the Holy Spirit—He shall make intercession at the Throne of God. I shall never be led into God's second-best when the Holy Spirit will present me before the Throne of God in prayer and prays through me. There is a fellowship; do you know that wonderful fellowship of the Holy Spirit? There is a communion; do you really know this Person, this Third Person of the Trinity? There are thousands who are talking much about the Holy Spirit in this great hour when the Holy Spirit is being poured out upon the entire world, who are experiencing this great movement that the world is calling the 'charismatic movement,' but there is something that millions are not experiencing—there is a fellowship, a communion. "I pray not that thou shouldest take them out of the world, but that thou shouldest keep them from the evil" (John 17:15). We need this training. We need these things to make us strong, but He will keep us from the evil one. There is a communion, a constant communion in the loneliness of the night and when there isn't a star in the sky. When the waters are so deep that they are about to overflow, you are not afraid—there is communion there. When all the gates of hell are allied against you, there is quietness, communion, and fellowship. That is what Paul was talking about. O, the mercy of the Lord Jesus Christ and the love of God, the Father, and the fellowship and communion of the Holy Spirit—more than just an experience of a few minutes' time, more than just the one experience, but a constant abiding presence of the Holy Ghost. 'When the enemy shall come in like a flood, the Spirit of the Lord shall lift up a standard against him' (Isaiah 59:19). HE WILL DEFEND US!

"We stand secure, sure of the price that was paid. It wasn't easy, and it wasn't just for a moment—and it was something more than speaking in an unknown tongue. It was something more than an outward expression or manifestation. I am speaking of something that is deep and abiding, and thousands of God's children will live and die and never know what I am talking about and never experience it. It is the greatest experience and the greatest life in the world.

"Down to the grave that you might come forth alive, and He bringeth you forth alive, and you grow in His glorious resources, and you are never defeated, never! Never in your own strength, for in your own strength, you are weak, but you draw on His resources, and all that is His is yours, and you keep drawing on His resources. And, you do that which you could not do in the natural. You tap His resources for love, loving the unlovely and unloved.

"Remember that before Jesus came to earth in the form of flesh, He offered Himself to God the Father through the Holy Spirit. When Jesus came up out of the water of baptism, the Holy Spirit came upon Him. What a glorious moment when the Three Persons of the Trinity were present, and God, the Father Himself, spoke and said, 'This is my beloved Son, in whom I am well pleased' (Matthew 3:17). No man who has ever lived or who shall ever live in the future can plead ignorance as to who Jesus really is; for God Himself said of Him, 'This is my beloved Son, in whom I am well pleased.' At that moment, the Holy Spirit came upon Jesus, anointing Him, filling Him, equipping Him with power for the glorious miracles that were to happen in the ministry of Jesus here on earth with the manifestation of the power of the Holy Spirit; Jesus did not do those miracles in His own strength. That was the power of the Holy Ghost. Jesus knew it, He was well aware of it, and when He left this earth, He gave to the church the greatest gift that was possible for Him to give. Don't miss it, whatever you do—I would get down on my knees and plead with you. Don't be afraid of the Holy Spirit. If Jesus could trust Him, and Jesus had everything at stake, surely you and I can trust Him.

"If Jesus staked everything He had on this mighty Third Person of the Trinity, then surely you and I can accept Him. For Jesus, when He went away, gave to the church the greatest gift that was possible for Him to give. There was no greater gift that Jesus could give the church than the gift that He gave: 'And ye shall receive power after that the Holy Ghost is come upon you' (Acts 1:8). It is the same power that was manifested during His ministry, the same power that was manifested through His life as He lived in the flesh and walked the shores of Galilee. He offers to us the same Person, the same glorious gift of the Holy Spirit, the gift that the Father gave to Him.

"The church is about to leave; this glorious body of believers, the bride of Christ, is about to leave, and the only restraining force in the world today against unrighteousness is the Holy Spirit. I would not want to be in the world for five minutes after the Holy Spirit leaves. He is the restraining force in the world about us. He is getting the bride of Christ ready to meet the Bridegroom. This living body of believers is being perfected, and that is why we are living in such a glorious and exciting time. You may not understand what is happening to you as you experience the power of the Holy Spirit; you are only aware that something is happening. It is because we are living in an exciting hour when God is getting the living church ready to meet the Bridegroom.

"The Holy Spirit is being poured out in such a beautiful way in this hour of restoration when all the fruits and gifts of the Spirit are being restored to the church. It is thrilling, it is exciting, and that is the reason for these miracles which we see. I know better than anyone else that I have nothing to do with these miracles of healing. Kathryn Kuhlman has nothing to do with what happens in the services. I stand in awe as anyone else in the great congregation who has never seen a miracle until that hour when they are face to face with that supernatural healing of that body, with the giving of sight or whatever the miracle maybe. No one is more awed than Kathryn Kuhlman herself, for I know better than anyone else that I had nothing to do with what took place in that physical body. These healings go beyond the realm of faith.

"We are living in a time of great mercy and great love. The beautiful tenderness of the Holy Spirit, when He melts hearts, heals bodies, comes upon one as he sits in the audience and is not able to understand. Sometimes, there is a great heat that comes upon that one, a strange and different kind of heat, consuming and burning, yet so different from anything one has experienced before. Then, sometimes, the Holy Spirit comes as a gentle coolness, a wind, yet a different kind of wind, and one senses a presence that is so real that if you turn quickly enough, you will see Jesus. This wonderful communion—you only begin to live when you know Him."

As the Spirit leads, Kathryn begins to call out healings. The ushers move up and down through the aisles, urging the cured up to the stage. Kathryn encourages them to try their newfound health. Crippled children rise and run across the stage. The deaf hear. Blind eyes are opened for the first time. Goiters disappear before your eyes. Wheelchairs are left behind. Those who have been healed flood the stage, anxious to testify of God's healing grace. Something incredible is happening.

As they come forward and claim their healing, Kathryn lifts her hand, and they fall back onto the floor under the power. "We give you the praise and the glory. Dear Jesus, I worship you. The power of the Holy Ghost is going through this body. The power of God is in this place." The experience sold many, even more than the miracles. Often, a relative of those healed came with them to the platform, and they too fell under the magnificent power of the Holy Spirit. Those skeptical in the beginning left unable to deny God's mighty presence. Whenever those under the power came to, their thankfulness directed at Kathryn was never accepted. "Don't thank me. I didn't have a thing to do with it. Kathryn Kuhlman couldn't heal anybody. This is God's mercy. Thank Him."

Several hours later, you realize how merciful He is. Those who came without expectations, who didn't believe in God at all, were among those healed. It makes no difference what race, religion, or class is represented. Whether or not you believed when you came, you have now witnessed the power of Almighty God, and you want to know Him.

"The greatest miracle of all is spiritual healing—that new birth experience; come now. Here they come, Jesus, for that new birth experience. Forgive their sins—the greatest ministry in the world for all eternity, complete security. Come—Jesus says come. The Holy Spirit says come. There is power in the name of Jesus. Come—adore Him. Worship Him; still, they come—come on."

Hundreds, then thousands, give their lives to the only power greater than themselves. With grace on their faces, they leave the auditorium, a new man, a new woman, set free from the bondage of sin and rebellion—into the glorious wonder of the Christ that now lives in them. Hallelujah.

KNOW THAT

The miracles sometimes overshadowed Kathryn's gift as a teacher of the Bible. Her teachings were in-depth studies presented in such a simple way that a layman could grasp and hold on to the fundamental truth of something as difficult as the rapture.

The first time Larry Alborn attended Kathryn Kuhlman's Tuesday night Bible study, he found the salvation he had never heard of in the Lutheran church he had grown up in. For the next seven years, he only missed three Tuesdays. "People came for the miracles on Friday, but Kathryn had so much love, and her Bible study was charged with love. It was always fresh manna. I was hungry, and it was so good—there was never a bad service. I took notes from this great feeding of the Lord. It was so quiet; there was such decency and order. One thousand eight hundred people would be there on a Tuesday night. It was quite remarkable."

Kathryn's teachings were frequently interrupted when she delivered some divine truth; she wanted to make sure you received it. She would pause, look inside the depths of her mind as though it was the first time she had received that particular revelation, and lift her hand—reaching out to you, with her index finger pointing to heaven. She snaps her fingers and looks into your spirit, commanding, "Know that ... know that. Believe that. It's just like that."

And for Kathryn, it was. She believed God's Word to be the absolute authority, infallible, and more up-to-date than tomorrow's newspaper. "I'm glad I'm stupid. I used to envy men with all their degrees, but I'm just stupid enough to believe every promise in God's Word and act upon it. That is the secret and power of my life and this ministry. I'm glad I never wrote a book on theology. I'd only have to recall it every week!

"No one has seen love. No one has seen the wind, but we see the results and force of them. It takes the sunshine and the rain and sometimes heartbreak for the sun to shine. We wear smiles as a mask, a front, when deep inside, we are not quite right. There is a way, a solution. No one needs to be defeated. Know that!

"I am trying to help those at the end of the day when they need to laugh and know they are doing a great job. I try, so in the last days, the work has been done, and they are ready to meet God. Once I buried the wrong man. I told the mourners how remarkable the woman was, and it was a man. But you see, the Lord honored my prayer anyway. God has kept His promises and covenants since the seed of Abraham. It doesn't make any difference to God what church you join; He cares what is right in your heart. The greatest place in the world is the center of God's will.

"The church has never been more challenged than today, and the church is not meeting the challenge. In the New Testament, the Christians were turning the world upside down. Today, the world is turning Christians upside down. A church is an organism, not an organization.

"God is exactly what He has always been. Don't blame Him for the chaps in the world; man has free will. God never sends a man to hell. Man does. By choosing to be lost, he determines his destiny.

"Only one can say, 'My church'—Jesus Christ. You don't join. You are born into it: that wonderful new birth experience where you surrender body, soul, and spirit. Are you willing to die to your career for God, to have that heavenly Father relationship and fellowship with the Holy Spirit? That convicting power lies within the abiding wisdom of every believer—the regeneration of salvation. If you are not sure and you want Him to guide you, for as many are led by the Spirit, He will intercede for the saints in prayer, according to the will of God. Oh, to know the mind of God—only the Holy Spirit knows.

"The Bible is unlike all sacred books—the authority of prophecy. The fulfillment of prophecy is evidence for the supernaturally inspired work of the Holy Spirit. There are twenty-five predictions in the Old Testament of Jesus Christ; twenty-five predictions of death, and every single one was fulfilled.

"One cannot accept the Old Testament and not the New Testament or the other way around. The Bible is the revelation of one person—Jesus Christ. When He came to Bethlehem, He came to die. The religion of that time didn't accept Him. They were expecting a king, and the circumstance of His birth was not such as they deemed worthy.

"This nation is crumbling. We cannot be like an ostrich and put our heads in the sand. I am proud to be a child of God first and proud to be an American second. World leaders are sensitive to the fact that something is happening, and we may be on the threshold of the greatest war, the final war, that will end all wars.

"I give you the Word of God. It comes from the highest authority in heaven and earth. It is a fool that takes disagreement with the Word of God. God will cross every T and dot every I. Flesh and blood has not revealed it, but my Father. There is no substitute for that I give to you, beloved child of God. Don't ever apologize for being a Christian!

"It is no time to compromise, my friend. As surely as there was the first coming, there will be a second, but Christ's body is never divided—as the body is one and has many members. Jesus revealed to Martha before He raised Lazarus: I am the resurrection and the life. Whoever lives and believes in me shall never die (See John 11:25).

"We are living at the end of the time of the Gentiles. Whatever the future holds, or whatever you feel about it, Israel will come out on top. God must keep His Word. The covenants must be kept, and the prophecies must be fulfilled.

"We should not be ignorant concerning those asleep. In 1 Thessalonians, Paul tells us that those who are asleep in Jesus, who died in Christ, shall rise first. Papa and Mama will know the resurrection life, rising up, one mile outside Concordia in that little cemetery. I have relived that moment so many times.

"Child of God, precious saint of God, let not your heart be troubled; for Jesus said, 'In my Father's house are many mansions: if it were not so, I would have told you' (John 14:2).

"There are two stages of His coming: 1, for His saints, and 2, seven years later in bodily form with His saints. The dead in Christ will rise first—those born into the body of Christ. Jesus Christ will meet His saints in the air in the great catching up, and His feet will not touch the ground.

"There is hope in Jesus Christ. No Christian dies. Wherefore, comfort one another with these words. One day, in the twinkling of an eye, like a thief in the night with no great fanfare, the unbeliever will be quieted in an instant. The trumpets will sound; the dead in Christ will rise. Next, His bride, the church, will meet Jesus in the air, caught up in the clouds. When the Holy Spirit leaves, He cannot go without those who are a part of Him. Know that.

"After the rapture, there will be seven years of tribulation on the earth. The world will never come to an end; however, God cannot look upon sin. There has got to be judgment. There will be judgment. Beloved, this is the Word of God. Millions of people all over the world will watch the manifestation of God's power.

"People will turn to God, to the spiritual—Jews and Gentiles. All have a capacity for God and things of the Spirit. People will all be conscious of His power and know that Almighty God still rules and reigns. Some will see the very thing I am talking about for the first time.

"When Jesus said 'verily,' it meant 'very important.' The fig tree is the symbol of Israel as a nation. Jesus said, verily I say to you that generation that sees this shall not pass away before the rapture (See Matthew 24:34). God will not leave this earth without a witness. He has always had a witness.

"The living will be taken up like Elijah. Elijah never tasted death—he just went walking one day and never came back. The Lord just took him. The Mount of Transfiguration of Matthew 17 was a wonderful rehearsal.

"In the last chapter of the Old Testament, the last two verses promise God will send Elijah back; we have not seen the end of Elijah. In His earthly covenant to the Jews, there will be two witnesses. They are the two olive trees—like a candlestick to light the way. Moses is the other witness that will be on the earth for the last three years of tribulation.

"The first three years will grow darker by the minute. Moses and Elijah are the forerunners before Jesus comes to the earth for the second time. In that hour, the whole world will acknowledge the Son of the living God as the true Messiah ... know that!"

Many of Kathryn's followers in Pittsburgh also attended Sunday services an hour-and-a-half away in Youngstown, Ohio, at Stambaugh Auditorium. Everett and Myrtle Parrott were impressed with a young man named David Verzilli when he sang *When Jesus Came* at one of their meetings. They told Kathryn about him and sent him to one of her meetings. Kathryn said, "I understand there is a young man named David here. David, where are ya?"

Once again, he sang *When Jesus came,* and Miss Kuhlman was so blessed she said, "Anytime you are around here, you can sing for me."

David felt a call on his life, but his Italian mother didn't want to give up her boy to go away to Bible school. Mrs. Verzilli prayed and pondered. Relatives said, "Don't send him. He's anointed, and it will spoil him."

The next thing they knew, Mama turned on the radio and heard Kathryn say, "Mama, send that boy to Bible school!" Mrs. Verzilli had never mentioned it to anyone outside of the family. She was too embarrassed to. David went to Bible school, and his first job lasted twenty-two years. He went to work for Kathryn Kuhlman. "Those were wonderful days. Truly, they were the high watermark of my life in my years of ministry. It was a sovereign work of God's eternal grace that brought Kathryn Kuhlman into being. A message and messenger who defies all logic. She didn't have the background or training. Today, everything is working towards men who are adept at everything. Everything that was Kathryn was given by God, even her administrative abilities. Truly, her ability to communicate was so anointed and dynamic that people found her irresistible.

"Nothing was counterfeit or copied. If it were not real, she'd put her finger on it instantly. She needed and wanted reality all the way. It's something that's left the people who were in the glory of all of it a little lost. They can't seem to adjust to anything else, and that's not good.

"After all these years, I still work with people who say, 'I miss it so much. I just can't get what we had.' It must have been like that for those who taught the Gospel after Jesus left the earth. They just couldn't get to the feelings of touching the hand of God through mortal man."

Men, like David Verzilli, are left to lead them in the truth. "The Lord allows these things to happen so we can move on to another level—to forget the messenger and cling to the message." It's difficult because David knows firsthand just how remarkable the messenger was.

"Sometimes, I walked away and wondered if my feet were touching the floor. We ate up every word. It was just exhilarating. Kathryn was so yielded—a mouthpiece of God, every word clothed with the anointing. Powerful. Arresting. A Pacesetter.

"Her spirit of discernment in the services was remarkable. God would show her things, and you knew it was the Holy Ghost. Sometimes, I see things today that scare me—people trying to imitate. If it's there, it should be real. Right after she died, they tried to put a red wig and dress on me, saying, 'You're the next Kathryn Kuhlman.' 'No! I'm just David,' I told them. They tried to groom me for the miracle services, but I had no enabling like Kathryn. I thank God that I was not deluded. The allure and grandeur were there, but you had to be built like Kathryn—it was her entire life.

"Sometimes, we think we're doing things in the Spirit and come up with pie on our faces. Kathryn hit the mark. She always struck oil. She went with it when she felt anything. When she walked on the platform, she was in the Spirit with the presence of the Lord and a commitment to meeting the needs of the sick and afflicted. We usually reserved thirty to forty minutes for praying for the sick, but nothing was set. The Holy Spirit was in control; no manipulation of music was necessary. Sometimes, she would come on the platform and say, 'People, the anointing is on us so great, I cannot even sing a song. The power of God is in this place right now.' You would look up, and it would be two hours later. That is a commitment to a calling—no facade, just one filled and yielded to the Holy Spirit.

"It was a thrill to work with her for twenty-two years. She allowed me to preach and teach the Bible study in four different cities. She never questioned me; she had complete confidence in my under-standing of the Word and never took issue with anything I said. When she left to go to the world, it was almost too little, too late. Perhaps, she should have done it ten years earlier, but before she would leave us, like Franklin, the building would almost have to cave in.

"Kathryn was the real thing, no doubt. She shined on the radio where she had a definite ministry teaching on parables—filled with true meat and depth that fed the soul. Kathryn could be stern, but you couldn't help but love her. She would scold me, but in the end, those who were devoted to her stayed with it no matter what she did. She expected everyone to be as committed as she was—SOLD OUT FOR GOD—a unique person beyond belief.

"One time, I was at Syria Mosque with the two thousand people downstairs. There were no television monitors, only loudspeakers from upstairs. We sat, looking at a vacant platform. I thought, *Lord, What I wouldn't give to talk to these two thousand. How can they get anything?*

"They just hear a voice. It was wintertime, and suddenly, I felt like someone opened a huge door and let the wind come in. I stood up abruptly. If you were sitting next to me, you probably thought I was crazy. I looked up and asked who opened the door? Twice I asked; then I sat down, embarrassed. Everyone was still seated; there was not a movement until suddenly again, the whole place was filled with the wind that swept across it. I realized it was the power of the Holy Ghost. I cannot tell you what I saw because it was that very moment when Kathryn began praying upstairs. People were leaving crutches behind, walking. There was no screaming, no hollering, nothing. They were walking up the great stairway to give their testimony. Streams of people leaving canes and crutches behind.

"I thought I was in the millennium. I thought I had just raptured. In an instant, God healed all these people in one sweep of His glory. There was not a door open. It was the power of the eternal wind of the Spirit healing His people. One experience confirmed the reality and anointing of Miss Kuhlman's ministry like nothing else ever. I live and die every time I tell the story. I feel the Holy Spirit wrap His arms around me and fill me with a fresh anointing.

"Miss Kuhlman had such a heart for young people. She reached out to them and could identify with the youngest up. The whole place exploded with joy to see her heart and devotion to babies, young children, and teens. If she were alive today, there would be a spiritual emphasis for the youth; she always found a spot for them. Seeing a need for revival among the youth today, she would commit. They would talk to her readily. She would draw them like a magnet.

"She would point that finger and look at you with those blue eyes that pierced the soul; hot preaching, but it made you go home and meditate. She'd say, 'Stay in the will of God, no matter what, and you'll stay in blessing.'"

David Verzilli takes these words to heart and continues to be a blessing by carrying on the work he had started even before Kathryn directed his path to attend Bible school. For many years after Kathryn went to be with the Lord, David would continue to meet fellow ministers across the country who were awed by the way God used the woman he was privileged to work beside for twenty-two years.

People in Youngstown express regret that they were too young to be a part of the ministry their parents and grandparents loved so much. David once said, "Sometimes you look back and wonder, was it a dream? It was wonderful—so wonderful."

Paul Dilena was a captain on the New York Police Department when he met Kathryn Kuhlman. He and David Wilkerson, the founder of Teen Challenge and focus of the film, *The Cross and the Switchblade,* went to Pittsburgh to meet her in the early 1960s. The author of *Run Baby Run,* Nicky Cruz, was also involved in the outreach ministry that dared to go into the ghettos and meet the gangs of New York City.

Paul's first impression was, "How much the congregation loved her. She was ordinary; only she had Holy Ghost charisma. She was so human and down to earth. There was an aura around her, like sunshine to rain, where you walked into the umbrella of the Holy Spirit."

Kathryn gave the initial money to develop Teen Challenge and several hundred thousand dollars to give it wings to fly. It became the most talked-about happening in the tri-state area. It was nothing short of sensational when seven to eight thousand teens gathered once a month to share the good news that ended their drug habits and their emptiness.

Kathryn saved one of the brochures distributed by the Kathryn Kuhlman Foundation to those young men and women. It is interesting how they apply today. Except for the 60's expression, "Be Keen," the message would be received by the troubled, lost teens of today who are up against the same battles.

"It's no proof of courage to drive dangerously. The big sound of a loud exhaust does not make you a big man.

"It's smart to show your driving skill, not seek a driving thrill—or chill.

"There's no joy in smashing your girlfriend through the windshield or waking up in traction yourself. The smart teen gets home in one piece, without a scratch on his boiler. It's no proof of manhood to take advantage of a girl and leave her with broken dreams and a ruined life. A real man (or woman) has respect for the other. Happiness and contentment and self-respect—come only the right way. Sex today will sting tomorrow. Stolen kisses and dishonest love are bittersweet. Look ahead and be a real person. You don't prove you are clever by your ability to light up a cigarette, down your liquor, or shoot a fix. Your body is a marvelous machine—don't gum it up with nicotine, alcohol, or dope. Stay in shape. Eat right, sleep right, live right. The sensible teen says no and stays on the go. You don't prove your intelligence by outsmarting somebody, by lying or cheating, living like a louse. Honesty is still the best policy. God knows your every act, word, and thought. Someday, He will call you to account for the way you are living. The smart one is the straight one. Living up your life to the fullest is lining up your life with God. TEEN CREDO:

"I am a creation of God, made in His three-part image. Therefore, I respect my body, my soul, my spirit. I keep my body clean and well cared for, unspoiled by liquor, nicotine, or dope. I keep my soul pure and decent—my spirit open to God, ready to hear and obey His voice.

"I am a person for whom Christ died, shedding His blood on the cross at Calvary, making atonement for my sins, providing me with His righteousness, opening a door for me into the presence of His Father. Therefore, I surrender my life to Christ, open my being to the influence and direction of His Spirit, ask that He cleanse away my sins, and make me His child through the miracle of conversion.

"I am a child of God, a member of the heavenly family, born again by the divine Holy Spirit, and indwelt by that Spirit who gives me the power to live righteously in this world and to be effective in my witness for Christ and my service for God. All that I have—my mind, my strength, my time, my money, my abilities, my affections—belongs to my Master, and I am happy to devote my entire life to His service and His pleasure. Doing His will and making Him happy is the highest aim of my life.

"I am a representative of Christ in this world; therefore, I live in such a way that I will glorify Him and point all men to my Savior. I will permit the Holy Spirit to fill my heart with the love of Christ that I may pour forth that love to others. I will let Him use my hands as an extension of Christ's hands to do good to all; my lips as the lips of the Savior to speak words of love and kindness; my life as a means of letting Christ live again in this world—through me."

Kathryn would moderate the service and let David Wilkerson take over the preaching. He spoke the language. One night, David, the independent young preacher, announced it was his last. Kathryn almost fainted. It was a complete surprise and disappointment. She was hurt, but Kathryn knew she had done her part. She carried on and acted like it never happened and left it in the hands of eternity.

David learned some very valuable lessons from his days with Kathryn Kuhlman. He shared them with biographer Helen Hosier. Being so young, there was a lot to learn from the famous woman preacher in Pittsburgh. The first time they met, David was backstage and accidentally heard Kathryn praying before the service; he saw Kathryn's inner humility. The flamboyant package became irrelevant. She listened to her heart and told him, "You can't give to anyone else more than you have yourself. Every morning, the first thing I think about is I wonder what's going to happen today." Kathryn rose with the sun each day because she was afraid she might miss something.

She stayed prayed up, taking her secret closet everywhere, praying without ceasing—anytime, anyplace. That way, she was always ready— always prepared.

But the most valuable lesson was how Kathryn kept up the unbelievable pace without tiring—without burning out. It happened one night when a young David tried to bow out of an invitation for dinner with an excuse of weariness. Kathryn was raring to go. She asked if he knew his Bible, did he preach under the anointing this morning, and this evening. Naturally, he answered yes to all three.

"Well, isn't the Holy Spirit supposed to be in us a quickening Spirit? The same Spirit that raised Christ from the dead. If He dwells in you, He shall quicken your mortal body, by His Spirit that dwelleth in you. Isn't it reasonable to believe that if you're preaching under the anointing that He's going to be in the process of quickening you? That is the secret to my strength.

"People don't realize that, but I am dependent on the Holy Spirit, and when the Holy Spirit is moving through me, He gives me unction. He's in the process of quickening my physical body so that if I exercise faith, I can have it and claim it!"

Kathryn believed anything you see is yours—absolutely anything is possible with God. You must acknowledge the revelation to receive it. If you see it, it's yours. She asked David, "Do you see it?" He did. "Good. Do you acknowledge it?" He did. "Good," she said. "Let's go eat."

David Wilkerson was still tirelessly ministering at Times Square Church in New York City as well as building ministries throughout Texas until his untimely death in 2011.

CHANGING OF
THE GUARD

"**G**reat souls by instinct to each other turn, demand alliance, and in friendship burn" (Joseph Addison). The year was 1973, and it was off to a bad start. Kathryn's commitment was complete, and if you were not as committed as Kathryn, it could prove to be a problem. As the ministry grew, Ruth's responsibilities increased tenfold. It was more than a full-time job to keep up: juggling sixty television stations, all of the monthly events in Los Angeles, and being a good wife. Ruth was near burnout. Her patience and tolerance were not what they had been.

Kathryn seemed resentful of Ruth's close relationship with Dino. Since they both lived in California and Kathryn was only in town once a month, the two had become good friends. Ruth and Gene had no children, so she looked after Dino like a protective mother.

Kathryn and Ruth were too much alike. They were so much alike that Kathryn gave Gene Martin one of her business cards with a personal inscription on the back. It read, "Ruth and I are one! Always remember that! Love, Kathryn." Both had take-charge, type-A personalities with tremendous responsibility and drive. They both commanded attention without asking for it.

They started to aggravate each other. Kathryn liked to know everything, and Ruth didn't have the time to go through the chain of command in Pittsburgh for things she already knew the answer to. Kathryn was listening to the needling of another's suggestion and, without notice or explanation of any kind, replaced Martin Advertising with Dino's brother-in-law Paul Bartholomew.

It was probably the worst decision of Kathryn's life. At least her first bad decision to marry Mr. became the very thing through which she saw the face of God. Through her obedience to that vision, millions were blessed. Kathryn must have kept the file of correspondence between her and her closest friends, Gene and Ruth Martin, as a reminder of what can happen when an impulsive act of insecurity and manipulation for control is exercised.

It would be unfair to expect any human being to be without fault. Look at the people in the Bible. In our frailties and insecurities, it is our faith that makes us whole. Kathryn never claimed to be anything but human, and to believe any spiritual leader is without faults and frailties is denial, and that is dangerous to everyone involved.

Later on, this very act could be interpreted as reaping what you sow. The work of ministry can be all-consuming, and that precious quiet personal time alone with God can get lost. You no longer hear that still quiet voice. You hear the flesh instead. This was an extremely difficult period of Kathryn's life. Her calendar, her body, and her mind were overbooked to a dangerous level.

No matter what the call, we are not created to be machines pushed to the maximum level of our ability. Grace, power, and love cannot abound in one hundred miles-an-hour lifestyles. There is no soul immune to the wages of exhaustion, bad decisions, bad health, and more often than not, bad blood between themselves and those they love. Kathryn wanted the whole story told for a specific reason—so others could learn from her mistakes as well as her success.

Ruth and Gene were devastated; they were in shock. For years, Kathryn's ministry had been of the first considerations of their life, and now, with no regard to not only their professional relationship but the personal relationship they had shared for over a decade, it was a real-life nightmare.

They took a vacation and searched their hearts and spirits. What was right in the eyes of God? After complete humiliation, going beyond the call of duty, Gene and Ruth graciously turned the business they had developed over to a man with no prior experience. He was an educational administrator whose only qualification was a degree in theology and being Dino's brother-in-law. He would eventually influence Dino in a heartbreaking decision.

Kathryn had complained a few months prior about the commissions received by Martin Advertising, stating some people would do it as an "act of love." Martin Advertising was well-paid, but Gene was not paid at all for all the meetings he set up. So, essentially, Kathryn had two full-time people for the price of one.

Surely, it was only a ploy to avoid the real issue because Paul Bartholomew's base salary was extremely larger than the position he left behind in New York. It was equal to about the same amount both the Martins received after expenses.

The Martins sent Kathryn a letter, thanking her for the pleasant years they had enjoyed as part of her staff. "Your ministry is one of the greatest of our times, and we suspect that it will not be long before you see a service in which every person will see a miracle." The closing is the same one Kathryn used in a letter to them eleven years ago. "May we never lose sight of our earthly life, striving diligently to fill every hour with our best service for the Master. May we devote our lives with such sacrificial service that our works shall live beyond the day when our voices shall be hushed with the last silences."

Shortly thereafter, the Martins received a handwritten letter:

"I sincerely apologize to both you and Ruth for my lack of conse-cration and a complete 'death to self,' where I am not 'hurt'—where I can rise above anything—and not let it affect me. I am sure there is such a place in the Lord. The last thing in the world that I want of myself is to be 'small' about anything.

Kindest Personal Regards,

Kathryn Kuhlman."

Devastation is ever so deeply felt when it is from one of your very own, whose heart and soul operated in beautiful synchronicity led by the Spirit of God. Wounds from a friend can be trusted, but the healing process takes time. A couple of months later, another handwritten letter arrived:

"Dear Ruth and Gene,

Sunday is Easter—there will be the communion service. I would be less than the person I should be if I did not apologize for any misunderstanding.

Everything has a small beginning, and I am sorry that we were not wise enough to take care of those 'little things'—those personal hurts—before they grew so large!

I Still Love You,

Kathryn."

Other sentiments were expressed in the closing lines of business correspondence. Key heartfelt phrases in their correspondence, over the years, were accented by the use of all capital letters.

"WE WILL ALWAYS REMEMBER THE PLEASANT TIMES WE HAD TOGETHER, TOO...."

The "too" indicates the times of this letter—right before the split.

"I WOULDN'T HAVE MISSED IT FOR ANYTHING!!! MY APPRECIATION FOR YOU IS ALWAYS SINCERE."

We forgive, but do we forget? Are we, as our Creator, able to forgive in such a way that offenses are forgotten as far as the east is from the west? It is a matter of the heart. All offenses come from the heart. Man looks at the outward appearance, while God looks at the heart. It is the heart that changes one's countenance, whether it is good or evil.

Gene continued to act as the Director of Foreign Missions, and the two that were one remained friends—though at a different level. Gene would no longer devote his energy to setting up Kathryn's miracle services.

Maybe the whole thing was a blessing in the end. The Martins would finally have time for their ministry and each other. There was life outside of Kathryn, and they had missed a great deal of it. They still loved Kathryn with a pure heart.

The miracle services didn't run as well without him. The order that was so important to Kathryn was second nature to Gene. He was "the solid rock." Others who attempted to fill his shoes never quite hit the mark. The Kathryn Kuhlman Foundation began calling, trying to negotiate his return.

Finally, Kathryn had a mutual friend call on Gene at home—a wealthy automobile dealer the Martins had introduced to Kathryn years before. He had been active in many ministries and was on the Board of Regents at Oral Roberts University in Tulsa, Oklahoma.

Three men had attempted Gene's job in three months and failed to please Kathryn. "Well, it would have to be different," Gene answered. "I can't work without a salary on love offerings that may or may not come." He was happy not to have the responsibility. The friend left and, an hour later, called to say Kathryn wanted Gene back. He agreed to try three meetings: Portland, Sacramento, and San Diego. Within ten minutes, Pittsburgh was calling. Maggie and Maryon went on about how horrible it had been; they hired inexperienced men with no hook-up to local pastors. It was difficult enough even with those things. Of course, these men didn't pump Kathryn up after the meetings either.

The three meetings turned into Gene's continued commitment as Kathryn's advanced man for the rest of her life. Gene recognized that Kathryn needed someone who understood business—someone who could deliver bad news and someone who had their own money to travel and assist Kathryn in ruling the roost. Gene was suggesting the man Kathryn sent to bring him back, who met all the qualifications—Tink Wilkerson.

Dana Barton and Sue Wilkerson were both raised as active members of the Assemblies of God churches in Tulsa, Oklahoma. They were attending Charles Blair's church in 1958 when a pretty, young, blonde missionary came over to make friends with their two little girls, Susan and Debbie, who were all dressed up. She was outgoing, and the girls immediately took to her. It was the beginning of a lifetime friendship between Ruth and Gene Martin and Tink and Sue Wilkerson.

In 1966, the Wilkersons were visiting Ruth and Gene in California. They turned on the television to watch a new program of a ministry the Martins were involved in. Tink and Sue looked at each other. "Oh brother, this must be a joke. That woman is just too much—that speech impediment, the way she talks. Who is this woman?"

The Wilkersons' background was extremely conservative, and Sue was quite sophisticated. They had never seen anything like this before, but one thing they were sure of was the discernment of their friends, and the Martins spoke highly of this Kathryn Kuhlman—a preacher from Pittsburgh, Pennsylvania.

Tink is the only son and namesake of D. B. Wilkerson. When he was six months old, his grandfather was playing with him, dangling his pocket watch on the crib. Tink grabbed it, threw it across the room, and broke it. "Well, you little tinker!" his grandfather said. The term stuck. When Tink hired an ad agency in 1967 to promote his automobile dealership, they liked its uniqueness and decided to shorten it to Tink.

Tink's father was a prominent automobile dealer in Tulsa whose business and generosity towards ministry carried over to his son. Tink's mother, Jeanine, was a well-known prophetess—one of the very few women Kenneth E. Hagen allowed to take the platform.

Tink was active in Oral Roberts University as a member of the Board of Regents for sixteen years. His generosity over the years reflects an eye for investing in the right ministries—if you base success on becoming well-known—names like Oral Roberts, Kenneth Copeland, Gene Scott, Carlton Pearson, The Spurlows, T. L. Osborn, and many others. Little did he know that their single biggest investment in ministry would be to that strange redheaded woman on television in Gene and Ruth Martin's living room—or that they would be branded as the scapegoat from a web of vicious rumors that continue to this day.

Judgment and condemnation start in our minds, and we write them in our hearts when we judge something we don't understand, something that defies logic. The devil's advocate becomes more enticing than the single truth. It gives us something to think about, talk about, and the next thing you know, one person's misconception is accepted by many others as the truth. Judgment, ill will, and hardened hearts become vessels of unforgiveness and cast a shadow over what was once a bright and shining star.

Kathryn was never able to deliver bad news. It was accepted and understood that others would be responsible for such things: Maggie, Gene, and later, Tink. Tink and Sue began attending Kathryn's meetings in the early 1970s. They were amazed at the dedication and integrity of this anointed woman. They found her quite fascinating and started working on bringing her to Tulsa. In 1971, Tink introduced Oral Roberts to Kathryn after a meeting at the Shrine Auditorium in Los Angeles. Kathryn had sensed a rivalry between them; they were the most well-known in the healing ministry at this time, but Oral was humble.

If there was any conflict, it was resolved at that moment. She looked into the heart of the man. The two became friends, and Kathryn came to Oral Roberts University several times. When Oral Roberts University became fully accredited, they gave the first honorary doctorate to Kathryn Kuhlman—Doctor of Humane Letters. Kathryn represented the finest of the healing ministries of Jesus. "We wanted the world to be reminded why ORU was established, that it was more than an academic institution." Oral said, "The one person in the world who epitomized all we believe in was Kathryn Kuhlman."

Kathryn came to the Civic Center in Tulsa for a miracle service in the fall of 1972. Nine thousand people attended, uniting all denominations for the first time. Tink donated office space to set up the service and helped with connections around the city. By now, the Wilkersons were well-acquainted with Kathryn and her staff at the foundation.

Kathryn's right hand, Maggie Hartner, sent them a thank you note for the Christmas present they had sent her.

"Dear Precious Wilkersons,

You do the nicest things. The beautiful clock is a knockout, and I love it. I have it so I can see it all the time, and it just shines with love. Thank you from the bottom of my heart.

Love,

Maggie."

Tink and Sue shared Kathryn's love of the finer things in life and the joy of giving them to others. Sue and Kathryn became close friends. Ruth and Maggie were wonderful, but it was different. They also worked with her, and the mix of business and pleasure was not quite the same.

Kathryn and Sue never discussed business. Sue knew nothing of it. She was a caretaker who had devoted her entire life to being the best wife and mother possible. As Tink's success grew, Sue's knowledge and appreciation of the finer things was apparent. She was regal, quiet, and reserved—the woman behind the successful man, who provided the stability needed to survive in his fast-moving business world. She looked like she walked right out of the pages of *Town and Country* magazine. She was flawlessly put together: slender with long, rich dark brown hair, worn off her face to show her olive skin and hazel eyes, and dressed in $2,500 Adolfo suits with only the finest in complementary accessories and elegant jewelry.

Kathryn admired her style and quiet demeanor. Sue preferred to be in the background. They were both extremely private, and their friendship was unique. Saturday mornings became their regular time to chitchat about their week. Kathryn trusted Tink and Sue. She had seen Tink's ability to handle difficult situations and his talent for overseeing details. In September of 1974, Kathryn sent a letter to the Wilkersons:

"Dear Tink and Sue,

You outdid yourself, Tink! I couldn't begin to enumerate all the things you did, the details you handled without anyone knowing … but it all went into making the Tulsa service the most perfect service we have ever experienced!

Words are cheap, I know, but I want you both to know that I appreciate you, admire you, and love you more than ever before!

My best love and prayers,
Kathryn Kuhlman."

Everyone sacrificed for Kathryn, for the Lord. Kathryn came to depend on the Wilkersons, and in the last year of her life, they sacrificed business and personal relationships to take care of her. Someone had to. She was getting weak physically, and her body couldn't keep up with her schedule. They spent their own money and gave 100 percent to taking care of Kathryn.

Tink was as generous as Kathryn, and she liked that she didn't have to pay him. They were friends, not employees. She never paid them, but gave them presents and treated them well. Kathryn was jovial most of the time, and she loved Tink's sense of humor—that mischievous little edge that led to fun and laughter. Kathryn and Sue shared a love for nice things and enjoyed conversing about their knowledge of them. In the end, neither of them attached themselves to earthly treasures. Sue was a lady in waiting to Kathryn, who just happened to wear $100,000 worth of jewelry. She could anticipate exactly what Kathryn wanted—whether it was the right first-class hotel or the right pastry at the farmers market.

Most people didn't realize how much Kathryn counted on them. They stayed in adjoining rooms with the door open, so Sue could check on Kathryn throughout the night. Soon, everyone was whispering behind their backs. "Who is that couple with Kathryn? They are everywhere she is." Even her closest friends and staff members resented them; they didn't understand how weak Kathryn had become. Kathryn needed them physically, mentally, and emotionally. She needed someone outside of the never-ending business to take care of her, so she could enjoy the end of her life. She knew, though she never complained. Instead, she would say, "Kids, let's stop here for a minute and window shop." They didn't realize it at the time, but Kathryn was in pain.

Kathryn called them "kids" because they took care of her as though she were their mother. They knew she wasn't well; she had difficulty sleeping, having to stay elevated on four or five pillows to breathe. The pastry chef at the Century Plaza Hotel knew that Room 1812 was waiting for fresh pastries and coffee by 5 a.m. Breakfast was at nine, and she needed fuel to get going.

One of her favorite places was the farmers market—a Los Angeles, California, landmark that just happened to be right down the street from CBS Studios. This outdoor sensory adventure, with row after row of friendly vendors, offered instant satisfaction, with ethnic taste bud sensations alongside vibrant displays of fresh fruits and vegetables. People watching was at a premium with the indoor tables that draw from the multicultural city. The farmers market in Los Angeles is one of the few places where young and old, rich or poor, the famous and the wannabes come together to relax and enjoy the simple pleasures of life.

Kathryn liked to arrive early for a fresh danish from Dupars and then piddle around before having some pizza. She was not one to eat much at a time; instead, she would eat a little every few hours with a late dinner. When the Shrine service was over, off they would go to the Bel Air Hotel to eat. After dinner, she would say, "Let's drive to Newport Beach." She was always on the move, never wanting to stay in any place for very long. It kept her mind off herself and her heart. Tink still shakes his head in wonder as he describes the persona of Kathryn. "Wherever we went, heads would turn, and the conversation would come to a halt when Kathryn walked in the room. Kathryn had a mystique that she carried anywhere she went; besides what was going on inside of her, her look, mannerisms, and the way she talked intrigued everyone. She gave so much of herself away. That was the joy of her life—compassion, commitment, never self-seeking, but reaching out to others. On or off the pulpit, Kathryn Kuhlman was the real thing—a Trojan warrior for God—one of the greatest. She played it straight. Her happiness was found in the healing of others. I've never seen miracles before or since like those with Kathryn. She called them out so specifically; it was amazing. She spent her entire life working herself to death for God, with not one moment of regret. She was the happiest in the service of others.

"One night in Pittsburgh, we were sitting at a red light when Kathryn looked out the window and saw a beautiful woman in a fur coat coming out of one of the finer hotels. She was drunk, unable to walk straight, and the doorman was pointing down the street. Kathryn got out of the car, went and talked to the woman, and gave the doorman a $50 bill to get her a cab ride home. When people approached her, she was always cordial. Her commitment made her what she was. Kathryn was never too busy to listen and pray with anyone, no matter where; she cared about drunks, prostitutes, and degenerates other people wouldn't touch."

PEACE IN THE MIDST OF THE STORM

*E*arly in 1975, the walls began to crumble all around her. Her trusted pianist and companion, Dino, was feeling trapped. He missed the companionship of women his age and was thinking of his future. Of course, none of the women he chose were good enough for Kathryn. Probably like a rebellious child with an overprotective parent, Dino chose an unlikely candidate for marriage—a former showgirl and ex-girlfriend to the brother of *Playboy* magazine's Hugh Hefner. Kathryn gave him several ultimatums over the last year, and Dino started to feel insecure about his financial future.

Kathryn knew the pain of marrying the wrong person, and she let it be known. She was protective of her investment, not the financial but the spiritual and the personal, the effect it would have on her ministry. Everyone knew she had practically adopted Dino. She recognized his potential if he stayed on track and in God's will, and she recognized the heartache this marriage could bring. She had not forgotten her years in the desert.

Dino sought council from Paul Bartholomew, the brother-in-law he had suggested to replace Ruth Martin. This was the family Kathryn thought Dino needed to feel at home in California, but ironically, it was the family Kathryn brought in to keep Dino grounded.

Ruth Martin loved Kathryn and would never have done anything to hurt her, but Paul Bartholomew had a seething hatred for Kathryn that he had been working on for some time. It was fueled by Dino's stories of her affluence and control, as well as the lack of respect and attention Paul felt he deserved despite making far more money than he'd ever made in his life.

Paul drew up a contract for Dino and arrived unexpectedly at the Century Plaza Hotel to personally deliver it to Kathryn. Dino was scheduled to play at CBS the following day, and Paul's innuendo to sign it, if she expected Dino to play, did not sit well with her. She called Maggie, who suggested they bring in Paul Ferrin. Paul, the talented pianist, whom Kathryn already knew in San Jose, California, had married into the Anderson Family of Denver. Kathryn agreed, and Maggie called Paul, who flew in the next morning.

Kathryn met Paul Ferrin at the First Assembly of God in Memphis. The church was like a second home for the Martins for many years, and Gene talked Kathryn into an afternoon and evening service. Kathryn did not bring Dr. Metcalf, and Paul directed the choir. Kathryn was very pleased. Paul told her he had been offered a position in San Jose, California as the minister of music and asked her to pray about it. Her response was, "Good, you do that, and someday we will work together."

When Dino arrived, he saw Paul Ferrin. Paul had been Dino's friend since he was a teenager. Dino had stayed in their home, so he knew how talented Paul was. His problem was not with Paul, so he turned away and walked straight into Kathryn's dressing room.

"Well?" he asked, standing in the doorway.

"Well, what?" Kathryn responded, never getting out of her chair.

"Did you sign it?"

"No, and I don't intend to. You know you can't pressure me like that. You've had things good. Too good."

"What's that guy Ferrin doing out there?"

Kathryn smiled. "You didn't think I would leave myself uncovered, did you? I've been at this a lot longer than you have. Now you're through. Finished. Get out and never come back." Dino had underestimated Kathryn. In her generosity and openness, he saw the vulnerabilities few were privy to. In his blind love for Debbie and blind guidance from a brother-in-law with his agenda, Dino bit the hand that fed him. That brief conversation in Kathryn's dressing room brought an end to seven years of nurturing friendship and trust. The two never saw each other again. The saddest part was that the worst was yet to come.

With a schedule no ordinary human could keep up with, let alone a sixty-seven-year-old woman with a heart condition, Kathryn pressed on. Among her current ventures were her television show, other television shows, the Shrine Auditorium, Pittsburgh, Youngstown, and other meetings. Once again, she had no choice but to act like it never happened. On the outside, she was fine. But inside, physically and emotionally, she was dying. Kathryn loved Dino. She would miss him. She needed a companion, someone she trusted to bounce things off of and laugh with—someone to have fun with, only this time it would not be someone she paid.

Without Dino, there was no point keeping Paul Bartholomew. He was overpaid and not liked by anyone in the organization. On February 15, she fired him as her administrator, but unfortunately, his contract as her television syndicate was good for almost another year.

Five days later, on February 20, her beloved choir director of thirty years, Arthur Metcalf, had a heart attack and died exactly one year to the day before Kathryn's heart stopped beating. In two weeks, Kathryn lost two key people and fired another. She needed a rest, but staying busy left her no time to think about the pain: physical, spiritual, and emotional. She pressed on, giving her very best on every occasion.

Paul Ferrin received a call from Maggie. "Kathryn said she won't have anyone but you direct her choir." Kathryn wanted Paul to resign from the church in San Jose, but Paul loved them, and he could see Kathryn was not well. By the grace of God, the church allowed him to do both. He fell heir to both playing the piano for television and directing the choir for the Shrine services as well as other miracle services. Paul was also happy to accompany soloist Jimmie McDonald—something Dino felt was below him. After Kathryn passed, Paul Ferrin said this about his time with her:

"The Holy Spirit laughed more with Kathryn than anyone else. There was a physical transformation when He came upon her. When the Holy Spirit left, she was just like other people. She was the greatest woman who ever lived—absolutely a pleasure to work with. We never disagreed. It was the most exciting year of my life."

Kathryn was surrounded by people who loved her, who understood her pain, and who admired her determination to release the past and forge ahead so that others would have a future.

PEACE IN THE MIDST OF THE STORM

Paul Bartholomew went to Pittsburgh in March to negotiate a settlement. He was threatening to sue for breach of contract, and in her weariness, Kathryn was considering paying him off. In April, Tink and Sue took their sick uncle to one of Kathryn's miracle services in St. Louis. Kathryn prayed for him and asked Tink to come back later. "Shut the door; I have a problem," she began. Tink could see her stress level was at the max. She had no strength left to fight with. "I just want it to end. I don't care what it cost. He wants $120,000, and it would be worth getting rid of him."

"Well, Kathryn. I'm not going to argue with you, but it sounds like blackmail, and that would just be the first of a series of payments. Sue and I are on our way to Hawaii, but we will stop and see you in Los Angeles on our way back. You let me know, then I'll be happy to help you in any way I can. You know that."

When the going gets tough, the tough get going. Only the strong survive. The show must go on. You can't keep a good girl down. She's a real trooper. All these were a key part of the makeup that enabled Kathryn to get past the hurts and heartaches, the loneliness and disappointment, for there was one and only one thing Kathryn could not live without—the presence of the Holy Spirit. In His presence, there is fullness of joy—there is peace and harmony. There is forgiveness that allows one to act like it never happened because, in the truth of the action thereof, it did not. To harbor those feelings would bring devastation upon a life's work that was dependent on His presence to heal the damaged goods of a worldly system.

No place on earth is any worldlier than Las Vegas, Nevada, Kathryn's next stop. "Sin City"—a twenty-four-hour gambling resort with flashing lights and flashier women. Church life and morals were certainly not a consideration of most visitors. Mayor Oran Gragson invited Kathryn after he and his wife visited one of the services at the Shrine Auditorium. He told the City Council they needed to bring her to Las Vegas. They declared Saturday, May 3, Kathryn Kuhlman Day. The city promoted it; even the gambling casinos and nightclubs went along with it.

You see, Kathryn was unique among the ministries. It made no difference to her if you were a drug dealer, a drunk, a prostitute, a stripper, or a blackjack dealer. All she saw was a child of God she needed to bring home. There was no condemnation—only love. When asked about the city, Kathryn replied, "I don't think there is any more sin in Las Vegas than in Los Angeles. It just seems to be more publicized here. This is the most unorthodox ministry in the world. We don't care if you are a Protestant, Catholic, Jew, or Gentile. God doesn't care, so why should we. They had a Catholic Mass for Kathryn Kuhlman yesterday. Before I leave, they'll probably invite me to the synagogue ... and I'll go!"

Eight thousand attended one of the most incredible services in history. Announcements had been made in nightclubs. Notices were posted in the dressing rooms of strippers; casinos hung posters in their main lobby. The day before, the priest of the largest Roman Catholic church in town held a special mass for the service. Chartered buses came from Reno, Phoenix, and Dallas. Chartered airplanes flew in from everywhere to be a part of this amazing event.

A magnificent choir of seven hundred voices and instruments filled the city auditorium with the beautiful ushering in of the Holy Spirit. Kathryn warmed up the crowd with her usual down-to-earth style that made everyone comfortable. She wanted them to know that she was one of them—a real human being who laughed and cried, and she wanted them to know that she was just as amazed as anyone else when people were miraculously touched and healed.

She called Sunny Simons, a famous Las Vegas showgirl, to the stage. Sunny had been healed of multiple sclerosis at the Shrine Auditorium, and she and her husband, a casino operator, were now praising God. Sunny was one of their own, and her opening testimony set the stage for believing in God and miracles.

Kathryn talked to them about the love of God and the Lordship of His Son, Jesus Christ—a simple message of hope, acceptance, and salvation. Suddenly, the Holy Spirit came upon her, and she began pointing and calling out healings all over the building. These "words of knowledge" were a gift unlike any others in our lifetime have seen.

The stage quickly filled with those who had come forward to testify. A woman who brought her son from Denver with the right side of his body paralyzed now stood weeping and amazed.

Every trace of the paralysis was gone. She stepped back for Kathryn to interview her son and collapsed on the floor. Kathryn stopped and smiled. "Don't touch her. That's the power of God; it's also proof I don't push people down like some critics say I do." The crowd laughed with her.

An Agnostic scientist testified he had been deaf in both ears when all at once he could hear perfectly. "I had lost faith in everything!" he cried. "I did not believe when I came here today, but now I believe."

An eleven-year-old boy confined to a wheelchair for three years was gleefully running back and forth across the stage. Kathryn sighed, "I would have come to Las Vegas just for this one little boy."

A woman who left her wheelchair behind grabbed a man on the platform and waltzed around the stage. "Only in Las Vegas," Kathryn said as she shook her head and chuckled.

Five hours and many miracles later, Kathryn called on the thousands present who had just witnessed the amazing love of God that heals believers and nonbelievers, young and old, Mormons and Jews alike, if they wanted the wonderful assurance of salvation. "Wouldn't you like to know your sins have been forgiven? Don't come forward unless you're willing to give your heart to Jesus." She was pleading, her face wet with tears. They were coming by the hundreds, then thousands, from every corner of life in Las Vegas: gamblers, strippers, prostitutes, chorus girls, and anyone who wanted to be born again.

She led them in a single prayer of confession and consecration. "Don't think of the sins you've committed. Think of the wonderful grace of the Father and the love of the Lord Jesus Christ."

Eight thousand people disappeared into the city lights of Las Vegas. They had never seen anything like it before. Kathryn Kuhlman had defeated Satan in his backyard with a simple message of love and dedication to the only business on earth that mattered—the treasure of the human soul.

She flew back to Los Angeles and was resting at the Century Plaza when Tink called on his way home to Tulsa. "I think you may be right. Can you come by in the morning, and we will talk about it?"

The plot had thickened. Paul Bartholomew was now threatening to expose a tell-all manuscript called *The Late Great Kate,* alleging misconduct within Kathryn's ministry. He was threatening to sue and go to press if he wasn't paid off. Kathryn knew she had made a mistake, but you can't go back; you go on, and whatever the cost, she couldn't bear to think of a scandal this late in life.

She had come too far, and so many could be hurt. Through the discernment of the Holy Spirit, Kathryn knew what was coming.

God chose twelve. Surely the smartest was Judas. He was the treasurer. If Jesus Christ couldn't choose, far be it for us too. Kathryn was human and accepted the situations without expressing regrets. What troubled Judas was the recollection of the sweetness and goodness that had been shown to him, the one who had hurt him most.

Kathryn was in Niagara Falls when the *Los Angeles Times* called to get her response to a lawsuit filed by Paul Bartholomew in the Los Angeles Superior Court and to Dino and Paul's allegations of inconsistencies between her professional image and her personal life. "Her double standard of living had taken its toll on my conscience," Paul said. "The walk-in vault in the basement of her Fox Chapel home, expensive art, and antique collection, and jewelry worth more than a million dollars."

Dino and Paul gave the same interview to *People* magazine. Kathryn was known around the world, so a scoop like this was good news for them. Their words were like razors to her wounded heart. The heart of a fool is in his mouth, but the mouth of the wise man is in his heart. Kathryn defended the allegations graciously and concluded the interview with the truth: "I have to live with myself. My life is an open book. I understand there is a manuscript called *The Late Great Kate*. Well, I am very much alive!"

Meanwhile, only six weeks prior, Paul Bartholomew had been trying to hire Myra White, one of Kathryn's West Coast secretaries, to work in Dino's new Hollywood office. He told her he had written a book about Miss Kuhlman and was carrying it in a briefcase every-where he went and that he never let it out of his sight. Paul said he didn't want to publish it if Miss Kuhlman would just talk to him. Myra concluded Paul was looking for a go-between for a payoff. It was inter-esting to Myra, who had overheard a conversation in Paul's Newport Beach office almost two years before. "When I am no longer working for Miss Kuhlman, I can collaborate on an article." This was the black-mail Tink had predicted and not something that had just come up since Dino and Paul's dismissal.

Kathryn was at the Full Gospel Men's Association meeting the following day when Gene Martin noticed one man that didn't quite fit in. He went to the police, who told him the man was a process server. Gene took action and instructed the ushers to form two lines around Kathryn as she came off the stage. Kathryn wasn't served, but she was concerned somebody was up to something dirty. Tink and Gene tried to reassure her and got her to her apartment in Newport Beach to rest.

She lay there all alone with her thoughts. *How could Dino do this? Paul meant nothing to her, but Dino ... why?* Was it all over Debbie and her refusal to accept their marriage? If only he could understand how much she had lost when those who loved her advised her against marrying the wrong man, and still she didn't listen. How could she expect that Dino would? How could she cast the first stone?

It's easier to take the advice of those who agree with you than to hear a painful truth. The Bible says you shall know them by their fruits, which is the testimony of their lives (See Matthew 7:16). Can one filled with hate guide you on love? Is one in turmoil able to lead you in peace? If you look for bad, then surely you will find it, and likewise, if you look for good, it will find you.

Within a couple of weeks, the stress led to a brief stay in the hospital. She chose Tulsa because Sue's brother-in-law was on the board, and they could keep it quiet. She thought they could drain the fluid off her ankles, which were extremely swollen. After they x-rayed her heart, the cardiologist informed them that surgery was needed to repair her defective mitral valve and that it may be a month, six months, or a year, but she would have another attack. Kathryn refused. She was scheduled more than a year in advance, and there was too much work to do to slow down for any surgical procedure.

Hospitals can be very dangerous places, especially with a common name like Thomas. Johanna Thomas was the name Kathryn used when she checked in at any hospital. One morning, Tink arrived early to check on Kathryn. He walked into her room at 6 a.m. just as they were coming to take her for surgery that was intended for another patient named Thomas. "What are you doing?" Tink asked. "She's not scheduled for surgery." Thank God he showed up in time. There was no telling what unscheduled surgery Kathryn was headed for.

Kathryn wouldn't listen—not to her body or the medical professionals. She was a ticking time bomb who refused to slow down long enough to have the surgery that could have extended her life. She had seen so many miracles, and surely God would heal her heart so she could continue the work.

Kathryn was at the pinnacle of her career, and she was going out in a blaze of glory. There was no way she was going out with a dark cloud over her head. One way or another, this lawsuit would be settled and laid to rest. Then maybe she could have the surgery she needed.

Upon her release, Kathryn spent a few days at the Century Plaza Hotel accompanied by a full-time nurse. Kathryn told Tink to call his attorney Irv Ungerman from Tulsa and get him out here now!

Tink went to work. He hired the prestigious LA law firm of Gibson, Dunn, and Crutcher and a real-life James Bond, whom we'll call #1, who followed Paul for weeks—watching and waiting for the perfect opportunity to seize the briefcase without being seen. True to his word, Paul carried it everywhere, eating with it between his legs protecting the intimate, detailed manuscript he had written about a woman he knew only as a business associate—and Kathryn was all business.

Even with the girls at the foundation whom she had known for years. Someone else was feeding him information—and had been for some time. #1 met with Kathryn on several occasions, assuring her it was only a matter of time. He installed a security system in her Newport Beach apartment to help her rest. He was not a believer, but as Kathryn told him about meeting the Pope, she said, "Oh, you just can't imagine what it was like."

He smiled and said, "It was probably like I felt when I met you." They had a great connection, and he loved her. He saw her vulnerability and her heartache. It only inspired him more. He was determined, and finally, the opportunity came. After weeks of following and observing the habits of Paul Bartholomew, fate stepped in.

Paul pulled up to a small outdoor kiosk to have a key made. The briefcase was in the backseat. He got out of the car and walked up to the window and pulled out a key. The man at the window turned around to cut a duplicate while Paul went back and sat on the hood of the car. As the key machine ground ... bzzzzzzz ... #1 slid to the passenger door, picked the lock ... bzzzzzzz ... reached around, unlocked the back door ... bzzzzzzz ... slid the briefcase out, shut the door ... bzzzzzzz ... and locked it back. Silence. Duplicating the key was the exact cover to the second. As Paul paid the man, our hero, #1, slipped away in an instant as though he was invisible to the hustle and bustle all around him.

There was a strange breeze as he sat cool, calm, and collected, watching Paul get back in his car and drive away. #1 drove to a secluded location and opened the briefcase. Jackpot! There, inside the briefcase, was the working copy, as well as the finished manuscript, of *The Late Great Kate*. He shook his head in disbelief. Why would anyone write such false allegations, such trash? Supposedly, incriminating photos of Kathryn with a bottle of champagne and Kathryn in a bathing suit with a cover-up so it looked like she had on no bottoms. *If this is the best they could do,* he wondered, *they must have been pretty hard up. Who would even believe this guy so filled with ill will? Thank ... God? Yes, thank God ... I mean, that was pretty amazing back there, even for me.*

Kathryn was on stage at the Shrine Auditorium. The code word for a successful retrieval was "Pay Dirt." A note with those words was passed to her. She opened it carefully and lit up like the brightest star in heaven. It was a fabulous service. She was full of light, back to life, and the secret agent, #1, watched as a beautiful little blind girl saw an angel of light for the first time. No longer cool, calm, and collected, he too felt tears roll down his cheek. He'd been all over the world, but he had never met one like Kathryn Kuhlman.

Tink passed a second note. "Don't say anything to anyone until we get it settled. See you at the hotel." Kathryn went straight to the

Century Plaza and paced the floor. There was the secret knock, and she opened the door. Tink stood in the hallway, dressed in a trench coat and dark sunglasses. He handed her the briefcase. Kathryn roared with laughter and danced in circles as the weight of the world was momentarily lifted from her slender shoulders.

#1 watched, thinking, *this is my reward. Look at that smile!* Tink cut up the photos, flushing them down the toilet so quickly that it stopped it up. There, Tink was on his knees, all dressed up, wearing his diamond rings, digging in the stopped-up toilet. The visual made Kathryn, Sue, and the invisible man who saved the day forget the weeks of waiting.

Kathryn never read the manuscript. She was only interested in getting it away. It wasn't that she had done anything wrong or had anything to hide. Scandal and mudslinging were not her style. Her life spoke for itself. She would not allow anyone to destroy what she had given her life for.

Page one of the manuscript told the story from beginning to end. The opening paragraph reflected the author's disdain and judgment, hearing Kathryn's voice on the radio long before they ever met—that of an educated mind who deemed her style as below his, but not so low that he could resist her lucrative offer of employment. Decisions made on money alone were destined for failure. Their business relationship began and ended on the same note—it was all about money, and the love of money is the root of all evil. If you make it your God, it will plague you like the devil, and sin is sure to follow.

#1 knew this guy couldn't imagine what he had done with it. Had he left it somewhere? In a parking lot? He thought he had put it in the back seat. *Man, this must be getting to me,* he must've thought. Maybe he even had some chest pains himself. #1 decided not to let him get off that easy. He called Paul using an accent of a country hick. "Uh, hey, man. I found yer briefcase and ... uh ... I want to know, man, this thang—it says *The Late Great Kate*. Are ya plannin' on killin' this lady?"

"Oh no, of course not," Paul replied, "but I need that briefcase back. I'll pay you for it; what do you want?"

"Well, uh, I dunno. It looks like uh purdy nice briefcase. What'll you gimme?"

"How about $250? I'll meet you right now."

A $450,000 lawsuit was just reduced to $250. That got under the skin of #1. *This guy must think everybody's a fool.* "I'll think about it ... maybe I should call the police." #1 hung up the phone. *Yeah, let's see him sweat a few bullets, see how he likes it.* The charade continued for a few days as the price and the tension escalated. #1 was satisfied with another job well done and headed off to his next assignment.

The lawsuit was promptly settled and laid to rest in early September for approximately $85,000, which went to Paul Bartholomew to buy out the television syndication contract. Dino and his wife Debbie were paid $10 to sign their releases. Just like Kathryn's marriage, their marriage ended in divorce, and Dino spent his time in the desert for his involvement.

It was disturbing that twenty-three years later, many of those who were interviewed blamed Dino for Kathryn's death. It was a terrible blow, and the stress at that time in her life was the last thing she needed. But Kathryn's heart condition had been diagnosed twenty years before by a doctor in Washington, D.C., whose business card was still in her wallet.

She was deeply hurt, and it truly broke her heart. A spiritual wound cuts just as deep as a mortal one. Kathryn, in all her pain—physical, mental, emotional, and spiritual—understood that Dino, too, was human, and as such, we err. To err is human; to forgive is divine. Kathryn's wallet contained all her identification and one photograph taken in 1974: a photograph of a handsome, young Greek man she loved as a son—Dino Kartsonakis.

Years later, Dino came to terms with his actions and wrote an open letter of apology:

"Dear Kathryn,

This letter I've wanted to write to you for a long, long time to say the things I was never able to say to you. I've held this within me, and now I'm determined to express through this letter how much you've meant to me and how much you have influenced my life and ministry.

You've been a major influence on my life. By your example, far more than by what you said, you taught me how God could mightily use individuals who commit themselves to Him.

The other day, a man who had been a faithful follower of yours approached me after a concert. 'Dino, I feel that same power and anointing in your music that I have felt in our beloved Kathryn's life and ministry.' He didn't know it, but he couldn't have said anything more wonderful to me.

Since you died, many Kathryn Kuhlman clones have come on the scene. I've said, as I'm sure many of your thousands of followers have said, this can't be. There was only one Kathryn.

Please forgive me for my part in the misunderstanding between us and our sad partings. It has been fourteen years since you left this world, and I'm fourteen years older and, I hope, wiser and less rambunctious.

Sometimes, especially when I start getting discouraged, I think of you up there watching me. If you can see what's going on in my life, I hope you're pleased.

And finally, Kathryn, you used to say, 'When I see the Lord, all I'm going to say is, I've tried.' When I meet God, I also want to look at Him and say, 'I've tried.'

With love forever,
Your friend Dino"

The sentiments were touching and sweet. If only Dino hadn't waited fourteen years to express them. If only he had asked for Kathryn's forgiveness, apologizing for the pain he had brought to her heart. Time is so precious, and tomorrow may never come.

We have to exercise the wisdom of God's Word on matters of the heart. If you are at the altar and have fought against one another, leave your gift at the altar, and be reconciled that you may give with a pure heart. Therein lies the will of God for all those who know and love Him—that you may receive all the blessings He has in store for you.

To be in the presence of one who hears His voice—to be led by one who is in His spirit—is not enough. It's like turning on some televangelist to touch God. That is the testimony of that person's relationship with God. It does not make it ours by osmosis. Our relationship with Him is the defining aspect of our every thought and action. It explains how we see people who work in ministry every day but act no differently than those in the business world: they are counting on the blessed assurance of someone else's faith, believing that by serving God's anointed, it supernaturally rubs off on them.

It is a sad misconception; for a while, good deeds can make you look holy in the eyes of man, but they won't get you into the gates of heaven. Fair warning is given to those who walk the walk and talk the talk for all the eyes of man when in that day God has to say, "Depart from me, I never knew you" (See Matthew 7:23). People led by the Spirit do not enter into a conspiracy for selfish reasons against one another. No good can come of it. In the understanding that we all fall short, we forget condemnation and look for restoration in the love of God that forgave us when we were the ones who fell short.

Kathryn's understanding and acceptance of that simple truth were a gift to all those who knew her. "Sometimes, I think the reason I have such a depth of feeling for people is that I can forgive so easily. I know I've been forgiven, so much so that it is easy for me to forgive others.

"Maybe that's the reason I see the tenderness of the Lord, and that's the reason I know His great compassion. It's more than theology with me, and so when anyone knows my background and what I've been through, then they understand me better. But I don't talk about it."

God can forgive you. You can forgive yourself—but you cannot ask the forgiveness of someone who has already entered into eternity.

If you don't express the words in your heart as you feel them, you may never have another opportunity to do so. Seize the moment, swallow your pride, and move on to a higher level of peace amid the storm.

BUILDING FOR
ETERNITY

*O*ral Roberts was blessed with one last visit from Kathryn Kuhlman. Over the years, she had a profound effect on the student body as well as Oral himself. "I revere her life, her ministry, and her legacy more and more. Kathryn's ministry affected me personally most positively. She lived in the presence of God. I directly witnessed miracles in several services in different cities, including Tulsa. I saw crippled people's bodies come loose, stand, and run through the audience. There were many others, but that particular manifestation of God's miracle power touched me most. I saw none like her, but I see the power of God that was on her upon many others today. Among those specially called in the miracles and healing ministry, I rank her at the very top. Her prayer still rings in my ears and my spirit: 'Holy Spirit, let me never disobey my Lord.'"

With the lawsuit settled, Kathryn prepared what she apparently knew would be her last message for the students of Oral Roberts

University. The new chapel, seating four thousand, was full. She spoke in the past tense to them as a body representing a family. "Just know, it was the Holy Spirit, and Kathryn Kuhlman was only the vessel He worked through." It was as if to say it was finished.

"The world called me a fool for having given my entire life to one whom I've never seen. I know exactly what I'm going to say when I stand in His presence. When I look upon that wonderful face of Jesus, I'll just have one thing to say: I tried. I gave of myself the best I know how. My redemption will have been perfected when I stand and see Him who made it all possible."

At the close, she appealed to the students to come forward and commit their lives to Christ. In the unity of that declaration, all four thousand came forward as one, falling on their knees and praising God in their prayer language as the Holy Spirit swept through the building and filled their hearts. Kathryn had prophesied many times. "One of these days before Jesus returns, there will be a service where every person present shall be healed." She always said the greatest miracle was the spiritual one. All four thousand united in harmony with the Holy Spirit was a parting gift to the handmaiden, who had given all to one she'd never seen.

On her way home, Kathryn made another last visit to her special place on earth, in the little town of Concordia, Missouri. The driver drove to the house on St. Louis Street, where she had been so happy as a child, playing on the front porch waiting for Papa to come home where she would run to his arms. She thought about the basement, where Mama had disciplined her so many times. Poor Mama, she had been such a handful; how things had changed.

In 1948, after one of Kathryn's services, Mama had come backstage. "Kathryn, I want what you have." Kathryn prayed and laid hands upon her mother, asking that God would baptize her in the Holy Spirit. Emma Kuhlman went out, slain in the Spirit, and began speaking in unknown tongues. From that time on, Kathryn and her mama shared a new relationship—one the people of Concordia thought strange. The two would walk arm in arm to go get a coke, laughing and cutting up like two teenage girls. Kathryn had helped Mama a lot in her later years, but Mama passed away in 1958 at the age of eighty-six. Kathryn filled the Baptist church with flowers and wore a big black lace hat. Rumors spread through the town that for several days, Kathryn left her casket in the living room of the little house on Orange Street, just like they had done with Papa.

How she wished she could lay her head on Papa's shoulder one last time or hold Mama's hand. She walked up to their graves in the beautiful little cemetery outside of town. The breeze caressed her face, and the sweet voices of the birds in the towering spruces reminded her of a simpler time when Papa could heal any sickness and dry every tear—a time before commitments and a ravaged, worn-out body took their toll.

She looked to her heavenly Father and spoke to her natural one. "Now, I won't be buried here beside you, but I know you're not here anyway." She began to sob. "I'll see you soon. I'll see you soon ... oh, dear Jesus, I'm coming home ... but not yet, not yet." She knelt down in front of the large standing granite marker above both of their graves that were simply engraved "KUHLMAN." Papa and Mama had individual markers at their head. She nodded her head in approval. "Yes, I did well." She had already chosen her own marker, which was much simpler, but Papa and Mama ... well, they deserved the best.

She rallied her strength and collapsed into the limo. She closed her eyes in silent prayer. "Just let me make it long enough to rebuild my integrity before the people of the world ... just let me make it to Israel."

Tink and Sue were now with Kathryn full time, and resentment was growing among the troops. In Kathryn's mind, she was placing her confidence and trust in the man who had saved her ministry's reputation, as well as hundreds of thousands of dollars—all through Tink's wisdom in hiring a great legal team out of Los Angeles and his unconventional Agent #1.

Pittsburgh was wondering why Kathryn didn't turn to them. They had been her dedicated, loyal staff for so long. With Kathryn gone so much, Maggie had assumed the head position, and she had done a wonderful job. Kathryn loved Maggie, but at this point, she considered it a business friendship, and what Kathryn needed most right now was to escape the pressures of the never-ending business. Even when Maggie traveled out of town, she worked and stayed in the hotel while Kathryn and others shopped and went out. She was responsible for handling the money and couldn't go.

Kathryn intimidated people unintentionally, and even those closest to her were sometimes afraid to express an original thought. But, with Kathryn gone, Maggie called the shots. Maggie was concerned about the future, about "Pastor" as she called Kathryn. She slipped and told David Verzilli, "Kathryn is not well. She took one bite and sent the whole meal back. She just couldn't eat." It was true, but somehow when Kathryn took the platform, energy would flow like a river.

It seemed nearly impossible to tell Kathryn no. One evening, one of the women walked into the foundation offices and found Maggie crying. She had fallen in a department store, broken her ankle, and Kathryn had just told her to fly to California. Once again, Kathryn expected everyone to be as dedicated as she was. After all, she had preached six nights in a row with a broken leg. "Well, just tell her no," the woman said. Maggie looked at her as if she were out of her mind. "You just don't do that," and Maggie didn't. She dragged herself to the airport and flew to California.

One time, Maggie was with a group of people and asked, "Pastor, would you like some hot chocolate?"

Kathryn answered, "Maggie, you've known me almost thirty years, and you still don't know I don't like hot chocolate." It was a small example of the distance coming between them. Maggie was trying to protect the foundation, and Kathryn was trying to protect her personal privacy and leadership that called all the shots, regardless of her health. They loved and respected each other too much to allow a disagreement, and each one played out their roles to the end.

Tink and Sue accompanied Kathryn on tour through the South during the month of October, and Kathryn began to share her funeral requests with Sue. She was very specific. Her resting place would be at Forest Lawn Memorial Park in the majestic rolling hills of Glendale, California, a suburb of Los Angeles where Aimee Semple McPherson, Humphrey Bogart, and Mary Pickford were buried. She had purchased plots for her and Myrtle in the late sixties. She carried her Forest Lawn identification card in her wallet, and her personal photographs contained a picture of Kathryn standing on her plot, along with Gene and Ruth Martin in the beautiful grounds that surrounded a magnificent towering marble sculpture of Christ above a waterfall in an evergreen alcove.

The service would be in the Wee Kirk O' the Heather, a quaint little reproduction of Annie Laurie's church in Scotland where stained glass windows told her story of love. It was just around the bend from Kathryn's final resting place, the Court of the Christus.

"I want all roses, nothing else, and I don't want anybody looking down at me and making some big fuss. That's why I bought that private lot—so people wouldn't come to worship it like some shrine the way they do, Aimee. Get Oral to do a simple service, nothing grand. Paul Ferrin will arrange the music. Leave that to him. Let's start the list. I want to invite ... and promise me you will always take care of Myrtle—always. I don't want her to worry about anything."

Kathryn also began to reminisce about her life, especially the great loves of her life. There were three—Papa, Mr., and the one man that never left her—the Holy Spirit. He was the man behind the woman, the one who took her from the obscurity of Twin Falls, Idaho, to the World Conference of the Holy Spirit. She was so looking forward to the trip to Israel, which was only a few weeks away.

"You know, both my falls were over men, and both times the bad press almost cost me that which was most dear. My life would be meaningless, of no value to myself or anyone else, if I ever lost the Holy Spirit. If I ever go out on that platform, and He's not there, I'll never go again. Without Him, I'm sunk, and my life is over."

Kathryn would cause a riot everywhere she went, especially in California. The attention didn't stop her from sharing her hours of laughter and tears as she relived her life. She would take a deep breath, "Oh, I was so in love with that man," and giggle. "He had the most beautiful feet in the world. Lottie and I would just go on and on about how handsome and dashing my 'Mr.' was." Then the tears would fall.

"Can you imagine telling the love of your life goodbye, getting on a train, never knowing if you would ever see him again," and then she would stop and stare, blankly lost in the moment. "And I never saw him again." Kathryn never got over Burroughs A. Waltrip, "Mr.," and she carried the pain of it until the day she died. She never spoke of the happy times—that would be even more painful.

Sue was as private as Kathryn. She understood what it was like to hold so much inside. Kathryn needed a friend she could trust with the most intimate details. Sue never betrayed that trust—not even with Tink. And Tink—well, he was as loyal as Kathryn, and the two of them really knew how to have a good time.

Kathryn felt good about her life. She had given 1,000 percent in her commitment to her call. She never said anything about a successor; it didn't even seem to cross her mind. Who could? Only God could choose one—just as He chose her. The foundation was taking in a million dollars a year, and television costs alone were $30,000 a month.

Kathryn was tired, too tired to deal with anything. "You handle it, Tink. I can't. Just take care of it." They were in charge, and they got the blame. Kathryn didn't allow anyone to dictate her path. You followed her instructions—it was her way or the highway. You could not change her mind or tell her what to do. She had built the ministry by listening to her heart—to God, living in the company of the Holy Spirit. Why should she listen to flesh and blood? It worked well, and there was no reason to change this late in her life.

November was near, and Kathryn breathed a sigh of relief; then, she got word that Dan Malaehuk was planning to charge $35 extra for people to attend her service. She felt he was exploiting her for his own good, and her red-headed temper flared. She went ballistic. Tink knew to stay out of her way; he hunkered down and waited for the tornado to pass. She yelled in the receiver, "You listen to me. People have already paid to come to that seminar. Now, you can just forget that, or I'm not about to come! This is the only conference I attend, and I'll not have the Holy Spirit or I exploited." Silence. Tink waited and watched Kathryn in control. Dan Malaehuk knew better than to tangle with Kathryn. Her discernment was amazing, and she put an end to the whole idea. People were afraid of her strength. Her persona couldn't be questioned. You couldn't tangle with Kathryn Kuhlman—you could never win. It would be like trying to tangle with God Himself.

Kathryn and the Wilkersons boarded the airplane for the seven thousand-mile flight to Jerusalem. As they took their seats in first class, she rested in God's grace in spite of physical pressure. Kathryn had made it; she was on her way to her final destination. Once again, as the lead speaker at the second annual World Conference on the Holy Spirit in Jerusalem. Whatever it had cost, any price was fine. It was well worth it.

Kathryn leaned her seat back and closed her eyes. Her mind began to replay the first World Conference on the Holy Spirit. It was a part of history. The largest overseas delegate in the history of Israel had come together to pray for peace in Jerusalem. Six thousand people from forty nations watched as the same God who healed in Kathryn's services across America brought healing back to the homeland of His Son. "At some point, you will call on God and ask for a miracle. Let's forget whether we're Jews or Gentiles. There is one God, one Son."

Sixty-seven Jews came back to Christ that day in Congress Hall. Kathryn left the stage, walking amongst the crowd as the Holy Spirit covered the building with God's love—healing hearts, bodies, and wounded spirits. Men and women were slain in the Spirit until 1:30 in the morning. The anointing was so strong that people had been healed and slain as they watched the film clips.

"One last anointing precious Holy Spirit, you have been so good to me ... I see your Son, the Mount of Olives, the Garden of Gethsemane, the Via Dolorosa ... and the cross—your greatest miracle of all. How you must have felt to know the only hope for mankind would be through the death of your Son."

She drifted off, resting in the arms of the one who would never leave or forsake her. They arrived in Tel Aviv, and Kathryn was exhausted. Everything seemed difficult, as though darkness was trying to shut out her last bright light. She wanted to preach on prophecy; the consensus was for something less volatile in the political climate than taking sides with the Jewish cause.

Although she had no fear, Kathryn reluctantly gave in. The night before her scheduled appearance, Kathryn met with a Finnish group of five hundred when there was only room for a hundred. One woman was dying of cancer, and her last wish was for Kathryn to pray for her.

Kathryn prayed for about fifteen minutes, and later, the woman died. Gene Martin had always kept things like that from her, knowing how much it could hurt her; this time, local police came and took Kathryn's passport as if she were responsible.

Tink was really nervous, wondering if they would get out of the country, but Kathryn never showed fear. The police came and talked to Kathryn. An Oral Roberts University graduate student who spoke Hebrew came to her rescue, and the passport was returned the following morning. Kathryn never showed any concern—just acted like it never happened.

Kathryn didn't allow herself to be put on a pedestal, and she opposed other ministries being torn down "out of jealousy or incompetence." Kathryn had no problem standing up for the underdog. She overheard two things that she didn't let slip by. One was a comment about the quality of Pat Robertson's suit. Kathryn went to him and encouraged him just in case he, too, had heard it. The other was a decision not to give a group of youngsters called "Terry Law and the Living Sound" enough time in Jerusalem. A cardinal had helped Terry get into communist countries for a series of concerts, and Kathryn felt he had something important to offer. Terry and the Living Sound did get their time—a full thirty minutes because Kathryn stood up and announced it. What could they do?

The final blow came the evening she was to appear. She paced in a dark tunnel below the stage for an hour-and-a-half, crying out to God, begging and pleading for the anointing and the strength to make it through. Dan Malaehuk interrupted her to apologize for the news; Kathryn would have to work with an interpreter. "You know that I don't do that ... I can't."

He explained they didn't have a choice. Finally, Kathryn told him to have the interpreter greet the Israeli people, and she would only speak for ten minutes and go directly into the miracle service. Ten minutes became an hour and fifteen minutes, and some of the Israelis walked out, unable to understand. She was waiting for the Holy Spirit to come upon her; only God could heal. She called forth healings, and as always, there were miracles. Even with all the difficulties and disappointments, the handmaiden of the Lord had done what she came to do.

Kathryn's emotional highs were fleeting, and after they were over, she liked to do something fun. They flew to Rome, where Kathryn loved to shop at Angelo's and have custom clothes made. She insisted Tink and Sue order some too. They were winding down, enjoying a relaxing vacation. On Sunday, the Pope addressed the people in Vatican Square. They strolled up and listened. Tink could sense Kathryn surveying the crowd. She was in her element. Like an entertainer, the crowds made her come alive. She was hooked, and she needed to be ministering. She turned to Tink and Sue, "C'mon, kids. We gotta go. I'm ready to go home."

"What's the hurry, Kathryn? We just got here." They headed home with three free days to prepare for Kathryn's ten-year anniversary at the Shrine Auditorium.

People arrived the night before and slept in lawn chairs to guarantee their seats. Everything was perfect. Myrtle sat proudly in her favorite spot on the balcony. She told the lady next to her, "You know from the time Kathryn started in a little storefront, there has never been an empty seat." Seven thousand faithful followers celebrated and rejoiced at all the miracles and wonders that had taken place in this building.

Kathryn was especially happy. Her electric blue eyes danced as she looked across the familiar faces in the crowd. She had lifted them up, and she had encouraged them through their doubt and fear until they too believed in miracles. God had certainly done a mighty work in downtown Los Angeles, and she was grateful to have been a part of it.

THE HANDMAIDEN

The service was wonderful. Afterward, she sat in her dressing room, sipping orange juice. She caught a glimpse of herself in the mirror—she had finally gotten old. The stress of the last two years had taken a toll on her health, and it was showing on her face.

She sat motionless for the longest time, looking right into the mirror as though it were talking back. "Yes, I have fought the good fight." For several years, she had carried the poem *I'm Not Growing Old* by John E. Roberts. She knew it by heart.

> *They say that I am growing old;*
> *I've heard them say it times untold,*
> *In language plain and bold—*
> *But I'm not growing old.*

> *This frail old shell in which I dwell*
> *Is growing old, I know full well—*
> *But I am not the shell.*

> *What if my hair has turned gray?*
> *Gray hairs are honorable, they say.*
> *What if my eyesight's growing dim?*
> *I can still see to follow Him*
> *Who sacrificed His life for me*
> *Upon the cross of Calvary.*

> *Why should I care if time's old plow*
> *Has left its furrows on my brow?*
> *Another house, not made with hand,*
> *Awaits me in the Glory Land.*

BUILDING FOR ETERNITY

What though I falter in my walk?
What though my tongue refuse to talk?
I still can tread the narrow way,
I still can watch and praise and pray.

My hearing may not be as keen
As in the past it may have been,
Still, I can hear my Savior say,
In whispers soft, "This is the way."

The outward man, do what I can
To lengthen out this life's short span,
Shall perish, and return to dust,
As everything in nature must.

The inward man, the Scriptures say,
Is growing stronger every day.
Then how can I be growing old
When safe within my Saviour's fold?

Ere long my soul shall flyaway
And leave this tenement of clay;
This robe of flesh I'll drop, and rise
To seize the "everlasting prize."
I'll meet you on the streets of gold,
And prove that I'm not growing old.

THE HANDMAIDEN

Kathryn had arrived that morning exhausted, barely able to drag herself there. Sue had flown home to Tulsa, and Kathryn was straining to get herself ready. Alone in her dressing room, she sat still praying for strength when she heard the choir singing "Hallelujah." She rose, restored to the youthful exuberance and physical transformation that left age and weariness behind. Replacing it with childlike faith and a face that made her so beautiful.

The Holy Spirit never failed her—not once. No matter how tired, how troubled, or difficult the circumstances, as the earthly vessel yielded to the author and finisher of her faith, only the power of the Holy Ghost was needed. "Thank you, Holy Spirit. I give you praise for this day." A peace came over her; she was alone with the love of her life. She lifted her head and raised her arms. "Precious Jesus, I have finished the work you gave me to do. I sought you with all my heart where you planted your words. How I love your people. Thank you, thank you, Lord. Wherever thou leads, I will follow. I ask but one thing ... take not Thy Holy Spirit from me."

Only a few volunteers and ushers remained. The seven thousand people had gone back to their world in the city of angels, renewed in the strength, encouragement, and euphoria of God's eternal love; they were inspired by her words of faith, hope, and healing.

Kathryn was in the deep and private communion with her best friend, the Holy Spirit. A gentle breeze surrounded her, and those with discernment of the Spirit dared not interrupt, and they watched as the two joined together for the last walk out of the dressing room where she had prayed so fervently, dying to self for ten years. The Holy Spirit was real to her. More real than any person she knew. Kathryn died to self every time before she opened the door that led to

274

thousands of lives being made whole physically, mentally, emotionally, and most of all, spiritually.

She pulled the curtain aside, looked onto the platform, and turned
to her Comforter. He took her by the hand. "Let's go," He spoke to her
very soul. "Let's go, that we may see what God has done and rejoice.
Rest in thy life, my humble handmaiden, for thy words have been
steadfast and blameless." Time stood still as moment by moment,
step by step, section by section, the Shrine Auditorium came to life as
the visions of Sundays past resounded in her heart. The end of an era
stood before her. Meetings were scheduled for a year in advance, but
Kathryn knew that she knew. She said goodbye to the Shrine Auditorium—thankful for all God had done, grateful to have been a part, and
weary for a place to lay her head.

In 1975 alone, Kathryn traveled out of the country to London,
Rio De Janeiro, Canada, Jerusalem, Argentina, and Venezuela on top
of her normal schedule at the Shrine Auditorium, CBS, Pittsburgh,
and Youngstown. There were also meetings in New York, Michi-
gan, Rhode Island, Massachusetts, Oklahoma, and Missouri. Even a
young, robust preacher on fire for God would be tired. The Spirit lives
forever, but the body of this frail sixty-eight-year-old handmaiden
of the Lord had burned the candle at both ends for many years. Her
body was more like 108 years old, and eternal rest was the only rest
Kathryn understood.

THE LONG ROAD
HOME

*K*athryn called and asked Tink to please fly Sue out to make her feel better. Even though Sue had barely been home for months, she caught the next plane out. Kathryn was asleep when she arrived at the Century Plaza Hotel Sunday evening at about 7:30 p.m. Kathryn rested on Monday, and on Tuesday, she met with Dick Ross, her director at CBS, downstairs in the Garden Room. She asked Sue to take a table nearby and keep an eye on her in case anything went wrong.

Tink and Sue were sitting nearby when Kathryn suddenly ran for the ladies' room. Kathryn was as white as a sheet and began to vomit. Sue helped her up to her room, and Tink asked Dick Ross to handle whatever decisions that needed to be made for the next two days of shooting. Tink just hoped and prayed Kathryn could make it.

Tink called Kathryn's doctor in Tulsa. Since Kathryn was breathing alright and sleeping, he thought she might have the flu and called in some prescriptions. The following morning, Kathryn insisted on getting dressed and going to CBS. Everyone else was ready to work, and her guests had flown in from around the country. Sue helped her get dressed, taking several breaks for Kathryn to sit down and rest. Finally, with Tink on one arm and Sue on the other, they started down the hall. Again, Kathryn had to stop several times.

At CBS, things were no better. Kathryn nearly fainted, and Tink and Sue were getting nervous. They put in a call to Oral Roberts. "Oral, Kathryn is so weak that she might not make it through this series of half-hour tapings; we are very concerned and want you to join us in a special prayer." Oral felt like he needed to call Kathryn back. Tink helped Kathryn to the phone.

He heard her weak voice in the background. A word of prophecy came to him, and he said, "Kathryn, there's darkness all around you." There was. "Yes, I feel it," Kathryn said. Then Oral saw a shaft of light, and the shaft of light was blowing the darkness away and engulfing Kathryn.

She whispered, "Yes, I know ... I know."

"Kathryn, you are going to make it through this telecast, aren't you?"

"Oh yes, I'm going to finish it." And finish it, she did. All four shows that day.

No force of darkness could stop her, even in the devastating weakness of her earthly form, but for the first time, she told Dick Ross to scrub the screening. She just couldn't make it through another two hours. "If I can only make it through tomorrow," she told herself as she lay in bed that night. "I always finish what I start—just one more day."

Kathryn returned to CBS one last time and finished all four of the thirty-minute *I Believe in Miracles* television programs, but there would be no grand party as there had been for the milestones along the way. Photos of the close cast and crew celebrating her 150th and 300th shows revealed a comforting look on the faces present, which one is not accustomed to seeing in the hectic pace of television where every moment counts. Her joy spilled over, and her faith gave rest to everyone around her.

Kathryn, being the consummate trooper, smiled and oozed enthusiasm even on the last shows. One of the last was with Dr. Thomas, pastor of the First United Methodist Church of Tulsa, Oklahoma. He had been a brilliant attorney when God called him into the ministry, and he was struggling. One night in 1972, Kathryn walked arm in arm with him for hours in Tink and Sue's basement, praying for the Holy Spirit to fill his life and ministry. It had set the struggling church on fire when Kathryn came to teach a two-day seminar on the Holy Spirit. She introduced Dr. Thomas as "One of the greatest theologians I know, a man of keen intellect." The woman without even a high school diploma taught men with the highest intellect to see the simple truth of God's Word.

Kathryn wore a green chiffon pulpit gown with her beautiful pave diamond heart necklace. At a glance, she looked like she was okay, but when you really looked past the message at the messenger, you saw a face swollen as if to swallow up the light from her blue eyes.

She collapsed into bed on Thursday as soon as they reached the hotel. She had finished one more great event of her life. Ten years of miracles were told to the millions watching. It would have taken a lifetime to tell them all, but there was no life left.

Early Saturday morning, Sue went in to check on Kathryn, who was exhausted and pale; her swollen ankles and abdomen were in constant pain. She was barely able to eat and rest; she just wouldn't let up. Nobody could convince her to slow down. Sue found her lying half-dead sprawled across the bed in her Century Plaza Hotel room. "Kathryn, you know that we have to do something. You are going to die if we don't get a doctor."

Tink contacted a mutual friend who recommended Dr. Carl Zabia of St. John's Hospital in Santa Monica. Dr. Zabia agreed to stop by on his way to the hospital. When Dr. Zabia arrived, Kathryn was close to terminal with congestive heart failure. Her heart was huge, and she was short of breath. He took her medical records to review on the way. He called an ambulance and told Tink he would see him at St. John's. Tink told Kathryn the ambulance was on the way. It was the only time when Kathryn got mad at Tink and Sue.

She absolutely refused to ride in the ambulance. They would take her in the car. They wrapped Kathryn's arms around Tink's neck, and together, they staggered down the hall, dragging Kathryn along.

Once downstairs, Tink paid the ambulance to lead them to the hospital, where they promptly put Kathryn in one of the emergency rooms. Dr. Zabia had been waiting for the ambulance for some time and was furious when Tink finally found him. Shouting obscenities over the confusion, Tink could only reply, "I have no defense. If she lives, we will talk about it." Later, when Kathryn was stabilized, Dr. Zabia understood what Tink was up against. "Miss Kuhlman is a very strong woman!" He had tried to unsuccessfully get her age out of her, something he was experienced in since so many celebrities lived in the Santa Monica area.

Maggie sent Dr. Richard O'Wellen of John Hopkins to check things out. He read Kathryn's chart and asked questions, leaving the impression that Kathryn might not have been in the best of hands. Kathryn was furious, and when Maggie came to visit, she barely even spoke to her. Maggie sat in a waiting room down the hall just so "Pastor" would know that she was there.

Kathryn had not endeared Tink to the foundation. She had him call in almost daily, instead of herself, to see what was going on, and naturally, they resented an intruder into their close circle. The more they resisted Tink, the more Kathryn resented them. It was simply an unfortunate misunderstanding. Kathryn had not been honest about how weak and sick she was becoming and how much she needed the company and comfort outside of the responsibilities the foundation held. If they questioned Tink, who was only following her direction, Kathryn took it personally—they were, in essence, questioning her, and she started to distance herself from them. When you are in a weakened condition, small things become big, and big things become small.

Kathryn bounced back. Dr. Carl Zabia was quite taken with this dynamic patient. "In all her pain, she remained cheerful, and all the nurses loved her and gave her special attention. She made them laugh. Any normal person would be extremely limited with severe heart failure. It was super heroic for Kathryn to be able to handle her schedule. Such dignity ... she would never admit to feeling bad."

For twenty days, Tink and Sue arrived at 7:30 a.m. and stayed with Kathryn until 10:30 p.m. Kathryn didn't want them to leave.

Kathryn charmed all the doctors and nurses, acting as nothing had ever happened. Dr. Zabia would walk in, and Kathryn would throw up her hands, "Oh, how is my favorite doctor in the whole world today?" She was full of joy and made a real impact on everyone.

As soon as she felt a little stronger, she would lay on the charm and ask, "Dr. Zabia, can't you just let them take me out for a little drive? I'm so tired of these four walls. Please, it would be so nice." A few minutes later, Tink would wheel Kathryn down Wilshire Boulevard in her oversized sunglasses and scarf, looking like a celebrity in disguise. As soon as they got in the car, she lit up and said, "Let's go to the Farmer's Market!" Like a mischievous child, she would eat all her favorites, including everything she wasn't supposed to, like pizza and doughnuts. On the way back to St. John's, she would swear Tink and Sue to secrecy. "Now, you had better not say anything!"

They didn't talk about business. They talked about life and the true meaning of it, of love and loss, and of joy and pain. It was just what the doctor ordered—relief from the insurmountable pressure of a multi-million dollar foundation—with thirty employees, 100 television stations, radio, and 125 services a year that led to Kathryn's personal appearance each week before as many as 120,000 people. Only the faith of a child could manifest the energy necessary; any grown-up would know it was an impossible feat leading to sure physical death.

Kathryn's lack of education only helped to form her into a humble handmaiden who was never dependent on herself, but on the one with all strength, all power, and all wisdom. Kathryn was enjoying her last days and the company of the kids. Like any parent, she wanted to leave them something.

During this time, Kathryn asked Tink to have Irv Ungerman, his attorney from Tulsa, who had helped Kathryn negotiate her out-of-court settlement with Paul Bartholomew, fly out. She had some legal matters she wanted to take care of. When he arrived, she asked them to leave the room, and with respect to all her wishes, they left without question.

On December 11, Kathryn was released from St. John's to stay at the Century Plaza with round-the-clock nurses. She seemed not only to be better physically but mentally. There had not been twenty days of rest in her entire life, and it was clear she had been doing a lot of thinking.

Kathryn called Sue in one day to bring paper and a pen. The Century Plaza stationary was in her things with a detailed list of who she wanted to have and what at her funeral. Kathryn knew there was not much time left, and she wanted to be "the boss" of her life until the end. The last thing she wanted was somebody else making decisions for her.

She chose her burial gown—a beautiful flowing pale gown custom made for her by Tony at Profiles De Monde. She went over the list of funeral arrangements with Sue. On December 17, attorney Irv Ungerman flew in again to deliver the legal papers she had requested, namely a new will, leaving all her loved ones specific amounts with the balance going to the Wilkersons. It was certain to make a lot of people mad, but Kathryn was not concerned. It was hers to choose, and perhaps Tink and Sue had become the children she never had. They had sacrificed their own lives since May, devoting all their time to her needs and paying their own way. Keeping up with Kathryn was expensive.

Kathryn only drew a $25,000 a year salary, but the foundation paid all her expenses. Her salary mainly went for shopping for antiques and gifts but only if she got a bargain. Kathryn had inherited her beautiful home in Pittsburgh's affluent suburb of Fox Chapel, an extensive jewelry collection, as well as investments from her dear friend, Eve Conley. Eve, who treated her like a daughter, had enriched her life in so many ways. The walk-in safe in the basement held money that was so old that one hotel had refused it. When people mistook her lifestyle, it was only because they didn't understand all she had been given. It had made up for the one-dollar inheritance from her precious papa and enabled her to give rather than receive.

Kathryn trusted Tink and Sue with her life, and in the end, she made the decision to give her inheritance to the "kids" she never had. They were not perfect, but Kathryn adored Sue and loved Tink. They shared so many good times, and they had stuck with her during the bad ones, never questioning anything she said. They showed her the respect she deserved.

The stage was set for rumors of deception, even murder from the media and some of those who knew or thought they knew Kathryn but didn't really know the Wilkersons. Tink had inherited the position as Kathryn's hatchet man, and just as others before him, he found it to be a position that didn't make you popular with the troops.

To really understand the depths and strength of Kathryn's relationship to the Holy Spirit, you must step back in time to that Christmas in 1975. It was one of her favorite times of the year, and even though she was weak, Kathryn wanted to go home to Fox Chapel and visit. Tink flew her, along with two nurses to Pittsburgh.

On December 21, Tink loaded Kathryn into his new $750,000 private jet that he had planned to lease to the Kathryn Kuhlman Foundation. Only now, it didn't look like Kathryn would be around long enough to enjoy it. He and Sue had only been home thirty-one days since May, and the commercial flights were getting old for everyone.

On Christmas day, Kathryn called his cottage in Vail, Colorado, where he and Sue were spending the holidays. Kathryn sounded really bad. "Tink, you have to do something. I'm getting worse, and they are going to kill me. Please come get me."

She was probably flooded with well-meaning visitors who were rightfully concerned with her deteriorating health. Kathryn had always been able to hide her suffering and never liked anyone feeling sorry for her. Tink took a deep breath and prayed for God's direction. Dr. Bill Loughridge, the respected heart surgeon from Tulsa, Oklahoma, received an urgent call. Tink Wilkerson was well known in Tulsa, so he took the call.

"Bill, I need you to do me a tremendous favor. I need you to go to Pittsburgh with me in the morning and pick up Kathryn Kuhlman."

"I'm not going to Pittsburgh, and I do not even know who Kathryn Kuhlman is. It's preposterous for you to ask me to do that."

"Just listen to me for a minute."

"Fine! I'm in a meeting, so make it quick." Dr. Loughridge was pretty curt.

"I am sitting outside, praying. It came to me that Kathryn needs surgery, and I need to get her to Tulsa in your hands. This is why it is important we go."

By his own admission, at that time in his life, the handsome Dr. Loughridge was cocky and arrogant. His faith was in himself, and he did not need anything else. He had the whole world in his hands. He was successful, professionally and personally. Nobody told him what to do.

"No! I am going on vacation."

Calmly, Tink replied, "I really wish you would reconsider."

The next thing Dr. Loughridge knew, he was saying, "Do you have airline tickets?"

"No, I have an airplane. I'll pick you up at eight o'clock in the morning, and we will take the airplane and pick up Kathryn."

"Okay." Bewildered, he had made a complete change of decision; he told his wife, who really thought it was crazy. Trying to make sense of the whole thing, he could only offer, "Well, it seemed very important to Mr. Wilkerson."

When they reached Fox Chapel, Kathryn was semi-comatose and jaundiced from severe heart failure. Dr. Loughridge carried her from the car to the plane for the flight to Tulsa. He laid her across the back seat, not having much hope for his acutely ill patient.

Dr. David Copple admitted her into intensive care at Hillcrest Medical Center on December 26, under the name Johanna Thomas. Dr. Copple had seen her in July and had recommended surgery then. The following day, he called Dr. Loughridge: "I need you to come to see Kathryn Kuhlman with me. There is a big entourage up here, and we are discussing what to do. It looks like terminal heart failure."

When Dr. Loughridge arrived, he was met by Oral and Evelyn Roberts, along with their son, Richard, and his wife, Patty. Oral and Evelyn "loved her and considered her a dear, dear friend."

The Roberts, Wilkersons, and several doctors looked to him for an answer. Dr. Copple spoke the last thing he wanted to hear. "When are you going to operate?"

"I'm not!" Dr. Loughridge was again put out with someone else calling the shots. "Nobody knows what's wrong. She probably has a bad mitral valve, and until she is steady, I'm not going to operate."

Oral Roberts suggested they pray about it. The first time Oral attended one of Kathryn's miracle services: "God's Spirit came all over me as I saw God working tremendous miracles of healing through her. I wept and wept for joy and knew God had raised up this precious handmaiden of the Lord, one unequaled in my generation. She brought forth the word of knowledge greater than I had seen. I saw this gift of the Spirit in a new light and knew in my heart that God was going to release it to His people everywhere. Kathryn's ministry at Oral Roberts University stirred the arid faculty's students immediately to tears, to understand that God was visiting them, and they had not been the same since. We had a profound sense of gratitude to God and to Kathryn."

Dr. Loughridge remembered the embarrassment he felt when they all joined hands and began to pray. All he could think of was what the ICU nurses would think of a "big stud" like him needing to pray. When they started praying in tongues, he rolled his eyes and broke into a sweat, agonizing over how uncomfortable this was. When it was over, once again, God answered prayer, and out of his mouth came, "I'll call the operating room and schedule it this afternoon."

Knowing he was making decisions with no logical means, his partner shook his head and said, "Bill, you're crazy. She is semi-comatose."

The operating room was the strangest experience he had ever felt. For years, he could not speak of it without weeping. Even now, he fought back the tears. Spirit-filled cardiologist John Meriman was praying in his ear the whole time. "I wish he would shut up. This is so distracting."

Dr. Kemper Lain was assisting when Dr. Loughridge noticed an ethereal mist had filled the room. Everything felt as though he was in a dream state, removed from and even watching as though in a movie. It was not his hands doing the surgery. Through the misty fog, he exchanged knowing looks with Dr. Kemper Lain that something spiritual was going on.

From that day forward, through the Holy Spirit, Dr. Loughridge has never been the same. It was a deep, inexplicable experience that completely altered his faith and future. Today, he is a beautiful example of the peace and grace that come from above. As a thankful gesture for his epiphany, there were no professional fees billed to Kathryn Kuhlman from Dr. Loughridge.

It was a perfect surgery, but the medical team was concerned that Kathryn might never come off the heart and lung machine. She did easily. Overnight, she was out of heart failure and the next day, off the respirator. It was amazing. Kathryn improved over the next few days, and Dr. Loughridge had his first conversation with the patient he had become quite proud of. Only she did not reciprocate his feelings. She was angry. Why did he repair her heart? It was time for her to go home, and she was ready. He assured her that not only was she going to be fine, but she would be able to go back to her ministry or whatever she wanted to do. Kathryn was adamant. "I'll never leave this hospital alive." Perhaps it was God's timing. Kathryn's ministry was at its zenith. It would have broken her heart to see it disintegrate.

The next day, Oral Roberts told Dr. Loughridge they needed to talk. Kathryn had asked him "not to pray for her to be raised up but to release her to go to her heavenly Father." He was deeply moved and not offended as she would point a finger upward and, with tears, say, "Let me go." He honored her desire even though he wanted her to stay.

Dr. Loughridge saw Tink as caring and compassionate—generous, even to a fault. He was never ugly or short to anyone, including the CPA from Pittsburgh, but Kathryn had placed Tink in charge, so again, he got the blame.

Very few people were allowed visitation. Kathryn was specific about who she wanted to see. Tink and Sue, her sister Myrtle, and Gene Martin were welcomed. They were her trusted family. Others who had long worked with her were refused. Gene Martin came right after the surgery.

Dr. Loughridge assured him it was a miracle recovery. Kathryn never indicated to Gene that she didn't plan to live. She was drugged and whispered, "Get me out of here. Please, I want to get out of here." Gene knew it was not possible. He already had meetings set up for the coming year, including a tentative date at Madison Square Garden.

The last time he saw her, she looked beautiful. She was fully made up, and she said, "Open up the meeting places, I'm coming."

She was delirious, and just like Everett Parrott, her body and spirit craved preaching the Gospel. Gene kissed her on the forehead and said a prayer. With tears of joy that God had restored her, he left the country for Guatemala to assist the devoted people who had survived an earthquake.

Once she had made it, Kathryn trusted four people with her most personal moments: Gene and Ruth Martin and Tink and Sue Wilkerson. She was able to let her hair down and not be judged or advised on what was proper for a preacher lady. She could just be herself, and if she was flawed, oh well. They loved her anyway, and they never betrayed her trust by exposing some personal matter.

Years before, Kathryn had told Gene and Ruth that if her funeral was in Pittsburgh, she wanted a men's chorus to sing, *I Heard 1,000 Trumpets Singing Out His Praises.* She wanted three testimonies: Red Dalton, her catcher for three years, who was saved sitting at the end of a bar watching her telecast; one testimony of someone delivered from alcohol; and one great healing from a woman. No sermon; if she were eulogized at all, Gene would know what to say. And Jimmie McDonald was to sing *His Eye Is On The Sparrow.*

But Pittsburgh was not on her mind. She was furious when the foundation accountant, Walter Adamack, showed up to retrieve the signed checks Tink was holding. "Get rid of him," she told Tink. "Just tell everyone to stay away." Kathryn was fighting for her life, and business was the last thing on her mind.

Kathryn had never forgotten from whence she had come and who brought her to where she was. She loved her sister Myrtle and would put up with anything from her. Probably Myrtle was the only one Kathryn would put up with. They often spoke on the phone and saw each other when Kathryn was in California. Myrtle was a strong defender of Tink and Sue. "You just stay out of it. Kathryn trusted the Wilkersons. She knew what she was doing."

Myrtle came and stayed for a short visit. "Tink, she wants to go home. She's ready." When Myrtle left, Kathryn reminded Tink always to pay Myrtle's rent. For seven years, he did, and Myrtle just thought the apartments really liked her because everyone else's rent kept going up while hers stayed the same. She never knew. It was best that way. Myrtle called Sue for years, talking for hours just like Kathryn used to do. And when Myrtle died, she was buried in the same section of Forest Lawn as her little sister Kathryn—the one she had led to becoming one of the brightest stars in God's Kingdom on earth. Yes, she was proud—more proud of that than anything she had ever done.

On January 2, Kathryn's heart failed again after attempts to wean her off the respirator, and they had to perform a tracheotomy. Kathryn was rail thin with very little muscle tissue due to being undernourished and her severely enlarged heart. Kathryn was totally spent. Her body was worn beyond years from a lifetime of dedication to her call. The heart condition had been present for so long and was severely enlarged. Still, she pressed on, never complaining. In the following weeks, Kathryn continued to deteriorate, but the medical community had to answer its call to save lives whenever possible. In twenty-seven days, she endured six operative procedures. Finally, a very unusual situation occurred. Kathryn's will to die was so strong that a spontaneous twist of her colon produced septic blood poison.

A remark made on Dr. P.B. Jorgensen's examination report on February 12 would have pleased Kathryn. He described her as middle-aged. At sixty-eight, it was a compliment she would have loved. Unfortunately, that's where the good news ended. She appeared fully alert and not at all drowsy but somewhat euphoric. Plus, she wept readily when the question of her recovery was discussed. She demonstrated gross disorientation.

One of his closing comments indicated that which Kathryn had feared. Kathryn had expressed concern that she might have a stroke and become an invalid. She wanted to go home just like Mimi Anderson, one of the singing sisters from her days in Denver. Mimi was on her knees reading the Bible. When Kathryn got the news, she said, "That's exactly how I want it to be." But the doctor later stated, "There could be no doubt that this lady had suffered considerable diffuse [widely spread] cerebral damage, and most likely related to her episodes of prolonged hypertension [low blood pressure] and possibly some hypoxia [inadequate oxygen]."

Her never-before-seen medical records were a study in themselves. No one with a beating heart could read them and not feel sorry for Kathryn. She had suffered for years and never told anyone. There had to be times when she did not feel like doing anything, but God always energized her to do His work. For at least ten years, she had taken diuretics to reduce the swelling in her abdomen and ankles. She was careful to hide her condition from even those closest to her. It was super heroic to keep her schedule, especially that last year.

Seven specialists and all the modern medicine at Hillcrest Medical Center could not stop Kathryn from having her way. At 8:20 p.m. on February 20, 1976, Kathryn Johanna Kuhlman left this earth. A nurse present spoke of the room being filled with light, especially around Kathryn's face, as she looked to heaven with the face of a child in the arms of her loving Father. At that moment, Kathryn's fervent prayer, "Take not Thy Holy Spirit from me," was answered. They were together forever.

THE COURT OF CHRISTUS

"*K*athryn Kuhlman dies at 66," was the headline of the *Los Angeles Times* on the following morning, Saturday, February 21, 1976. They were two years off. Even in death, Kathryn kept the world guessing about her age.

On Tuesday, February 24, the memorial service Kathryn had specifically choreographed was held at the Wee Kirk O' the Heather in the Forest Lawn Memorial Park in Glendale, California. The early morning sky was overcast, and drizzling rain fell softly on the rooftop. Birds were singing just outside during the entire service. A blanket of roses covered the closed casket. Just as Kathryn had wanted, she was surrounded by a virtual rose garden. A set of tall, interlocking hearts made of pink roses was placed on the right side, where members of the Kathryn Kuhlman Foundation sat. They seemed to be a reminder of Kathryn's "Heart to Heart" talks that would continue on the radio for many years. They were also a replica of the hearts on Mr.'s Valentine.

The front of the chapel was filled with beautiful sprays of vibrant red and pink roses.

One hundred fifty of Kathryn's favorite people, still in shock that she was gone, slowly made their way into the quaint recreation where Annie Laurie found a treasure of comfort through God's love. In the belief that a heart filled with love knows no separation from those who live on in memory, inscribed above the chancel is 1 John 4:16: "God is love, and he that dwelleth in love dwelleth in God, and God in him."

Paul Ferrin softly played "Hallelujah" on the organ as people entered the Wee Kirk O' the Heather and took their seats. Jimmy McDonald's rich baritone trembled as he sang, "Thou hast taught me to say, it is well with my soul. Burden no more. Praise the Lord. Oh, my soul."

All those present joined in for the last chorus of "It Is Well with My Soul." Jimmy looked out among the crowd and took a deep breath. "The first time I met Miss Kuhlman, that was the first song I sang for her. She taught me more about God and the Holy Spirit than any other person I know. I am thankful to God that He loaned her to us for the time that He did. The legacy to us is to begin to walk and live in the things that we've seen as reality in her life. She believed in the simple Gospel and expressed it in her life. Sometimes the way did grow dark and dreary, but she knew God watched that little sparrow, and I know He watches me."

Why should I feel discouraged?

Why should the shadows come?

Why should my heart be lonely?

THE COURT OF CHRISTUS

When Jesus is my portion

My constant friend is He

I sing because I'm happy, I'm free

His eye is on the sparrow, and I know He watches me

The Reverend Oral Roberts led the prayer. "Let us stand. Our blessed heavenly Father, you're so real to us. You're closer to us than our breath, nearer to us than life, and standing here, we fill this whole place in light. By your angels, touched by the resurrection of our Lord Jesus Christ Himself, that as we continue in this word of faith and life concerning your servant Kathryn and our sister, we would draw, we draw from you for our own resources to be replenished, and for the light that lit her way to come into a brilliance that's never been known ... that's never been revealed before which we believe is beginning to happen. And now, as the Lord taught us to pray, let us pray."

In unison, the people prayed:

"Our Father, which art in heaven,

Hallowed be Thy name.

Thy Kingdom come, Thy will be done,

On earth, as it is in heaven.

Give us this day, our daily bread.

Forgive us of our trespasses, as we forgive those who trespass against us.

And lead us not into temptation, but deliver us from evil.

For Thine art the Kingdom and the Power and the Glory

Forever. Amen."

Oral continued: "'I believe in miracles because I believe in God.' In 1968, when I first tuned Kathryn Kuhlman in and heard her say those words and saw the smile on her face as she said them, the warmth that went through my body was indescribable. I knew it was the Holy Spirit. Three years before, I knew that the crusades I had been conducting in the big tents and auditoriums would come to a close, and the methodology of my ministry was switching to another stream of God's power. I knew it would switch, but I didn't know how God was going to do it.

"I had gone off television after having been on uninterrupted for over fifteen years, and now I was in that twilight period. *God, what are you going to do with my life? Are you through with my life? If you are, thank you for how you used me.* But deep down inside me, the flood of the Spirit was still flowing, and I knew He wasn't through with me. Then I heard these words, and it was as if God Himself had stepped out of heaven and put His hands upon me and gave me a new light, and I knew I was to go back on television.

"Kathryn, through the Spirit, touched me, and I got light. I had the privilege of telling her this so that she would know that her life had helped me find myself again. For I have been a person who always needed help to find himself, and usually, it was someone who knew God. God's always used people to help me find Him, and He helped me find my way back. It gave me a format that was utterly new in this country, and it caused a lot of controversies until people understood what it meant. From that, our ministry increased. Today, I am still in terrible awe of what God is doing in my life and that there is so much more than I had since 1968, but the turning point to point me back to find that new methodology belongs to Kathryn. 'I believe in miracles because I believe in God.' That was right. That was scripturally right.

It was right because it was not only a statement of faith from her, but it was based soundly upon the Word of God. It was a balanced ministry that God had given her.

"I did not have the privilege of knowing Kathryn personally. In the 50s, she honored us from time to time. She'd slip into our crusades and sit near the front. Frankly, I didn't know she was there most of the time. I first came to know of her through Rex and Maude Aimee Humbard, whose lives and ministry had been touched by this woman. They told me an incredible story, that they had her big tent in Akron, and when they were starting their work, Kathryn would come in Sunday morning at 6 a.m., and the tent would not seat the people. I told Rex that this could not be true, and he said, 'Oh yes, at 6 o'clock in the morning, six to eight thousand people!' Rex and Maude Aimee began to tell me other things, and I began to know through other people. Like Denise, my associate evangelist, who had met her and kept telling me about this woman I heard on the radio. She absolutely fascinated me because when someone would get healed in the audience, she had a knack, and she would begin to interview them, and when they would say how they were healed, she'd say, 'Are you really healed? Really? Really?'

"She had this rather theatrical way. I began to pick up the word theatrical from various friends. Those who were close to her said, but don't be misled by that. That was the woman, personally.

"In 1971, I said to my producer, who was also hers, 'Could you arrange for me to go to the Shrine?'

"He said, 'Of course,' and there I met Tink and Sue Wilkerson. Tink is on our board, a dear young layman, and he and Sue are so close, and they really had been going to her meetings, flying from

Tulsa to wherever she was, just for their own benefit, for their souls, and I could see the change. They led me to a seat on the balcony. It was a long way from the platform. As I sat there, some of my old partners were in the meeting, and they were coming over, pulling at my left and right. I called the usher and asked, 'Would you just let me have some peace? I came here to meet God, to worship God.' Now, I had never heard her personally until that day. I sat there on the edge of my seat. The service was going on, and the choir was singing. There was an order: I tell you about the organization. I began to realize I could learn something about organization, about running a meeting. And then she came traipsing out on the platform, and I used the word traipsing because it really explained what she did. She came dancing out on her toes; those hands were out, and the crowd rose, and I got swept up in it.

"Then we settled back down, and she made this statement: 'Kathryn Kuhlman is nothing. She cannot heal, she cannot do, she has never done anything. It is the work of the Holy Spirit!' The Holy Spirit—I wish I could say the term Holy Spirit like she always said it. She said it in the most familiar way because she knew who she was talking about. Then she preached. She must have preached an hour, and people were sitting there. I looked around, and it was a different audience than the one who came to my meetings. There were so many big people and a lot of so-called little people. In God's eyes, there are no big or little people. In our society, people are segregated big and little, rich and poor, but you could tell that this was an audience that had touched the so-called top people as well as the more common people like me.

"Then all of a sudden, a change swept over her being. You could see it from the balcony. She said, 'there was someone over on the left who was feeling the presence of God and that was being healed if you would stand and come forward.' I turned and saw a woman stand with a little child. The little child was on braces and crutches. That little thing stood up, and they were helping him to put one foot in front of the other, and by the time they got halfway down the aisle, they stopped. They took off the braces and took away the crutches, and the little child took a step and another step up to the big steps that led to the platform.

"People started to help, and Kathryn said, 'Don't help this boy. Let's see what the Holy Spirit has done.' When he got on the stage, he turned loose, and he didn't walk, he ran, and by that time, I was absolutely broken up.

"I knew that Kathryn Kuhlman was God's anointed vessel, and I was thrilled because as I sat there, I saw things that God hadn't done through me. I saw things that God hadn't done through anyone I'd ever seen! I rejoiced because my God was so great—He was greater than I could conceive Him. He was greater than she could conceive Him. He was greater than the Catholic priest on the platform could conceive Him, and the Methodists and all the Pentecostals and the Baptists—they were there, and they were all pointed out, in one way or another. I've never seen a group of Catholics and Pentecostals and even a Jewish rabbi come together. I knew that Almighty God had to do something awfully special to get all these people together, which I was witness to from up in the balcony.

"I thought this arrangement was quite well done. I was there to meet God. When it was over, I started to walk away. Tink came and said, 'She'd like for you to come behind the stage.'

"I said, 'Oh no, I can't do that because I've had meetings like this, before large audiences, and when I finished, all my strength left me. When the anointing left, I was let down, and I was weak, and I wanted to go to my room and lie down.'

"Tink said, 'Well, she's not like that. She's even stronger when she finishes.' She could turn around and have another four-hour meeting. For four hours, she had stood on her feet.

"I saw people smiling and nodding their heads. Anyway, I was worn out after four hours of sitting there on the chair, watching her stand there for four hours, remembering I had to have a terrific anointing to do, which I did, and you practically had to carry me out. She was stronger after it was over than she was when she started, so I wanted to see what God had done.

"I came into her dressing room and reached out my hand, and I heard these words coming out of my mouth, 'God has really raised you up as His handmaiden of the Lord. Your work has gone beyond mine, and I can't thank Him enough.'

"She said, 'Oral, I know who I am. I know who you are. I know what I am, and I know what you are. I know what I am in the Kingdom, and I know what you are. I know my place.'

"Then I said, 'You must be terribly tired?'

"She said, 'Oh no, I'm going out to dinner with some friends.'

"I said, 'Kathryn, you have something I don't.'

"She said, 'Oh, I feel great!' and she spun around. About that time, someone came into the room, and she stretched out her hand, and that person hit the floor. The same thing was going on back there in the little room, just like it was on the stage.

"Well, time passed, and she came to Tulsa. A young woman came to town in advance and asked if our students at ORU would help to form a choir, and of course, we were thrilled to do that because I recognized that God was in this woman. She was unique in my eyes, at least because God was using her in a different way. He had always used not only my voice but my hands. He didn't use her hands upon people. He used her hands stretched out, and He used her voice, but she didn't have to touch the people. God always had me touch the people, and when I didn't touch the people, there were never as many people healed unless my hands touched them, but it was the opposite with Kathryn.

"I began to see that God didn't use anyone's method. He has so many. Everything was arranged, and the meeting in Tulsa began at the Civic Center. That big building had been visited by people, like Elvis Presley and Lawrence Welk, and had been packed out by these people.

"Before the doors were opened at noon, there were more people outside waiting than there were seats, not counting standing room. So, later when the meeting started and we came, there were the pastors of Methodist, Baptist, various Catholic priests, and the heads of industry and oil companies. I looked around, and it was like the who's who of Tulsa. I'd been around twenty-five years, and never have I seen anyone who could break through such a barrier of society and bring together people in virtually every walk of life.

"Then the meeting started, and the first ones touched were the little Catholic nuns who fell under the power of the Spirit. You see, I'd never seen that. I knew those little Catholic nuns wouldn't fall under the power unless it was the Spirit. That was not their background. Later that day, I saw the pastor of the First Methodist Church who was there that day, Dr. Bill Thomas. When I saw the owner of the largest independent drilling company in the world fall under the power of the Spirit, I began to realize there was something beyond what you had ever known in your lifetime. I asked Kathryn since she was so super strong, since she never got tired. I asked Tink if he would see if she could stay over until Monday, and we would have a special Chapel at ORU.

"She talked for an hour and told us the story of her life. She was the daughter of the mayor, and she told precisely how she was reared and how God began to deal with her and how God chose her. She didn't choose God. God chose her sovereignty.

"ORU presented her with the first honorary doctorate because she epitomized God's healing power. She took it, held that piece of paper in her hand, and turned to me to say, 'I know what this means. You know Oral, you and I are one. We are one.' It gave me goosebumps because when she said it, there was a power in it that puts warmth through your body and light in your eyes and a song in your soul.

"What I'm saying is not new to you. I just wanted to say something personal. The Bible says that the Spirit spoke to St. John and told him to write these words: 'Blessed are they that die in the Lord for they shall rest from their labors and their work shall follow them' (See Revelation 14:13). I was there, nearby, when she died. In her living and dying in the Lord, there were some unusual circumstances about this and that, only two or three, perhaps four in the room know, and I think they should go into the record today.

"She had fallen in love with Tink and Sue. She found them at a time of great need. They were willing to leave their business in Tulsa just to give up whatever they were doing to help. I never knew such a will that a person could have. When it was her desire to be brought to Tulsa and put in the hospital, there was something about it that she wanted to be there. She called and asked Tink to bring her down, and her doctors asked me to stand with them on a difficult decision they had to make. Some twenty feet from her bed, five physicians joined hands, and the room filled with light. Kathryn would nod and look up, nod and look up. I didn't go back until Kathryn asked for me to come up. She put one arm out for me and one arm around Tink. I started to pray, but there was no prayer. Only words. She looked up with that smile, she must have gathered up all resources for that one smile, and then she fell asleep.

"She wanted to go home. The surgery was the most perfect ever on earth; it was the talk of the medical profession. Every surgeon, every doctor, and every nurse had a profound religious experience. When we were praying the big prayer, God revealed to me that within ten days, we would know the outcome, and on the tenth day, we did, at 4 p.m. In that prayer, we were praying for complete restoration. The doctors were working day and night to restore that great life to the platform. We had God's perfect total delivery system working virtually. Prayers were coming in from all over the nation—a world of telegrams coming, telling of people's prayers—our prayers, the prayers of our whole student body, the prayers of the people all over town, everywhere. When I touched that woman the last time in what we call the big prayer, the will of Kathryn was so powerful. I turned to Tink, and I said I've dealt with thousands and thousands of people in my life, but I never encountered such a will. This woman's will was so strong.

"Now, I know how she could stand up for hours. Now, I know how she could endure such pain and tiredness and never open her mouth, how she could stand whatever came against her. You know she was so generous ... then the news came that an indescribable peace had come over her, and she had just fallen asleep.

"Kathryn was alive more than anyone in this room. We were closer to the Holy Spirit than we had ever been, and we understood Jesus more than we ever had.

"Kathryn, we're glad you walked among us, and above all, we're glad the Holy Spirit is still walking among us, and we are one with you. Amen."

Silence and tears filled the little chapel as the ushers helped Kathryn's loved ones to the door to see a burst of sunlight peeking through the clouds; they breathed a sigh of relief as the memory of the legacy she'd left filled their hearts and soothed their spirit. The service continued as they drove to Kathryn's final resting place. The simple marker on her grave was exactly what she wanted.

KATHRYN KUHLMAN

I Believe in Miracles

Because I Believe in God

February 20, 1976

One sentence composed of the words she lived by—the words that formed her life and legacy: a humble handmaiden of the Lord who became the foremost female evangelist of the century.

BEYOND THE
BENEDICTION

$\mathcal{T}$he greatest tragedy in losing precious human life is the sudden focus on who gets what and why. In death, as in life, Kathryn was making headlines. Newspapers across the country focused on the amount of her estate as well as the drama of an unexpected new will. The new will was lengthy and specific. It would be impossible to dismiss Kathryn's obvious consideration and expression of appreciation to those she deemed worthy—she didn't base it on how long you had been with her. She based it on what she felt in her heart, her personal sense of appreciation.

On Sunday, April 11, *The Pittsburgh Press* ran a lengthy article giving the details: "$267,000 in cash bequest were provided, the largest being $50,000 to her sister Myrtle Parrott; $40,000 to Kathryn Kuhlman Foundation head Maggie Hartner; $25,000 to Kathryn's private secretary Maryon Marsh; $25,000 to Steve Zelenko, the head of her radio ministry; $20,000 to Charles Loesh, her handyman and chauffeur; $10,000 was given to Kathryn Kuhlman employees: Ruth Fisher, Margaret Dillon, and Youngstown preacher David Verzilli." According to the treasurer, Walter Adamack, the Kathryn Kuhlman Foundation was already operating at a loss barely sixty days after her death. It doesn't quite add up since they are still going twenty-three years later. A few of the foundation employees were disappointed that Kathryn hadn't left the bulk of her estate to the organization, and this became open season for manipulation of a press that is always sorting dirty laundry.

Myrtle Parrott knew her sister well, maybe even better than anyone. She and Kathryn were always close. Myrtle told a reporter, Ann Butler, that she was not surprised to learn of the new will. "So many of us loved her and loved the Gospel. I know she wasn't influenced ... she was always the boss. I want to emphasize that my sister told me personally that she had a great deal of confidence in the Wilkerson's, and I believed her."

Maggie said the five-member board of the Kathryn Kuhlman Foundation considered contesting the will but voted not to. "We felt it would have been the foundation against Tink Wilkerson, and that would have hurt Miss Kuhlman and the ministry."

"I've never met Tink," said David Verzilli, "but I really admire the man. Formerly, I was bitter. I felt he invaded Miss Kuhlman's life. But when she was ill, he took her in and gave of himself. I like that." He allowed Tink to come before the Youngstown congregation. Reverend Verzilli introduced Tink, "Here's the man we thought stole our pastor. I don't think that's right."

Tink faced the angry crowd and tried to explain. "Kathryn asked me to do a job, and I did the job she asked me to do. I did exactly what she wanted." Maggie was furious and scolded Reverend Verzilli for allowing Tink on the platform.

Ruth Martin agreed that Tink was on a mission. "Kathryn needed him very much. There was a crisis in her life about a year ago. She was alone, and she needed someone like him, who knew about business."

Tink made an offer everyone refused. "If anyone is concerned about what we've gotten, Sue and I will be happy to donate all of our residual to ORU providing the other benefactors do the same." When asked why Miss Kuhlman left nothing to charity or the foundation, Tink replied, "That's hard to defend. Kathryn had the feeling she had given her life to the foundation. There are many unanswered questions about Kathryn Kuhlman—many mysteries surrounded her."

Tink was the man Evangelist Kathryn trusted. The front-page headlines ran over from one side of the *Pittsburgh Press* to the other. It was Sunday, April 11, 1976, and reporter Ann Butler's interview must have raised some eyebrows. Tink and Sue sat on the curb outside the Fox Chapel home. They were in town to pack up and make preparations for the sale of the home Kathryn left to them. The article began, "Tink Wilkerson is a real likable guy. When he was talking to you in his soft, smooth, full-of-Oklahoma accent—pausing now and then for a genuine smile—honey, you can't help but figure him for any less than an honest-to-God, down-home, good old boy. His forty-four short, with a bit of a paunch and receding auburn hair. His freckled face is sunny and open, with greenish-gray eyes shining behind wire-rim glasses."

The extensive interview covered the events of the past nine months of Kathryn's life, including answers to the rumors. In answer to influencing Kathryn's life for his personal benefit, Tink said, "I don't think anybody ever had an influence on her. She never had a business manager. I had no financial dealings with her ... I expect that if I had undue influence, I would have tried to get her to leave it all to me instead of leaving some $250,000 in cash bequest to twenty employees."

Rumors began to circulate that Tink was secretly Kathryn's son. They both had red hair. Of course, his prophetess mother was less than pleased with the implications that her son had influenced Kathryn. "My son is no shyster. That woman just needed a friend. Tink didn't need a thing she had ... he was so kind. He treated her as a mother. He was strictly interested in the person and the ministry. He never expected, never dreamed of such a thing."

"She was a lonely woman," he added. "Most people wanted something from her other than just to be a friend. They wanted to be near her for healing, or for spiritual reasons, or to exploit her. Ours was a genuine friendship. So often, friendships are one-sided. But ours was always a two-way friendship."

One year later, in February of 1977, *The Pittsburgh Press* reported a final court inventory of Kathryn's wealth. The estate total was $732,543. Inheritance taxes of $115,000 were paid, $52,500 was paid to the Pennsylvania Inheritance Tax, $150,000 was paid primarily for hospital bills, and $100,000 was paid for estate closing cost, representing the legal fees in Oklahoma and Pennsylvania. That left $314,500 to pay $267,000 in cash bequest, and the remainder went to Tink and Sue—for less than $50,000. Some continued to portray them as the bad guys for taking money away from the foundation—money that Kathryn specifically wanted them to have, which was less than they spent the last year while taking care of Kathryn. What a terrible waste of energy and ill-will.

BEYOND THE BENEDICTION

Instead of taking money, Tink and Sue chose to keep pieces of Kathryn's antiques and jewelry collection and all of her most personal items that remain perfectly intact for such a time as this.

These were the precious pieces of history that allow you and me, for the first time, to see inside the woman who was known of and respected around the world—but was never really known until now. Until those few chosen extended family members, that have now gone home to be with the Lord as well, unified and shared what may have been lost forever—the essence of the real human behind the miracles.

In our weakness, we are made strong. In our frailties, we expose our true heart and soul, and in the end, what we leave is what we love. Kathryn's love for life and for her fellow man and woman—regardless of age, race, creed, class, or accomplishment—is a testimony of a real, true understanding of God's love for all His children. If more of us step outside ourselves, out of our safe little worlds with that level of love and commitment, there would be no war, no crime, no divorce, and no suicide.

Within a year of Kathryn's death, two biographies that were already in the works came out. *Kathryn Kuhlman: The Life She Led, The Legacy She Left* by Helen Hosier, which is no longer available, and *Daughter of Destiny* by Jamie Buckingham, which has always been marketed as the only authorized biography. That may be slightly misleading, according to several sources.

Kathryn would refer to Jamie as a "stage door Johnny" who they had to get rid of on numerous occasions when Kathryn would say, "I don't want to see him." She was very opposed to Jamie writing the book. In 1973, Kathryn told Dino, "I don't want Jamie Buckingham to write that book. He thinks he knows me, but he doesn't."

Kathryn had given Jamie several interviews, which are available at the Billy Graham Center Archives. Maggie worked with Jamie after Kathryn's death. Had she known all the awful things he would write, she would have never agreed to do so. Jamie had told one of Kathryn's closest friends, "If I don't get the interview, I'll make something up."

Kathryn's strength was threatening to some men; perhaps this was true of Jamie. He came to a lot of conclusions that everyone I interviewed disagreed with. He was not a part of her inner circle, and there was a great deal of supposition on his part.

Writers are encouraged to go for the controversy, and sometimes it leads to the jugular vein of their subject. Kathryn's discernment was on target again. The unflattering photo on the cover reflected the intent and some of the content. Although Jamie's book was not completely factual, he did offer the truest explanation of why Kathryn left no successor. "She knew exactly what she was doing—ending her ministry. Her purpose for being here was introductory. She was the John the Baptist of the Holy Spirit. Her role was to reintroduce the miracle power of God to a non-believing church. And as John left no legacy, neither did she."

"If I speak in the tongues of men or of angels, but do not have love, I am only a resounding gong or a clanging cymbal. If I have the gift of prophecy and can fathom all mysteries and all knowledge, and if I have a faith that can move mountains, but do not have love, I am nothing. If I give all I possess to the poor and give over my body to hardship that I may boast, but do not have love, I gain nothing.

Love is patient, love is kind. It does not envy, it does not boast, it is not proud. It does not dishonor others, it is not self-seeking, it is not easily angered, it keeps no record of wrongs. Love does not delight in evil but rejoices with the truth. It always protects, always trusts, always hopes, always perseveres.

Love Never Fails."

1 CORINTHIANS 13:1–8 NIV

In one year, Kathryn's message of love somehow was lost in the past, and the focus of the present was money. It was the Reverends Ruth and Michael Walney of Prayer Time Cathedral in Duquesne, Pennsylvania, who ran a tribute to remind us of this beautiful woman who gave her life to His work.

A Tribute to Kathryn Kuhlman.

"It's been one year since the passing of the wonderful preacher lady, Kathryn Kuhlman. It's strange when someone passes on that no thought is given to the good of a life she lived pleasing her God. Still, only the money and estate are brought to the front lines to be sifted and talked about—how much to this one and how much to that one is all that is considered, and to what purpose is all the controversy? Something we are sure that Miss Kuhlman was aware of—what she left and to whom."

To know Kathryn Kuhlman is to love her. I hope you feel that now you know her too, and in doing so, know and see all that is available to you. For Kathryn Kuhlman was a real person in flesh and blood just like you and me, with frailties, failures, and struggles—a woman whose life stood for something greater than self, personal accomplishment, and the approval of mortal men.

THE HANDMAIDEN

She was fearless, courageous, and miraculously committed to the love of people like you and me. What if we only had looked at her with mere mortal eyes? Would we still see, or even believe, some skinny little freckled-faced redhead from Missouri, with not even a high school diploma, leading us to see the deeper truths of life? Shouldn't we leave that to some great theologian or scholar with a conservative look and eloquent speech? Doesn't the world today tell us so?

In the natural, Kathryn was the most ordinary human being in the world, just like she said—just like most of us. Look what she became and what she accomplished when she chose to listen to God instead of men. So shouldn't we lay aside all of our preconceived notions about all men and women and learn to look with spiritual eyes—learn to look with God's eyes, eyes of love. Kathryn was one of His children, and she loved His Son. In God's eyes, Kathryn was a superstar, and so are you. You see, we have to look through spiritual eyes to see even ourselves as God sees us—a perfect creation that needs to come home, where we can be sheltered in His arms and fulfill the true purpose and destiny of our own lives.

Whether your struggle is with the love of self or lack of love, lack of faith in God or in yourself, Kathryn's life points the way to personal and spiritual freedom—yielding to the Holy Spirit in all things and placing all your trust in His Word and ways to guide your life.

This has been a life-changing journey for me. From the very beginning, there have been many moments when I heard the music from the *Twilight Zone* running through my head. Like the first time Tink Wilkerson came to my Dallas home to be interviewed—I had just stepped into the garage and set my favorite handbag down by the car. Later that day, I planned to drop it off for freshening up. I opened the garage door as Tink pulled up, and he stepped out of his Lincoln with the identical handbag. I was holding Kathryn's Louis Vuitton feedbag purse with all her personal IDs and belongings inside, just as they had been for twenty-two years.

Along the way, I couldn't help but notice that Kathryn and I had more than a few things in common. From mischievous children growing up in a small town—to strong, overly driven independent businesswomen in a man's world, choosing the wrong men, a serious case of denial about any kind of health problem, and a genuine love for all people.

Certainly, I do not compare myself to Kathryn, but I do believe God specifically brought me home to Texas for this very project. I first discovered Kathryn Kuhlman at a time when I was as deep in the world as you could possibly be without going six feet under. Drugs, sex, and rock and roll in the land of milk and honey were the privileges of my success.

Despite my bright smile and winning personality, there was this big empty hole that I never knew how to fill; I tried it all: psychologists, fortune tellers, palm readers, astrologers, self-realization mood elevators, uppers, downers, and in-betweeners. Running from that hole made me an amazing overachiever, and there was always someone willing to let me so they could reap the benefits. It was a pretty picture on the outside with an empty shell on the inside.

With all the worldly success, I still wanted to cry myself to sleep on many occasions—only no tears would come. In all my drive and determination, I had suppressed all real feelings. My whole life was an act, and it looked really good on the outside.

Then, I read about Kathryn Kuhlman—the remarkable woman who made God so real to me. She brought God's love and His Word to life. I had looked at the Bible many times before, but now, through the life of a very modern-day woman, I could see that God was real—and that He loved me and cared about me. Once I began seeking Him and applying the simple truths that only a child's mind could understand, I, too, understood. I had grown up too fast and joined forces with all the wrong powers.

I looked at her life, and I saw what she accomplished by simply applying all her energy to faith in God and taking His every Word as a literal promise. It became my heart's desire to develop a project on the life of Kathryn Kuhlman. In the process, by the grace of God, I have been made whole, and the joy you see in me comes from my heart and soul. Yes, Jesus is alive, and He lives in me. His Holy Spirit is with me anywhere I am. I have been blessed beyond belief. There have been personal miracles of healing that saved me from a gruesome surgery and complete restoration of all relationships that in the past had led me to seek counseling. I have seen miracles in the lives of people that I and others prayed for. My husband, Todd, and I came out of the entertainment industry and are now ordained ministers who share a wonderful relationship with each other and with God everywhere we go.

Only a few months before all this, I had written a letter to myself. It began, "I am less than nothing." I listed all my failures and short-comings; I knew God, but at that moment, I had lost faith in myself, and I gave it all to Him. I died to self—and look what the Lord has done. He can restore you if you'll just let Him, and all your pity parties will be packed away. Then one day, He will remind you of how far you have come and how much He loves you.

Her title was no more than that of any schoolteacher. Most of those who loved her simply called her Miss K. Twenty-three years after her death, her methods and influence are studied, analyzed, and copied by preachers, theologians, and sociologists. Her ministry goes on through the Kathryn Kuhlman Foundation and through her followers, old and new, who, like me, found a phenomenal example that led them to God's everlasting grace and purpose for their own lives.

Today, my life is a true testimony of the grace, forgiveness, and mercy of a loving God. When I tell you that I have perfect peace and that I feel like the most blessed girl on the face of the earth, please know that God spoke to me through the life of the foremost female evangelist of the century, Kathryn Kuhlman.

I will close with her words: "The secret of it all was my heart was fixed; I was loyal at any cost, any price. I spent my entire life searching for the Word of God—one constant prayer, always preaching with a burden for souls. I never desired to leave the things of God—not once was I disappointed in Him … never.

"My commitment was complete. Like the Apostle Paul, I was completely fulfilled in doing so. I didn't need anything else, so don't feel sorry for me.

"My joy is complete. I've often prayed that God will take me before this anointing lifts.

"There isn't a day in my life—and I say this with heaven as my witness—that I don't pray, 'Father God, you can take my last living relative, my last penny, leave me with one outfit and one pair of shoes … but take not Thy Holy Spirit.'"

THE END

BC TALBOTT

In her first published book, BC Talbott shares the compelling and beautiful story of Kathryn Kuhlman. Most of BC's career has been spent working within the entertainment industry in Los Angeles, California. Her experience has included working as an actor, singer, writer, and public relations executive in entertainment marketing. Over the years, BC has been recognized in Cosmopolitan Magazine and other publications as a leading female entrepreneur owning numerous successful companies. Today, she resides in Miami, Florida with her husband, Todd, and her two fur babies.

You may contact BC at bctalbott@aol.com